Marketing Management in Practice 2008–2009

Marketing Management in Practice 2008-2009

John Williams and Tony Curtis

ELSEVIER

AMSTERDAM • BOSTON • HEIDELBERG • LONDON • NEW YORK • OXFORD
PARIS • SAN DIEGO • SAN FRANCISCO • SINGAPORE • SYDNEY • TOKYO

Butterworth-Heinemann is an imprint of Elsevier

Butterworth-Heinemann is an imprint of Elsevier
Linacre House, Jordan Hill, Oxford OX2 8DP, UK
30 Corporate Drive, Suite 400, Burlington, MA 01803, USA

First edition 2008

Notice
No responsibility is assumed by the publisher for any injury and/or damage to persons
or property as a matter of products liability, negligence or otherwise, or from any use
or operation of any methods, products, instructions or ideas contained in the material
herein.

British Library Cataloguing in Publication Data
A catalogue record for this book is available from the British Library.

Library of Congress Cataloguing in Publication Data
A catalogue record for this book is available from the Library of Congress.

ISBN: 978 0 7506 8963 2

For information on all Butterworth-Heinemann publications
visit our website at http://www.elsevierdirect.com

Designed and typeset by P.K. McBride

Printed and bound in Italy
08 09 10 11 12   10 9 8 7 6 5 4 3 2 1

Contents

Unit 1 Management and marketing roles

Learning objectives

1.1 To describe the nature of relationships with other functions in organizations operating in a range of different industries and contexts.

1.2 To explain the importance of developing and maintaining effective relationships with people in other functions and disciplines.

The learning objectives are only partly covered in this chapter and they are a theme throughout the book. Other chapters will also be concerned with these objectives, particularly the chapters that focus on the use of teams and communications.

Key definitions

Accountability – The extent to which individuals and managers are held responsible for the outcome of the decisions they make.

Autonomy – Independence to make decisions within a decentralized working environment, where decision-making is passed down from the top of the organization to the lower levels.

Fads – Fashions that enter quickly, are adopted with great zeal, peak early and decline very fast.

Flat hierarchy – An organizational structure that provides a wide span of control within only a few layers of organizational hierarchy.

Global firm – A firm that by operating in more than one country gains R&D, production, marketing and financial advantages in its costs and reputation that are not available to purely domestic competitors.

Global organization – A form of international organization whereby top corporate management and staff plan worldwide manufacturing or operational facilities, marketing policies, financial flows and logistical systems. The global operating unit reports directly to the chief executive, not to an international divisional head.

International division – A form of international marketing organization in which the division handles all of the firm's international activities. Marketing, manufacturing, research, planning and specialist staff are organized into operating units according to geography or product groups, or as an international subsidiary responsible for its own sales and profitability.

Marketing database – An organized set of data about individual customers or prospects that can be used to generate and qualify customer leads, sell products and services and maintain customer relationships.

Market research – The process of (1) analysing marketing opportunities; (2) selecting target markets; (3) developing the marketing mix; (4) managing the marketing effort.

Marketing mix – The set of controllable tactical marketing tools, product, price, place and promotion, that the firm blends to produce the response it wants in the target market.

Market segment – A group of consumers who respond in a similar way to a given set of marketing stimuli.

Market segmentation – Dividing a market into distinct groups of buyers with different needs, characteristics or behaviour, who might require separate products or marketing mixes.

Introduction to the book

The coursebook is targeted at assisting you to pass the Marketing Management in Practice examination. The main focus of the CIM Professional Diploma Course Marketing Management in Practice is on the development and implementation of marketing plans at an operational level in organizations. The Marketing Management in Practice unit helps students to develop and implement marketing plans at an operational level in organizations. A key part of this unit is working within a team to develop the plan and managing teams implementing the plan by undertaking marketing activities and projects. Its aim is to assist students in integrating and applying knowledge from all the units at Professional Diploma, particularly as part of a team. This unit also forms the summative assessment for the Professional Diploma.

The syllabus is covered in eight units and these cover the main areas that contribute to effective marketing management. A marketing-oriented company needs to align its distinctive competencies with market opportunities but to do this effectively requires a team effort.

The structure of an organization can be a barrier to success if it separates one department from another. In some organizations, sales, marketing and customer service are organized as a team but finance, human resource management, research and development, production, purchasing and management all affect the marketing effort. To ensure that everyone is working to the same broad objectives as a team requires good communication and an awareness and respect for each other's contributions. The book looks at these key issues. Unit 1 introduces the broad subject of management in the context of marketing and marketing management. The diverse roles of marketing management and the various ways in which the marketing function is organized are discussed. Guidance on examination preparation will focus on the examination techniques that will maximize your probability of passing.

CIM Professional Marketing Standards

These set out a competency framework that can be used as the definition of marketing practice and the requirements of organizations that employ marketers. The framework has been developed in partnership with large organizations including multinationals, and is based on competencies defined through marketing job descriptions. This framework defines what marketers in organizations actually do, identifying the knowledge, understanding and skills.

What form do the CIM Professional Marketing Standards take?

The Standards are an easy reference matrix, combining six key marketing roles and four job levels. These are the the job levels and associated qualifications.

CIM Qualification	Job Level
CIM Professional Postgraduate Diploma	Senior (direct/guide)
CIM Professional Diploma in Marketing	Manager (manage)
CIM Professional Certificate in Marketing	Practitioner (do)
CIM Introductory Certificate in Marketing	Support

The marketing roles established through research are:

1 Research and analysis
2 Planning (at an operational marketing level or at a strategic level)
3 Managing brands
4 Implementing marketing programmes (of various types)
5 Measuring marketing effectiveness
6 Managing marketing people.

Marketing orientation

Marketing as a management philosophy and orientation, espoused and practised throughout the corporation, is being seen increasingly as critical to the success of any organization. Customer focus needs to be shared by the whole organization and should not be seen as just the responsibility of the marketing department. A marketing orientation involves multiple departments or functions sharing information about customers and engaging in activities designed to meet customers' needs. However, whilst a marketing orientation is seen as increasingly important, marketing as a stand-alone function in the typical organization appears to be more in decline.

A key element of a market orientation is intelligence-gathering about customer needs and preferences and what influences them. This should involve people throughout the organization but channelled for analysis towards a particular part of it. This may be carried out by a marketing department in larger organizations. In a business that has a marketing orientation the needs of customers and potential customers drive all strategic decisions. Everyone in an organization needs to be aware of the marketing message, visions, and goals of the company. Every contact with customers and potential customers, whether it's through advertising, personal contact, or other means, should carry a consistent message about the company and product. In effect, every employee is a sales person, and every employee is a customer service representative. Kohli and Jaworski (1990) define market orientation in terms of three dimensions:

1   The generation of market information about needs of customers and external environmental factors.

2   The dissemination of such information among organizational functions.

3   The development and implementation of strategies in response to the information.

Different orientations to the market

There are three main alternatives to adopting a marketing orientation. These are:

1   Sales orientation

2   Production orientation, and

3   Product orientation.

Sales orientation

Some businesses see their main problem as selling more of the product or services which they already have available. A sales-orientated business may pay little attention to customer needs and wants and does not try particularly hard to create suitable products or services.

Production orientation

A production-orientated business is said to be mainly concerned with making as many units as possible, aimed at maximizing profitability through exploiting economies of scale. The needs of customers are secondary compared with the need to increase output. Such an approach is likely to be most effective when a business operates in very high growth markets or where the potential for economies of scale is significant.

Product orientation

Products may be launched as fully up-to-date but, by failing to consider changing technological developments, or changes in consumer tastes, a product-orientated business may find that its products start to lose ground to competitors.

Managing people, teams and knowledge

This element provides the underpinning knowledge required for the selection, development and maintenance of effective marketing teams. Marketing teams are operating in an organizational and global context, and how different organizations adopt different approaches to marketing depends on their context and culture.

Key skills:

◆   Working with others

◆   Improving one's own knowledge and performance.

Managing marketing projects and activities

Managing the planning and performance of a marketing task by a team requires skills in planning, scheduling, directing, motivating and monitoring. The techniques of project management equip marketing managers to manage marketing activities and projects effectively.

Managing knowledge and delivering market research projects

Knowledge management is about people. People need to be motivated and enthused to share and exchange knowledge. This cannot be done by simply presenting them with a piece of IT equipment. It requires a cultural norm of open communication, informing and sharing knowledge, and motivating and rewarding knowledge-sharing that benefits the business.

Developing and implementing marketing plans

This element requires effective teamwork, and a good understanding of the marketing planning process and techniques to produce successful outcomes.

Awareness of similarities and differences

Examples from one sector may not always be appropriate for understanding what happens in other sectors. There are stereotypes about what happens in both the 'private' and the 'public sector' from within each sector. It is important to go beyond the stereotypes to look for similarities as well as differences. Not all private sector management is good and public sector management bad and vice versa.

Fads and fashions

Writing about management is prone to fads and fashions, with management gurus often very influential in disseminating ideas about what seems to be working. However, not all popular management ideas are effective. Some management ideas have had a negative effect on some organizations. In the early 1990s, the Chief Economist of Morgan Stanley argued strongly in favour of downsizing, saying that it was a cure for companies' problems. By 1997 he had changed his mind and argued, on the contrary, it could be a recipe for disaster. In 1982, Tom Peters wrote *In Search Of Excellence*, a book that identified 43 successful companies and gave reasons for their success over 20 years. However, many of the companies, ran into problems not long after the book was published. Peters apologized, saying that 'there are no excellent companies' and now says of his writing 'Some of my stuff is wrong. Some stuff is right, but I hope all of it is provocative.'

What is management?

Management is an inclusive term that is used in a variety of ways. Generally, it is the process of planning, organizing, leading, co-ordinating and controlling aspects of an organization's resources to achieve organizational goals. It is the organizational process that includes strategic planning, setting objectives, managing resources, deploying the human and financial assets needed to achieve objectives, and measuring results.

Competencies and standards that define a good manager

There are many sets of management competences and organizations sometimes develop their own or use generic management standards. Although the following example is taken from an NHS document it could be applied to many different sectors and contexts.

As an effective manager, you should be able to:

◆　　Lead a team effectively

◆　　Identify and set objectives

◆　　Communicate clearly

◆　　Manage resources and plan work to achieve maximum benefits

◆　　Make sound decisions in difficult situations

◆　　Know when to seek help and do so when appropriate

◆　　Offer help to those you manage, when they need it

◆　　Demonstrate leadership qualities through your own example

◆　　Manage projects

◆　　Manage change

◆　　Delegate appropriately – to empower others, to improve services and to develop the skills of the people you manage – without giving up your own responsibilities

◆　　Consider and act upon constructive feedback from colleagues.

Source: Management for Doctors (February 2006)

www.gmc-uk.org/guidance/current/library/management_for_doctors.asp

A manager assesses an organization's goals and resources, formulates a plan of action and implements it. Management functions are not limited to managers and supervisors. Every member of an organization has some management and reporting functions as part of their job. Different managers have different styles that are formed by their past experience, the nature of the tasks they have to undertake, the context they work in, and the expectations, capabilities and motivation of the people they work with. Studies of management behaviour show that there are wide variations both for the same manager from one week to another and between managers in similar jobs. There are also wide differences between managers' jobs in the same country as well as across countries. Individual influences such as gender, age, ethnic background, education, career experience and personality may also have an impact but there is no conclusive evidence about whether and how these factors influence management behaviour. The use of high performance work teams can result in changes to a manager's role. A manager may be required to adapt to change, provide vision and principles and align people towards a purpose, set direction and strategy. As teams take on more and more responsibility, a manager's focus may shift from controlling to motivating and inspiring.

The following case study provides an example of a modern conception of management.

Case Study: Siemans

Siemens AG is a global electrical and electronics business employing half a million people around the world. A key pillar of the Siemens' business strategy is the way it manages, develops and motivates its employees.

Fit42010 is Siemens' global Strategy. The four cornerstones of this programme are People Excellence, Operational excellence, Corporate Responsibility and Portfolio. The business strategy that relates to people management is referred to as People Excellence. The vision is: "To provide a people experience at Siemens that generates unequalled engagement, commitment and capability, delivering exceptional customer value and organisational goals"

People Excellence encompasses 5 key areas:

◆   Acquisition- Attraction, selection, integration, entry-level talent

◆   Identification- Performance Management Process, Succession planning, expert and functional careers, diversity and work-life balance

◆   Development- Management, graduate and trainee development

◆   Deployment- Performance management process, job evaluation

◆   Engagement- Leadership feedback, upward feedback.

and consists of four main elements:

◆   achieving a high performance culture

◆   increasing the global talent pool

◆   strengthening expert careers

◆   Siemens' Leadership Excellence Programme (SLE).

Central to People Excellence is the building of a high performance culture. Feeling part of a successful team is part of the engagement process. Siemens wants its employees to be involved in the business and to feel part of its success. Employees therefore need to know how they fit into the business. Targets for individuals are related to targets for the whole business. A high performance team is one in which all members of the team work towards shared targets and have a sense of shared responsibility for the results the team achieves.

Siemens' talent management philosophy involves making sure that every employee is provided with the guidance and support to achieve their full potential. Everyone has talent and matching talent with task is a business priority and source of competitive advantage. People Excellence supports the business by providing a framework to match talent with task – enabling people to make the best use of their talents, whatever they might be.

By applying the Talent Management philosophy managers are expected to engage and motivate employees throughout the organisation, regardless of hierarchy or organisational boundaries. Talent Management enables job enrichment, where individuals are encouraged to take on extra tasks and responsibilities within an existing job role to make work more rewarding. It also promotes job enlargement, where the scope of the existing job is extended to give a broader range of responsibility, plus extra knowledge and skills development.

Talent Management is a global philosophy that is a key part of supporting each of the elements of the Siemens' business strategy.

Activity 1.1

The case study identifies a number of key themes in modern conceptions of management, for example, fostering a non-hierarchical culture, customer focus, team working, listening, responsive and fast moving. However, this may be the theory of how management should be practised, an issue for all organizations is whether any of the theory is translated into practice and managers are held accountable for ensuring that it happens.

How would you characterize management in your own organization? Is it like this or is there a gap between the theory and the practice? If the latter, why does this happen?

Studying management

One of the key issues to bear in mind when studying management is that although it is possible to identify trends that are occurring in some large well-known companies, this does not necessarily mean that they are occurring everywhere in all sizes and types of companies.

Management roles

Henry Mintzberg analysed the nature of managerial work and concluded that management consisted of a mass of fragmented activities, constant interruption, pressure for immediate answers and reliance on word-of-mouth messages. Managers value 'soft' information, often acquired through gossip, hearsay and speculation. Consequently, important information for the organization is held not necessarily in the memory of its computers but in the minds of its managers. Mintzberg offered a view of management based on 'roles'.

Interpersonal	Figurehead	Performs ceremonial and symbolic duties such as greeting visitors, signing legal documents
	Leader	Sets the strategic direction of the organization, motivates managers and other staff
	Liaison	Maintains information links both inside and outside the organization
Informational	Monitor	Seeks and receives information, scans periodicals and reports, maintains personal contacts
	Disseminator	Forwards information to other organization members, sends memos and reports
	Spokesperson	Transmits information to outsiders through speeches, reports and memos
Decisional	Entrepreneur	Initiates improvement projects, identifies new ideas, delegates responsibility to others

Disturbance Handler	Takes corrective action during disputes or crises, resolves conflicts among subordinates, adapts to environmental crises
Resource Allocator	Decides who gets resources, scheduling, budgeting, sets priorities
Negotiator	Represents department during negotiation of contracts, sales, purchases, budgets

Figure 1.1: Mintzberg's managerial roles. *Source*: Mintzberg (1973)

Each of the ten roles covers a different aspect of managerial work. The ten roles form an integrated whole but different managers are likely to give greater prominence to different aspects of the job. For example, sales managers tend to spend relatively more time in their interpersonal roles, while production managers tend to give relatively more attention to the decisional roles. Mintzberg found that the amount of time spent in the three sets of roles varied with the level of the manager. For example, first-line supervisory positions are likely to have more decisional roles (at a day-to-day operational level). Senior managers spend more time on interpersonal roles. Middle managers tend to be more occupied with informational roles. Roles will also change with culture and organizational size.

Over the past two decades there has been a change in management practices in many organizations. This shift is based on a greater focus on customers' needs and aspirations, and engaging the commitment of all employees to meet those needs effectively. Typically, the organizational boundaries that used to exist between people are being replaced with internal networks that emphasize team working. Enterprises are being transformed from hierarchical organizations with simple jobs, to less hierarchical, more decentralized and network-oriented organizations with more complex jobs. Charles Handy in his book *The Empty Raincoat* (1990) has written about the future 'Shamrock' organization that would concentrate on fewer full-time people at the core whilst others had to develop 'portfolio' lives, a mix of different bits and pieces of part-time work. However, he felt that people were not being properly prepared for this kind of future.

Culture and language

What happens in one country may not be easily applied in other countries because it is difficult to transplant all the social and cultural conditions that make a particular initiative or innovation a success. In recent years, there have been many attempts to use Japanese management techniques with varying degrees of success. Much management writing is based on what happens in companies in the United States and the United Kingdom, so it is important to be aware of cultural differences and how other countries do things. What works in one context may not work as well in a different context.

When Parker Pen devised advertisements for its ball point pen they were meant to say 'It won't leak in your pocket and embarrass you.' However, in Spanish 'embararzar' means 'pregnant', not 'embarrassed' and the advertisement was translated as 'It won't leak in your pocket and make you pregnant.' In Chinese, the name Coca-Cola was translated as Ke-kou-ke-la to make it sound similar to the original. However, after printing its signs, the company discovered that, in at least one dialect the phrase means 'female horse stuffed with wax'. In Taiwan, the slogan 'Come alive with the Pepsi Generation' was translated as 'Pepsi will bring your ancestors back from the dead.'

However, language is only one aspect of culture. The term refers to complete way of life of a people: the shared attitudes, values, goals and practices that characterize a group; their customs, art, literature, religion, philosophy, and so on; the pattern of learned and shared behaviour among the members of a group.

Organization culture

Organizational culture is an amalgamation of the values and beliefs of the people in an organization. It can be felt in the implicit rules and expectations of behaviour in an organization where, even though the rules are not formally written down, employees know what is expected of them. It is usually set by management whose decisions on policy usually set up the culture of the organization. The organizational culture usually has values and beliefs that support the organizational goals.

The culture of the organization, if it is positive and helpful, can help to motivate staff or at least prevent them from becoming dissatisfied. If the climate does not satisfy the needs of staff, then it will probably cause dissatisfaction and so people would become less inclined to want to work towards achieving organizational goals.

Case study

Homebase is part of the Argos Retail Group, serving 1.5 million customers a year. The culture of an organization is the way that it and its people behave. There are clear guidelines which help to motivate staff. Homebase's values are as follows:

◆ Good service

◆ We put the customer first

◆ We succeed through teamwork

◆ We make it easy

◆ I make a difference

◆ The customer is our No.1 priority

◆ Look after our customers and they will look after us

◆ Everything we do must benefit the customer

◆ Treat customers as you would expect to be treated yourself

◆ Listen to our customers and go the extra mile.

We never want any customer to have a wasted journey. Empowerment means giving greater responsibility to staff. It is a good motivator. Homebase has a teamwork approach with regular meetings called 'huddles' where team-building activities and two-way communication take place. Empowerment encourages independent thinking and decision-making. Staff should think 'I make a difference' and can be rewarded with Homebase Recognition Awards like bronze – star, silver – hero and gold – legend. Gold is the ultimate award with only 16 awarded across the company.

Source: http://www.homebasecareers.com/hb/about/ourmission/customerfocused.html

Organizational culture is the pattern of shared assumptions, values and beliefs that govern behaviour within a particular organization. Assumptions are the shared mental maps or theories-in-use that people rely on to guide their perceptions and behaviours. Beliefs represent the individual's perceptions of reality. Values are more stable, long-lasting beliefs about what is important. They help to define personal and shared perceptions of what is right or wrong, or good or bad, in the world. Organizations have subcultures as well as the dominant culture. Some subcultures enhance the dominant culture, whereas counter-cultures have values that oppose the organization's core values.

Charles Handy (1993) reporting the work of Harrison suggests that organizations can be classified under four cultures. He felt that every organization was a different mix of the same four basic cultures.

Power culture

Handy describes this as the Zeus Culture, after the head of the gods, and is an organization dominated by the personality and power of one person, often the owner. The visual image is of a spider's web with power residing at the centre controlled by a single owner or a small group. Power and influence spread out from a central figure or group. The organization is dependent on the ability and judgement of the central power base.

Role culture

Handy calls this the Apollo Culture, after the god of harmony and order, and represents a culture dominated by rules and procedures. Work within and between departments is controlled formally by procedures, role descriptions, lines of authority and well-defined systems. Matters for decision have to be taken up the line and co-ordination is at the top by the senior management group. Role cultures tend to develop in relatively stable environments. The civil service and the IBM of the late 1980s are examples of a role culture.

Task culture

This is called the Athena Culture, after the warrior goddess. It is a culture that is suited to project work and is typical of consultancies and advertising agencies. The visual image used by Handy is a net with its vertical and horizontal lines and, not surprisingly, network and matrix organizations are examples of this kind of culture. People with the necessary skills, sometimes from different levels of the organization, are brought together to work on specific projects. The teams can be formed for specific purposes, disbanded, re-formed and reconfigured according to the nature of the work that needs to be undertaken.

Person culture

Handy calls this the Dionysius Culture, where the individual has the freedom to develop their own ideas in the way they want such as in an artist's studio, or a traditional university. In this type of culture it is difficult to manage individuals since there is very little structure and individuals are relatively autonomous to carry out their work in the way that they want. Some consultants, barristers' chambers and universities are examples of such a culture. Typically, individuals work on their own but they do find administrative support useful.

Organization culture

Every organization is different from every other one but they are all a mix of the same four basic cultures. The problem is that some organizations get 'stuck' in one of them instead of mixing all four.

Organizational culture is a form of social control and the 'social glue' that bonds people together and helps employees make sense of the workplace. Organizations need adaptive cultures so that employees focus on the need for change and support initiatives and leadership that keeps pace with these changes.

Organizational structure

Organization structure refers to the pattern of relationships among positions in the organization and among members of the organization. The purpose of structure is to divide work among members of the organization and co-ordinate their activities so that they are directed towards achieving the goals and objectives of the organization. Structure defines tasks and responsibilities, work roles and relationships, and channels of communication. It should embrace:

◆ Accountability for the areas of work undertaken by groups and individual members of the organization.

◆ Co-ordination of different parts of the organization and different areas of work.

◆ Effective and efficient organizational performance, including resource utilization.

◆ Monitoring the activities of the organization.

◆ Flexibility in order to respond to changing environmental factors.

◆ Job satisfaction of members of the organization.

An organization's structure is said to have two major components; these include formalization and centralization. Formalization is the extent to which rules and regulations are used to regulate behaviour. This is affected by the size of the organization because a small shop will not have as many rules as a hospital or an oil refinery. Centralization refers to where decision-making powers lie within an organization. In highly centralized organizations, most decisions are made at the highest level of management and these are communicated to other members. In a decentralized organization, the authority to make decisions is more widespread at all levels of management. Most organizations use a variety of these forms and may combine aspects of both for different parts of the organization.

Henry Mintzberg's view of organizational structure

Simple structure

Often a beginning organization, young, small, no sophisticated techno structure in a simple and dynamic context; strong power position of the manager. Company examples of this are landscape gardeners and website designers.

Machine bureaucracy

A clearly defined hierarchy with procedures and exactly defined areas of competence.

They have an impersonal and abstract division of functions and of forming of functions. There is an emphasis on standardization of the work, narrow specialisations and high degree of divisions of labour. There is an emphasis on creating formal relationships. Company examples are manufacturing companies.

Professional organization (also called professional bureaucracy)

Emphasis on standardization of skills, directed to standardized delivery of services to clients. Highly educated personnel with a lot of influence and authority with respect to their own work independently working, few middle management, and a lot of support for the professionals. Company examples include doctors, architects and teachers.

Division organization

The duplicates function as quasi-autonomous units, without the necessity to co-ordinate with the other units. It is exactly prescribed what has to be delegated to the divisions. The co-ordinating mechanism is the output and this output will be thoroughly controlled.

Company examples include Virgin and EasyJet.

Ad-Hocracy

Temporary collaborations, project organization, creative solutions for one-off, unique problems. This structure functions as ad-hoc teams in a throwaway organization. It demands of its workers a high ability to adjust.

Hierarchical models of organizations

- Responsibilities and duties are clearly laid down – strong on formalization and strong on centralization
- Specialized rather than generic roles
- Vertical rather than horizontal communication
- Decision-making is strongly centralized at senior levels of the organization
- Clear lines of accountability between different levels of the hierarchy
- Clear rules of procedure written down.

Collegial models of organizations

- Authority is generally through expertise and knowledge rather than necessarily through position
- Weak on decentralization
- 'Bottom-heavy' – large numbers with the same pay and conditions
- Common goals and purposes – people work together in teams
- Formal and informal opportunities to participate in the development of initiatives
- Employees are autonomous individuals needing a minimum of rules.

Handy's model of organizational culture can be put together with the formalization and centralization dimensions to form a matrix as shown in Figure 1.2.

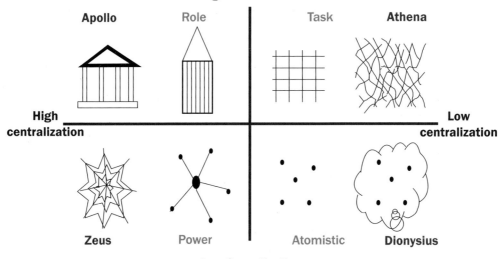

Figure 1.2: Models of organizational culture

The following case study identifies what is needed from an organizational structure and culture.

Case study: Tarmac

Tarmac operates both aggregate and building product operations internationally. It works in a wide variety of countries, including the UK, Poland, Spain, Romania, Turkey, Belgium, Germany, the Czech Republic, France and the Middle East.

Organizations like Tarmac are complex, and need a range of functions to support their efficient operation. These functions must communicate with each other and all share a common vision, linked to the mission statement.

Its mission statement is 'to be the first choice for building materials and services that meet the essential needs for the development of the world in which we live'. The statement is used to underpin corporate values, planning and culture in all of its functions.

Main functions

These are divided into business units, functions and support functions

Business Units	Functions	Support functions
Aggregate Products	Operations	Human resources
Building Products	Technical	Strategy, Marketing and Technical
International Business	Commercial	Finances (inc IT, Procurement & Supply Chain)

Functions

Tarmac's main functions are divided into operations, technical and commercial areas.

Operations

Operations involves managing raw materials, health and safety, the supply chain and production to make sure that customers' needs are met. It also manages the sharing of ideas across the company and sustainable projects. Operations are split into two areas. These are:

◆ Productions operation and management – making the wide range of products and services that Tarmac produces.

◆ Engineering – developing and maintaining the plant and equipment.

Technical

Technical staff solve technical issues, liaise with customers and ensure that products meet national and international quality standards.

Commercial

Commercial staff deal directly with customers and suppliers and take the lead on developing markets. The service aspect of Tarmac's operations is vital in both customer and supplier relationships.

◆ Customers are asked to suggest improvements. Good communication in both directions is seen as key. Tarmac has shown its commitment to customer service through its 'Customer First' programme.

◆ Suppliers are seen as strategic partners with which Tarmac can build long term relationships. This includes expecting the same high standard from suppliers as it promotes itself, including safety, value for money, innovation and ethical working.

Human Resources

HR makes sure that Tarmac's core values are shared across all staff. It carries out recruitment and selection and makes training and development opportunities available.

Strategy

Strategy, strategic development and strategic management are key roles in their own right. Additionally, various managers and levels of management are involved in many different ways. The management team undertakes a review with the aim to improve returns on investment and to identify parts of the company not performing as well as others.

Marketing

Tarmac's marketing team is involved in four key activities to help it achieve its mission statement:

◆ gaining insight into markets and customers' needs

◆ applying this knowledge to inform strategy development and marketing plans, and identify new product ideas and services

◆ managing the Tarmac brand image and external communications through a broad range of communication channels including public relations, advertising, website development, e-marketing, brochures and exhibitions

◆ leading internal communications through the company magazine, newsletters, intranet and conferences.

Technical

Through its technical team, Tarmac constantly looks for new and innovative solutions.

Finance

Any company with sales in the region of £210 million is a big business and therefore relatively complex.

A global business such as Tarmac also requires financial expertise in:

◆ foreign exchange

◆ export credit guarantees

◆ hedging of foreign exchange and interest payments.

Conclusion

Organizations like Tarmac are no longer mere factories or large-scale projects. They are organizations that have serious objectives tied to a commitment to achieving them. Tarmac is also dedicated to operating as ethically as possible.

Working in a multinational and multi-functional environment like Tarmac is varied. There are many departments that work together, e.g. an accountant working with an engineer, who in turn works with a production controller.

Source: www.tarmac.co.uk

Types of organizational structure

Functional

This type of structure groups major functions, for example information, finance, personnel and marketing. The advantages of this kind of structure are that it increases the utilization and co-ordination of groups of people with technical/specialized expertise. It can encourage sectional interests and conflicts, and make it difficult for an organization to adapt to product/service diversification.

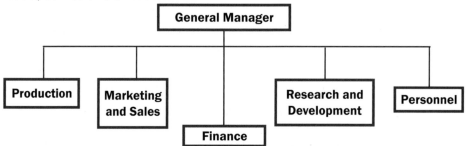

Figure 1.3: Example of a functional structure

Product/service

This is where there is grouping by service/product. For example, in the Health Service, the structure could have groupings around specialisms such as orthopaedic, surgical, psychiatric, and so on, rather than medical, nursing and paramedical functions.

This is an example of a large marketing-oriented organization. In this kind of structure, marketing is represented at board level and a Marketing Manager co-ordinates the marketing activity in the organization.

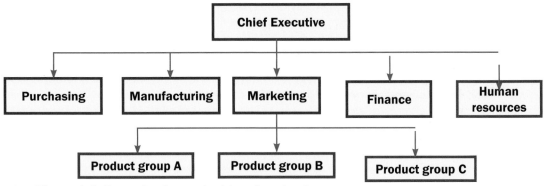

Figure 1.4: Example of a product/service structure

Geographical

A nationalized service develops regions or areas; for example, in the NHS there are District Health Authorities, Health Authorities, Primary Care Groups, Hospital Trusts, Primary Care Trusts and Strategic Health Authorities covering regional and local organizations. Such a structure should mean greater responsiveness to local/regional issues and different cultures, national/state laws, and so on. A potential disadvantage is the possibility of localities/regions conflicting with each other. The following two case studies are both examples of very different organizations with a geographical organization structure.

Case study

The Seventh-day Adventist Church is organized with a representative form of church government. This means that authority in the Church comes from the membership of local churches. Four levels of Church structure lead from the individual believer to the worldwide Church organization.

1 The local church made up of individual believers.

2 The local conference, or local field/mission, made up of a number of local churches in a state, province or territory.

3 The union conference, or union field/mission, made up of conferences or fields within a larger territory (often a grouping of states or a whole country).

4 The General Conference, the most extensive unit of organization, made up of all unions in all parts of the world. Divisions are sections of the General Conference, with administrative responsibility for particular geographical areas.

Source: http://www.adventist.org.uk/

Singapore Airlines uses a geographical structure because it perceives that this makes it easier to customize services to local markets and enable greater responsiveness to customers.

Geographical structures traditionally developed as companies expanded their offerings across territories. There was usually a need to be close to the customer, and to minimize the costs of travel and distribution. Today, the economics of location is important but information technology is making it less important in certain industries. The use of geographical structures depends on the industry. In service industries where the service is provided on-site, geography continues to be a structural basis for many companies. Sales forces and knowledge services like consulting were traditionally managed out of local offices, based on personal relationships and knowledge of the region. However, industry knowledge and expertise are becoming more important. Geographical structures are occurring in industries where the technology is creating a smaller efficient scale and flexible plants, and where customers demand just-in-time delivery.

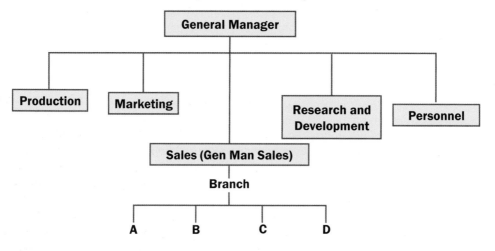

Figure 1.5: Example of a geographical structure

Division structure

This is where the organization is divided into divisions with devolved responsibility for the conduct of their business and financial performance, the grouping of services and/or geography and functionality (but often with functions such as finance, personnel and planning retained at headquarters). This can be suitable for international companies that are highly diversified, working in more than one country, for example, a pharmaceutical company with divisions in each country producing and marketing products developed by the parent company. Divisional structures can be tight or loose, that is, with varying degrees of central control and common service (finance, personnel, computing, etc.). Examples of this kind of structure are General Motors and GEC (United Kingdom).

The divisional structure is often developed in response to the difficulties associated with the functional structure. Divisions or business units are set out, each being regarded as a profit centre. Often the divisions are decided upon according to processes, geographic region, product type, or sometimes a combination of two of these. There is often diversity within a division which can be combated by subdivisions (e.g. product divisions further divided according to geographic region), or by having a functional structure within it. The main advantage is that each division can be managed almost as if it were a separate company, which helps to deal effectively with different products or markets. This division of the company can, however, lead to wasteful duplication of services. This structure is suited to companies which are able to very clearly distinguish between different divisions. When there is confusion as to which division should be responsible for something, it can lead to considerable managerial difficulties. Advantages include improved decision-making, accountability for performance and better co-ordination of functions. The disadvantage is that economies of scale can be lost and rivalry among divisions might be fostered.

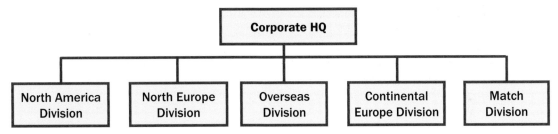

Figure 1.6: Example of a divisional structure

Matrix

To make use of both marketing and product know-how, modern companies establish a matrix organization. It should combine product and marketing know-how in a flat hierarchy that is flexible towards market requirements. The matrix approach involves organizing the management of a task along lines that cross normal departmental boundaries so that the ability of product managers and functional managers to communicate with each other is crucial. For example, a new product development team might be formed from an engineer, a research chemist, a marketing manager and a designer. In the matrix, individuals have two or more 'managers', for example, a sales manager will report to the marketing director and the product manager. Once the project has been finished, the team may be disbanded, with the individual members being drafted into other teams or absorbed back into the organizational structure.

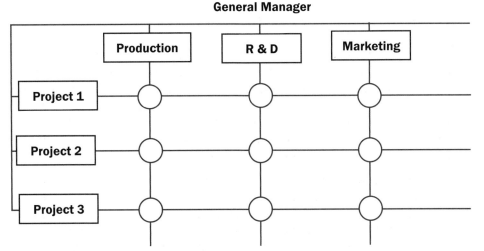

Figure 1.7: Example of a matrix structure

This kind of structure should ensure that the project is better co-ordinated than with four or five departments contributing occasionally. If many different project teams are organized, it gives more people an opportunity to use their capabilities. It emphasizes that project aims are all-important. The disadvantage is that individuals may suffer if both managers make heavy demands on them and there can be conflict between the project leader and the functional leader. Sometimes there can be a failure to provide clear lines of accountability.

Case study: BIC

A company's values should help to determine the way it behaves. BIC's values relate to its products, which are:

◆ **Functional** – designed to perform a specific function well, for example, to draw a line, produce a flame, shave hair. The key to achieving functionality is to adopt the most appropriate design, engineering and technology.

◆ **Affordable** – achieved by using appropriate design, materials production and distribution channels.

◆ **Universal** – capable of being used by anyone worldwide, for example, the ballpoint pen, the pocket lighter, the one-piece shaver.

BIC has three core categories for products, based on a global range, designed for mass appeal. BIC then helps local retailers to select the products that best suit their own customers' needs. Each of the product categories is managed by a Category General Manager, who has the overall responsibility for the marketing, development and manufacturing worldwide. In recent years manufacturing operations have been simplified and super-factories serve very large geographical markets. Product distribution is then organized by continent, with country managers reporting to their continental manager. The organization is a matrix structure based on two main lines of communication:

1   By product category

2   By geographical region.

It means that an employee working, say, in a pen manufacturing plant in France would be accountable both within the Western European division and the stationery category.

Source: http://www.bicworld.com/inter_en/index.asp

From the BIC case study it can be seen that the matrix structure is aimed at maximizing the benefits of strong product expertise with strong operational structures in each major geographical area.

The problem with all forms of organization structure is how to encourage people to feel that not only do they belong to their part of the organization but also to the whole organization. The Singapore Airlines case study provides an example of how managers are encouraged to have a company-wide focus. Do you have any similar policies in your organization? Do they work? Do they cause unanticipated problems, for example loss of expertise?

Modern management theories

The essential features of management and what makes a manager have not changed much since the early writers on management were expounding their theories. Clearly, in the last 100 years there have been major changes in the ways that people relate to each other and expect to be treated. The old style command and control approach where people were expected to do as they were told is inappropriate in most areas of work where people are expected to think for themselves and contribute their ideas on how work should be undertaken. What has changed in management is the emphasis given to different aspects of the managerial role and the evolution of management styles. The hardest part of managing is managing people whether this is employees or customers. Managing people is not easy. However, it can be done successfully and, like any skill, it is something that can be improved with study and practice. Not surprisingly, modern management theories tend to emphasize the relationship aspect of management and, in marketing, the concept of relationship marketing was popularized by Theodore Levitt in 1983. The following section looks at some theories which reflect modern ideas about how managers should manage the relationship aspect of their work.

Emotional intelligence

Emotional intelligence is relevant to organizational development and developing people because the principles provide a way of understanding and assessing people's behaviours, management styles, attitudes, interpersonal skills and potential. It is an important consideration in human resources planning, job profiling, recruitment interviewing and selection, management development, customer relations and customer service. The essential principle is that to be successful requires the effective awareness, control and management of your own emotions, and those of other people. This includes understanding yourself, your goals, intentions, responses, behaviour and understanding others, and their feelings.

The original five 'domains' of emotional intelligence are:

◆ Knowing your emotion

◆ Managing your own emotion

◆ Motivating yourself

◆ Recognizing and understanding other people's emotions.

◆ Managing relationships, that is managing the emotions of others.

More recently Daniel Goleman (1996) has reduced this to four categories:

◆ Self-awareness (emotional self-awareness, accurate self-assessment and self-confidence)

◆ Self-management (emotional self-control, transparency (trustworthiness), adaptability, achievement orientation, initiative, optimism, conscientiousness)

◆ Social awareness (empathy, organizational awareness, service orientation)

◆ Relationship management (inspirational leadership, influence, developing others, change catalyst, conflict management, building bonds, teamwork and collaboration, communication)

By developing their emotional intelligence managers can become more productive and successful and help others to be more productive and successful too. An effective focus on Emotional Intelligence should help to decrease conflict, improve relationships and understanding, and increase stability and harmony.

Four Dimensions of Relational Work

The Four Dimensions of Relational Work by Timothy Butler and James Waldroop was published in the *Harvard Business Review* in June 2004. According to the authors, managers can boost productivity by:

◆ Hiring the right employees

◆ Devising interesting work assignments

◆ Rewarding performance

◆ Promoting career development.

However, there are four types of relational interests and skills that need to be taken into account:

1 Influence

Professionals who enjoy developing and extending their sphere of interpersonal influence. They take pleasure in persuasion, negotiation and the power of holding valuable information and ideas. This is typically associated with roles such as sales managers and marketing managers.

2 Interpersonal facilitation

People that are attuned to the interpersonal aspects of work situations. They focus on others' experiences and behind the scenes they work to keep their colleagues committed and engaged so that projects run smoothly. This is typical for HR managers.

3 Relational creativity

People who are good at forging connections with groups of people through visual and verbal imagery. This is associated with advertising people and brand managers.

4 Team leadership

People with a strong need to interact frequently with other people (team members and customers) to feel satisfied. They thrive on managing and working through teams in busy service environments. This is typical for programme managers and managers of service delivery units.

These four dimensions are not discrete and someone may have skill in two or more areas or in none of them. Scoring high in one dimension may be detrimental to other areas and to certain types of work. All four types of relational work contribute to the bottom line and should be rewarded and different people will be motivated by different non-financial rewards. Managers need to attend to relational work since a strategy is only as good as the people and teams who carry it out.

The PAEI model

The PAEI model by Adizes (2004) describes the four key roles that make up a successful management team:

1   Producer
– The organization must know what results to produce (e.g. become properly positioned in the marketplace and management must ensure that the organization is constantly focused on those results and is driving to produce them). Of the many results an organization must produce, the most basic and most important are those that ensure it serves the needs of its clients.

2   Administrator
– The organization must be efficient and consistent in its production of the appropriate results. It does this by getting organized and establishing system pro-cesses and procedures which it follows.

3   Entrepreneur
– No organization can survive doing the same old thing. It must adapt proactively to changing markets and environments. The entrepreneurial role represents a focus on tomorrow, the empowerment of new ideas and sometimes taking strides to position the organization for a more successful tomorrow.

4   Integrator
– Successful organizations are born twice. Once generally as the outgrowth of one person's vision and commitment and a second time as a team. This role creates shared vision, teamwork and synergy.

When any role is weak the organization will be mismanaged. For example, low on entrepreneurialism means danger tomorrow, little creativity, and opportunity for competitors. Low on Aadministration means lack of control and inconsistency of results.

Insight: Social networking – a new marketing model

The emergence of social communities and the uptake of broadband means that people now spend more time on the Internet than they do reading print media. Globally, there are more than 200 million personal profiles on MySpace, Facebook, Bebo and YouTube. Customers are spending much of their time using a constantly changing mix of media. The media is not only fragmented, it has been for years, now it is completely fluid.

In social networking more than a quarter of people expressly use their sites to influence others. In today's cluttered world, people are increasingly turning away from traditional advertising and towards their peers for information and product recommendations. Social networking sites offer a facility for going beyond Internet pop-up ads, banners and skyscrapers. Here, brands and product owners have an ability to target their recipients based on demographics, psychographics, interests and hobbies. The customer is at the heart of your world, so create conversations, not just annoying pop-ups directing them to your website.

http://www.totalbusiness.org.uk/article

Strategist Gary Hamel and The Future of Management

Gary Hamel believes that developments such as social networking have a lot to offer modern approaches to management. In his book *The Future of Management* (2007) he sets out his view that traditional management models are reaching the end of their useful life and need to be replaced with approaches that exploit the creative potential of technology, particularly the use of the Web. To see the future of management, look to the Internet, open source, free markets and democratic institutions. In a world of accelerating change, the only antidote against irrelevance in the world is the capacity for fast-paced adaptation and change. The challenge is to think about how the new technology of the Web e.g. tagging, social networks, Wikis, etc. can be used to transform the work of management. In so doing, the divide between how people live in and out of the work context will be narrowed:

> *"For the first time since the dawning of the industrial age, the only way to build a company that's fit for the future is to build one that's fit for human beings as well."*

http://www.managementtoday.co.uk/search/article/735140/management-next-move/

Technology makes it possible to organize and manage in new ways. New tools enable the aggregation and amplification of human capabilities in ways that were never before imaginable or possible. The impact of the Web has made it much easier for people to achieve more collectively than they otherwise could individually. In traditional management models the type of people who are wanted are mostly docile, who do as they are told, who follow instructions and do not make mistakes. In the new world, companies are going to have to find ways of encouraging more value, more inspiration and more creativity from the people who work for them. People entering the employment market will be much more technology savvy and have different expectations. The power to allocate resources is going to be much more widely distributed in companies.

The outlines of the 21st-century management model are already clear. Decision-making will be more peer-based and the tools of creativity will be widely distributed. Ideas will compete on an equal footing. Strategies will be built from the bottom up. Power will be a function of competence rather than of position. To become inspired management innovators, today's managers must learn how to think explicitly about the management orthodoxies that bound their thinking — the habits, dogmas, and conceits they've never taken the trouble to challenge. For example, many people believe that it takes a crisis to change a large organization because in most companies the authority to set strategy and direction is highly concentrated at the top. As a consequence, a relatively small group of people at the top can hold the organization's capacity to change hostage to their own personal willingness to adapt and to change.

However, the reality is that most organizations are inflexible and innovation is something that happens at the margins. One of the reasons companies often get caught out is that it is difficult for talent and resources to be quickly reallocated around new opportunities. Existing arrangements have powerful constituencies who want to keep their resources and their people. The single, biggest challenge is to do something with the technology. We have to stop the IT people saying: 'Well, you know, we can't do that. It's going to take six months to get it done. You have to put in an order.' There is a danger that IT has become as much of a wet blanket on innovation as the legal department.

Insight: Half of employers ban Facebook

However, there is always more than one side to a question and using the tools of technology in the workplace is not universally accepted

Half of businesses are restricting employees' access to social-networking site Facebook, due to concerns about productivity and security, according to security vendor Sophos. According to the firm's research, 43 percent of workers polled said their employer blocks Facebook access completely. A further 7 per cent said access is restricted depending on whether it's required for a particular job.

'I think it's a growing concern for employers for a number of reasons,' said Graham Cluley, senior technology consultant at Sophos. 'The most pressing concern at the moment is one of productivity. Some people are spending an inordinate amount of time on non-work-related websites.' It is difficult to tell when people are using a social-networking site when they are sitting at a computer.

The issue of security was also raised by the Sophos research. In a separate poll by the company, 66 percent of workers said they are concerned about colleagues sharing information on Facebook.

Details such as employment history and mobile phone numbers have been found on the site and could be used for identity theft or to launch corporate phishing attacks, security experts warn. Sophos research found 41 per cent of Facebook users are willing to divulge personal information to complete strangers.

Of the 50 per cent of companies that allow access to Facebook, some view it as a valuable networking tool while others are nervous about the possibility of an employee backlash to a ban.

Marketing management

CIM's definition of marketing is 'The management process which identifies, anticipates and satisfies customer requirements profitability.' This process varies depending on factors such as the size of the organization, the sector in which it is located, the type of work role performed by the manager and the career experience that the marketing manager brings with them. Generally speaking, the smaller the organization the more multifaceted are the roles of the marketing manager.

The only certain thing about the term marketing management is that there are hundreds of interpretations of what it includes. The American journal *Marketing Management* describes its focus as:

> Strategic issues that marketing managers face every day. It covers brand management, CRM, product innovation, ROI, marketing effectiveness, and B2B — to help managers keep pace with this rapidly changing field. (2008)

http://www.marketingpower.com/content1050.php

However, not all definitions limit the term to strategic issues. In *Marketing Management* (2006), Philip Kotler and Kevin Lane Keller define marketing management as 'the art and science of choosing target markets and getting, keeping and growing customers through creating, delivering, and communicating superior customer value.'

In this view the scope of marketing management is quite broad and any activity or resource a company uses to acquire customers and manage the company's relationships with them can be considered to be part of marketing management. Thus, marketing management can imply managing all the factors that influence a company's ability to deliver value to customers and, therefore, it should be part of everyone's job description. However, some businesses have a more limited view of marketing and a marketing department may be responsible for little more than developing sales brochures and executing advertising campaigns. In a more limited sense the term 'marketing management' may mean only whatever a marketing department happens to do.

The role of a marketing manager can vary significantly depending on factors such as the size of the organization, its corporate culture, and the type of employment sector in which it is located. For example, in a large consumer products company, the marketing manager may act as the overall general manager of his or her assigned product category or brand with full profit and loss responsibility. In contrast, in a small company there may not be any marketing staff at all, requiring the company to make marketing management decisions on a largely ad-hoc basis.

In larger organizations, especially those with multiple business units, top marketing managers may need to coordinate across several marketing departments and also resources from finance, R&D, engineering, operations, manufacturing, or other functional areas to implement the marketing plan. In order to effectively manage these resources, marketing executives may need to spend much of their time focused on political issues and inte-departmental negotiations.

The effectiveness of a marketing manager may therefore depend on his or her ability to make the internal 'sale' of various marketing programmes equally as much as the external customer's reaction to such programmes.

Marketing management is the application of marketing techniques and the analysis, planning, implementation and control of programmes to create, build and maintain exchanges with target markets. The marketing manager has the task of influencing the level, timing and make up of demand in way that will achieve the objectives of the organization.

The activities that a marketing manager may be involved in are as follows:

◆　　Understanding the economic structure of an industry or sector.

◆　　Identifying target markets.

◆　　Identifying segments within a target market.

◆　　Identifying the marketing strategy which best fits the organization and its goals.

◆　　Marketing research to develop profiles (demographic, psychographic and behavioural) of core customers.

◆　　Understanding competitors and their products.

◆　　Developing new products.

◆　　Establishing environmental scanning mechanisms to detect opportunities and threats.

◆　　Understanding an organization's strengths and weaknesses.

◆　　Auditing customers' experience of a brand.

◆ Developing marketing strategies using the marketing mix variables of price, product, distribution and promotion.

◆ Creating a sustainable competitive advantage.

◆ Understanding where brands need to be in the future, and writing marketing plans to achieve goals and targets.

◆ Establishing management information systems to monitor progress and, if necessary, adjust the process.

One of the main responsibilities of a marketing manager is to identify the target market for products and services, devise strategies and select media that will reach and attract the target market. A marketing manager needs to work with a range of people inside and outside the organization on all aspects of marketing. Inside the company the marketing manager may work with the sales force, promotion manager, product development teams and market research. Outside the company this may involve advertising agencies, consultants and market research organizations. This means that marketing managers need to have good people skills. A marketing manager's responsibilities include large-scale customer relationship management, utilizing skills in customer segmentation, customer loyalty, customer satisfaction, database marketing and direct marketing. These jobs may require market research skills or they may be the responsibility of a market research manager.

Recent changes and future trends in marketing management

Across organizations there is more emphasis on developing marketing strategies rather than just using marketing tactics. The focus is on building brands through a co-ordinated integrated marketing strategy that involves all points of contact between the company and the public.

Other key features of change are as follows:

◆ Recognizing the lifetime value of a customer and retaining existing customers are key driving forces rather than just a short term focus on profit.

◆ Analysing how the whole value chain contributes to meeting the end customers' needs.

◆ Segmenting markets using a range of variables, such as usage rate, loyalty or benefit.

◆ Measuring performance by financial, strategic and marketing metrics instead of a sole emphasis on financial metrics.

◆ Placing an emphasis on satisfying all stakeholders not just shareholders.

◆ Making everyone in an organization undertake some marketing, not just a specialist team.

◆ Making greater use of cross-functional teams rather than functional divisions.

Marketing titles

Marketing titles and positions vary considerably along with the particular responsibilities that accompany them. They span a range of positions, including marketing director, marketing manager, sales manager, advertising manager, promotion manager and public relations manager. A marketing director is responsible for directing overall marketing policy.

Marketing managers work with service or product development, market research and others to develop detailed marketing strategies.

Marketing departments

Some writers argue for the value of the marketing function beyond an organization-wide market orientation, suggesting that they can and should coexist, and that the effectiveness of a market orientation depends on the presence of strong function that includes marketing. In this view the marketing function facilitates the link between the customer and various key processes within the firm. On the basis of an extensive study of managers across a wide range of business types and six different functional affiliations, Moorman and Rust (1999) drew the following conclusions:

1   Marketing is best viewed as the function that manages connections between the organization and the customer. The primary connections may be viewed as the customer–product, the customer–service delivery, and the customer–financial accountability connections.

2   The extent to which the marketing function manages these connections contributes to financial performance, customer relationship performance and new product performance, beyond the impact of an organization-wide marketing orientation.

3   The marketing function can improve its contribution to the firm by expanding its scope beyond the traditional customer–product connection to include more emphasis on service delivery and financial accountability.

Many marketing, sales and services departments still operate in a traditional, fragmented fashion with an assortment of advertising agencies, direct-marketing firms, market research companies, data wizards, PR spin doctors, corporate communications people, brand marketing and more. The traditional marketing structure can be slow moving. Some companies, for example Starbucks, have created fluid marketing organizations to enable them to spot opportunities, allocate resources quickly and move people in and out of teams according to their skills. All members are responsible for identifying opportunities and should receive the tools, the technology and the leadership needed to achieve results.

A marketing department should act as a guide and lead the company's other departments in developing, producing, fulfilling and servicing products or services for their customers.

The marketing department should have a better understanding of the market and customer needs, but should not act independently of product development or customer service.

It is important to gather information from many people within the company. Not only does providing input help the rest of the company understand and support the marketing efforts, it also provides some invaluable insights into what customers want and new ideas that may have slipped past the rest of the company.

For example, customer service personnel will have great insights into customer opinions and needs. Marketing is a team effort and whilst individuals may have their own goals and priorities if they don't also consider the goals of the company it may hinder efforts and make carefully planned marketing efforts fail. A marketing department studies the market and the customers, determines the best way to reach those customers and works with the rest of the company to help determine the new product needs of the market and represent the company in a consistent voice.

Sales and marketing

As mentioned above, sometimes sales and marketing are combined in one department, section or job description so as to avoid the damaging splits that can sometimes occur when they are separate. Sales and marketing teams should work together creating opportunities for new business, identifying new markets and gathering competitive intelligence. However, they may work quite differently. Sales managers direct the efforts of sales professionals by assigning territories, establishing goals, developing training programmes, and supervising local sales managers and their personnel. Sales teams need immediate information to close sales quickly whereas marketing teams are often focused on longer-term results. Differences in approach between sales and marketing can create barriers to sharing information and make it difficult to close sales.

Sales and marketing

A key aspect of developing and maintaining effective relationships with people in other functions and disciplines within the organization is how the sales and marketing functions work together. This is a critical relationship and can take different forms depending on factors such as the size of the company, number of products and services and the geographical reach of the organization. Greater complexity creates greater demands on the co-ordination of activities.

According to IT market analysis firm Aberdeen Group Inc., as much as 80 per cent of marketing expenditures on lead generation are wasted because these efforts are ignored by salespeople. Marketing teams overlook critical input from salespeople regarding customer data and needs. Marketing exists to support sales. A marketing department can develop a good product strategy, but it is up to sales staff to implement it. And when the marketing and sales departments fail to share the right information, the organization suffers.

Salespeople are required to spend the bulk of their time in the field meeting with customers, in the office on the phone, or at the computer. Marketing people are under pressure to solve challenges quickly and creatively while analysing the available information on the competition, the marketplace, the company's products and services, and the target audience. They rarely interact with customers, unless it is through second-party reports from surveys or focus group research. To succeed, marketing people and sales staff both need to be involved in the development of sales and marketing programmes and planning marketing activities – from product launches through promotional campaigns – If the sales force is not involved programmes are likely to fail. Sales staff need to share customer insights as well as candid information on the usability and effectiveness of marketing tools and campaigns.

Source: www.entrepreneur.com

Working across organizational boundaries

Marketing management has an important role in working across organizational boundaries to help prepare managers to develop strategies for their products and services, and incorporate marketing into the corporate strategy. This means that marketing managers need to work with, for example, colleagues from human resources and finance to deal with recruitment and the reward of staff as well as securing and monitoring budgets and expenditure. If a company has introduced a human resource management approach as opposed to a 'personnel' approach, a manager may find that many of the responsibilities that used to belong to the personnel department have been pushed across to line managers.

Case study: Argos

Argos is one of the UK's largest chain stores owned by GUS plc. In the late 1990s, a new boss set out to improve its performance by changing the business culture, that is, the values and beliefs shared across the organization. The new culture he wanted to promote was one that was based on:

◆ Good customer service

◆ Close teamwork

◆ Managers being given more responsibility

◆ All staff showing respect for each other

◆ All staff wanting to compete better and to improve the business.

The sense in which all employees feel that they work for one organization rather than a particular department or function in an organization is a key aspect of organizational success. A feeling that we are 'all in it together' based on good relationships is likely to be a more effective approach than one where there are a lot of internal rivalries and destructive competition.

Case study: Tesco

Tesco has a very flat organization. There are just six levels from the Chief Executive to the front line and there are no great hierarchies or job titles to complicate things and to keep people in their place. At any one time, Tesco is preparing one in ten people to come through, and people do come through from the bottom rung right the way to the top of the organization. There is a very simple management tool that helps keep the company on track. If you went backstage in any store, you would find a big chart on the wall. It is called the Tesco Steering Wheel. Why? It looks like a wheel, and it helps to steer the business. Tesco developed this management tool to emphasise parts of the business that do not figure in traditional accounting, such as corporate responsibility, employee trust and customer relations.

The Steering Wheel divides the business into four different sections – customer, operations, people and finance – which are monitored by managers with a traffic light system: green indicates that targets are being met and red flags up a problem. Each Tesco store has its own individual Steering Wheel. Performance is reported quarterly to the board, and a summary is sent to the top 2000 managers in the company to cascade on to staff. This is a clever way of linking strategy to day-to-day work. It is broken down into a number of performance measures which senior menagement monitors and reviews regularly. It is a simple system, so that every time they go in, staff can see at a glance how they and their store are doing, their particular contribution and the difference it is making. Tesco believes that this very simple idea helps everybody in the business.

http://www.tescocorporate.com/internalcontrolandriskmanagement.htm

Key marketing roles and tasks

Marketing titles and positions can vary among different organizations and sectors of the economy along with the responsibilities that accompany them. The marketing function can also be organized in different ways depending on factors such as size, management philosophy and type of business.

A summary of some of the main marketing management roles is shown below.

Advertising

Advertising managers may oversee account services, creative services and media services departments. Planning and managing advertising campaigns and briefing and managing advertising agencies are a key part of the role, particularly in larger organizations. In larger firms, advertising managers oversee in-house accounts, creative and media services departments. An account executive manages the account services department, assesses the need for advertising and, in advertising agencies, maintains the accounts of clients. The creative services department develops the subject matter and presentation of advertising. A creative director oversees the copy chief, art director and their respective staffs. A media director oversees planning groups that select the communication media – for example, radio, television, newspapers, magazines, Internet or outdoor signs – to disseminate the advertising. Assessing the effectiveness of advertising is often undertaken in conjunction with market researchers. In a small firm, managers may serve as a liaison between the firm and the advertising or promotion agency to which many advertising or promotional functions are contracted out.

Insight: How companies are marketing online

A McKinsey global survey of marketers shows that companies are using digital tools – from websites to Wikis – most extensively for customer service, least in pricing. Two-thirds are using digital tools for product development, almost as many as are advertising online.

Respondents consider online ads to be as useful for brand building as for direct response. Spending is expected to increase on all types of online advertising vehicles over the next three years.

In 2010 just over half of all respondents expect their companies to be getting 10 per cent or more of their sales from online channels – twice as many companies as have hit that mark today. And 11 per cent expect to be spending a majority of their advertising budgets online by then.

Most companies today don't integrate their online and offline marketing efforts; companies that use online tools across the full spectrum of marketing activities are much more likely to do so.

http://www.mckinseyquarterly.com/How_companies_are_marketing_online_A_Mc Kinsey_Global_Survey_2048_

Source: McKinsey Marketing Practice, 2007

Brand management

Brand managers design and enhance the brand image to support the marketing strategy and plans. They identify the issues to explore with consumers about their brand experiences, and they build the research capabilities to gather that intelligence. Then, with help from each of the company's functions, product development, manufacturing, marketing and sales, they translate this learning into specifications for product development and process design. They also fund the development of brand-building capabilities and track the performance of the functions they oversee.

The New Brand Management – Traditional brand managers are responsible mainly for managing promotions, advertising and relations with the trade. Often, they have neither the authority nor the skills to articulate the strategic, cross-functional, long-term perspective that is required. It takes someone with the power, skills, perspective and access to information necessary to drive the development of new products and the design of new business processes. What might the new brand management function look like?

Category Brand Management – Category managers patrol the boundaries and relationships among brands ensuring that a company's brands are not competing with each other.

Corporate Brand Management – A manager must have a holistic perspective on the consumer's experience and on the entire business system that defines a brand. The levels of managerial expertise are higher, and the stakes involved in launching, maintaining and evolving a brand are also higher today compared to the past.

Does this match up with your experience of brand management and brand managers?

Direct marketing

This develops the direct marketing strategy, ensuring it complements the overall marketing strategy. It requires an understanding of the various channels through which customers can be reached directly. It requires building, developing, maintaining and using large databases. Campaign results and trends need to be analysed and presented to senior management. External agencies need to be briefed and managed.

Market research

Virtually every company in the United Kingdom uses market research and it is one way of keeping the company in touch with its customers. It is often commissioned from external agencies. The main purpose of market research is to provide information about actual and potential customers to support marketing decisions. A marketing manager's responsibilities include large-scale customer relationship management, encompassing the key customer approach and utilizing skills in international marketing, customer segmentation, customer loyalty, customer satisfaction, database marketing and direct marketing. These jobs may be very intensive in market research skills or may be the responsibility of a market research manager. Within market research, firms or consulting firms, marketing research managers might specialize in market strategy (including new products and markets), customer satisfaction and customer segmentation (customer care in many consulting firms), service marketing, database or direct marketing and emerging technologies such as e-commerce.

Public relations

Public relations managers conduct publicity programmes and supervise the specialists who implement them. They provide advice about pitfalls to avoid and opportunities to pursue. A key part of the role is to monitor and assess PR activity to ensure that it is effective, for example, evaluating advertising and promotion campaigns to see that they are compatible with public relations efforts. Adverse publicity needs to be managed, and media coverage needs to be archived and distributed to managers so that they are aware of what is being written about the company. Keeping track of competitor activity, as reported in various types of publications, is also an important part of the role. Public relations managers may specialize in a specific area, such as crisis management, or in a specific industry, such as health care. They may produce internal company communications such as newsletters and liaise with financial managers to produce company reports. They can also have a role in drafting speeches, arranging interviews and maintaining other forms of public contact.

Product or service management

The original purpose in creating product or service managers was to have someone who would take full responsibility for an individual product or a portfolio of products or services. This meant that the role was there to ensure that important issues were not overlooked. Product management involves monitoring the performance of a specific product or service group in the marketplace. This makes it possible to avoid having a marketing department that focuses only on a few favoured products or services. The potential benefits of product and service management are:

◆ Expertise and know-how is acquired about all aspects of a product or service group.

◆ New product or service development is better oriented towards market requirements.

◆ A more cost-effective marketing mix for the product group can be developed.

◆ Changes in the marketplace that are relevant for the product or service group can be identified more quickly and acted upon.

◆ Someone is responsible and accountable for the profit generated by the service or product group.

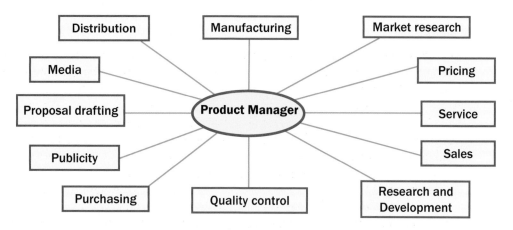

Figure 1.8: The cross-departmental role of the product manager

The product manager needs to co-ordinate all activities relating to the product and service. One of the problems often associated with the role is the lack of direct authority compared to functional department heads. This cross-departmental role means that a product or service manager often needs to work by persuasion rather than through direct authority to champion the product internally as well as externally. A service marketing manager's role is often parallel to that of a product manager. For example, on the service side of a computer manufacturer's business, the ongoing servicing of the product and customer over several years may be a much larger piece of business compared to the initial sale.

Case study: Gillette

Much of Gillette's success comes from its ability to develop the new products that customers want. Its first success was the safety razor, introduced by King C. Gillette in 1901. The challenge for Gillette is not only to continue to make shaving easier by producing efficient tools but also to make it as pleasurable an experience as possible. This means coming up with new ideas and then using modern technology to develop the products.

First mover

Over the years, Gillette has continued to be the first to market with a number of innovations, including the twin-bladed, the pivoting-head and the triple-blade razors. It produced the first razor specifically aimed at women. Being first gives Gillette advantages. The first mover, in a market can often win and keep a major market share before any competition arrives. Gillette is also a leader in many areas of operation which include Duracell batteries, Braun electrical goods, Oral-B dental products and the Right Guard brand.

Researching the market

Market research is used to find out what sort of products consumers might want. This may be either qualitative – such as working with small focus groups; or quantitative – involving large samples and the use of strategies such as questionnaires. After this, Gillette carries out technological research and development to test the viability of the new product. It will also carefully forecast the possible effect of competition and whether the product can be profitable.

Product development

Gillette's research has shown that it needs to develop shaver products for several distinct markets within the world shaving market – worth over £5 billion a year. It has targeted two main markets: systems and disposables.

◆ Systems are where the razor is bought to last with the customer, necessitating buying replacement blades.

◆ Disposables are where the razor is bought for limited use and then discarded.

Both sectors are then further divided into premium (top price and quality) markets and standard markets. Quality is all-important. Whatever market the razor is in, it must produce an efficient, clean shave.

Gillette uses market research to find out what people want and then develops these products. Much of its success comes from being a first mover.

Source: http://www.iabuk.net/en/1/casestudyhandbaggillettevenus.html

Promotion management

Promotion managers direct promotional programmes that combine advertising with purchase incentives in order to increase the sales of products and/or services. They direct promotion programmes combining advertising with purchase incentives to increase sales. In an effort to establish closer contact with purchasers, dealers, distributors or consumers, promotion programmes may involve direct mail, telemarketing, television or radio advertising, catalogues, exhibits, inserts in newspapers, Internet advertisements or websites, in-store displays or product endorsements and special events. Purchase incentives may include discounts, samples, gifts, rebates, coupons, sweepstakes and contests.

Not-for-profit marketing

Marketing is often criticized for promoting materialism and unnecessary consumption. However marketing can be good or bad depending on who uses it and to what use it is put. Many not-for-profit organizations routinely use marketing to further their mission and goals. Not-for-profit organizations have more 'key publics' that they need to consider compared to commercial organizations. These can be classified as:

◆ **Beneficiaries** – People who benefit directly from services.

◆ **Funders** – Funding may be offered and received from many sources. The people providing the funding may have different motives which may raise ethical issues when deciding whether or not to accept funds.

◆ **Internal staff** – These may be mostly volunteers who undertake the work for a variety of reasons and motivations. This can alter the manager–employee relationship and, for example, volunteers may not want to undertake certain tasks. The manager may not have much leverage beyond personal influence and persuasion. This may be an issue if levels of customer service are compromised by an unwillingness to undertake certain tasks.

Social marketing

Social marketing involves the application of marketing principles and techniques, developed in the private sector, to social issues. It has been defined as 'the design, implementation and control of programmes calculated to influence the acceptability of social ideas and involving considerations of product planning, pricing, communication, distribution and marketing research' (Kotler and Zaltman, 1971). They argue that every organization performs marketing-like activities and that marketing has evolved from an economic discipline to one concerned with the relationships of organizations in the broadest sense.

It should be clear that in many organizations, the effective performance of marketing roles requires good working relationships with a wide range of people inside and often outside the organization. This means that there is also a need to develop a range of other social skills as well as marketing expertise. Marketing managers need skills in the following areas:

◆ Communication

◆ Project development

◆ Team leadership

◆ Delegation

- Time management

- Working across organizational boundaries

- Negotiation and conflict resolution

- Project planning

- Managing people

- Performance management

- Coaching.

Case history : The value of marketing in the NHS

Effective marketing is an essential ingredient of a modern healthcare service, regardless of whether it serves NHS or private patients. Those who regard marketing expenditure as an unnecessary diversion of funds away from frontline services should consider four important arguments:

- Patients are increasingly well informed about healthcare matters. Access to the Internet has fostered an appetite amongst the public to obtain a wealth of information about their condition and the latest developments in clinical practice. They expect to participate actively in their programme of care, and not be treated as passive recipients. This demand for information is why organizations as diverse as charities, professional associations, local government and trade unions will all commit resources to marketing activity.

- The Choice agenda has empowered patients, and their advisers, with the ability to select where they wish to be treated for their ailment. This restructuring has introduced a degree of competition between providers, and those who are not able to engage with a sufficient number of patients will experience financial and operational consequences.

- Providers that fail to communicate with their customers will not accurately appreciate their needs and expectations. This will lead them to offer inappropriate services, inadequately attuned to what their customers require. Effective marketing is not the production of glossy ads or catchy lyrics – it is fundamentally about achieving insights into needs and expectations in order to shape an organization that is capable of meeting and exceeding them.

- Marketing can be a loaded word in the modern culture, and the activity is perhaps best considered as communication. Healthcare services have a greater complexity of stakeholders than almost any other type of body – patients, relatives, referring clinicians, SHAs, PCTs, voluntary groups, political and community leaders and theDepartment of Health. Each of these is a legitimate audience for communications. In the modern world, where individuals are exposed to hundreds of branded messages every day, these stakeholders will all expect communications to be clear, accessible, appealing, and professional.

At the present time, the 'marketing mix' that is employed contains nine elements:

- Market research

- Face-to-face engagement
- Brand and visual identity
- Open days
- Advertising
- Electronic media
- Brochures and leaflets
- Sponsorship
- Public relations.

The first two categories relate to understanding needs and expectations; the rest relate to proactive communications. Forward-minded organizations will also construct feedback loops so that activity can be continuously improved in light of comments and reaction from stakeholders.

http://www.netcareuk.com/netcare/uploads/mediadiscussion/NHSMarketingBrochure.pdf

Activity 1.2

What information is needed for effective marketing management in your selected organization? In some ways market research is easy, as it is most often conducted under the control of the marke,ting function. However vast amounts of information are collected by modern business systems (e.g. electronic point of sale for supermarkets) and in other parts of the organization. Review how information collected outside of the marketing function is used in it. How appropriate is the nature and quality of the information? Is it received in time to integrate with the organization's marketing research? Do the 'part-time' marketers appreciate their role in this marketing process?

Corporate Social Responsibility

The values and standards of companies is of interest to a wide variety of stakeholders, for example, consumers and employees, investors and legislators. A MORI poll found that four-fifths of the public believe that large companies have a moral responsibility to society – a view with which many industrialists would probably concur. But the majority of the public also believe that large companies 'don't really care' about the long-term environmental and social impact of their actions. (Reputation and Corporate Responsibility, MORI, January 2003)

In recent years, companies have taken the offensive in promoting themselves as socially responsible organizations. It is now commonplace for large companies to report on this aspect of their work as a major aspect of how they want to communicate their values to their various stakeholders. However, there are also sceptics who doubt the real intentions of organizations as outlined in a report from Christian Aid.

Insight: The true face of corporate social responsibility

Christian Aid calls for laws to make multinational companies meet basic social and environmental standards in poor countries.

Christian Aid is calling on the politicians to take responsibility for the ethical operation of companies rather than surrendering it to those from business peddling fine words and lofty sentiments. The image of companies working hard to make the world a better place is too often just that – a carefully manufactured image – says 'Behind the mask: the real face of corporate social responsibility', a new report from Christian Aid. Its target is the burgeoning industry known as corporate social responsibility – or CSR – which is now seen as a vital tool in promoting and improving the public image of some of the world's largest companies and corporations.

'Some of those shouting the loudest about their corporate virtues are also among those inflicting continuing damage on communities where they work – particularly poor communities', says Andrew Pendleton, senior policy officer at Christian Aid and author of the report. Legally binding regulation is now needed to lessen the devastating impact that companies can have in an ever-more globalised world. 'Behind the mask: the real face of corporate social responsibility' demonstrates how over the past decade companies have used an image of social responsibility to oppose regulation and convince governments in rich countries that business can put its own house in order. The report concludes that the voluntary approach to improving corporate behaviour is wholly inadequate and that international legally binding standards are now needed.

www.christian-aid.org.uk/indepth/0401csr/index.htm

Sometimes managers make decisions which conflict with their own or society's values because of what they see as the pressures of the business world. Doing the right thing is one of the most crucial questions that managers have to face. Is it a manager's job just to maximize profits? Or should managers be concerned with using their organization to carry out other social responsibilities such as supporting education?

Increasingly, businesses are seeing that behaving responsibly *is* good for business and the public relations benefits can be great if a company is able to secure media coverage for its initiative. Obviously, businesses do want to claim that what they do is driven by a desire to be seen to be behaving ethically and responsibly and, to that end, there is no doubt that some people are beneficiaries of these kind of actions.

Case study: Amway

In 2005 Amway UK launched a three-year corporate partnership with UNICEF UK, having already established a relationship at Euro-pean level. Under their pledge to 'Help children live better lives', Amway UK is now working to raise funds for immunisation programmes around the world. All Independent Business Owners' (IBOs) donations and profits from the sale of greetings cards and gifts online go directly to UNICEF. Money is also being raised by more than 100 Amway employees. Amway has developed its Global Cause strategy to raise around £350,000 a year every year until 2010 to help combat children's diseases. In 2005 it became an official corporate partner of UNICEF, setting up a close long-term relationship.

The strategy has the interests of Amway's various stakeholders in mind:

- Amway: it helps to grow the business
- IBOs: want Amway to be a caring organization
- Customers: want the businesses they deal with to be responsible
- Staff: want to work for a responsible organization
- UNICEF: want to work with a business that shares their values and helps them raise funds
- Amway supports UNICEF through sales of items such as greetings cards, wrapping paper and children's toys. In addition, its staff are involved in fund-raising events.

Clear communication helps the strategy to run smoothly. This includes: face-to-face communication – regular meetings between the various partners; printed material: public relations and online.

Source: http://www.thetimes100.co.uk/studies/all-studies--amway--11.php

Summary

- Marketing departments can be organized by:
    - Function
    - Geographic area
    - Products or brands
    - Matrix
    - Corporate divisions
    - Global aspects.
- A marketing manager needs to work with a range of people inside and outside the organization on all aspects of marketing.
- The marketing manager is involved in a wide range of activities, particularly in small organizations.
- The marketing function is organized in different ways in different organizations, depending on factors such as size, geographical spread, management philosophy and type of business.
- A matrix structure is suited for collaborative working focused on projects that cross normal departmental boundaries.
- Managing effectively requires knowing yourself, and effective managers understand how their behaviour affects others and are able to adapt their style to the context in which they work. Personal management skills are common to all management jobs at whatever level.

Further study

Kotler, P. (2005), *Marketing Management: Analysis, Planning, Implementation and Control*, Harlow: Financial Times/Prentice Hall, 12th Edition

Websites

Management Learning website: http://managementlearning.com/art/culttsoc/index.html

Reports, books, newsletters or websites on permission-based e-mail marketing:

www.email-marketing-reports.com/report_imt1.htm

Connected in Marketing – dedicated to e-marketing: www.cim.co.uk/ece/cfml/index.cfm

What's New in Marketing Newsletter? www.wnim.com/issue13/pages/index.htm

Free articles: www.marketingprofs.com/intro.asp

Free marketing articles: www.bizweb2000.com/articles.htm

Hints and tips

◆   Where possible, include examples from the marketing press, textbooks, journals and the Internet to support your examination answers. This is one way of demonstrating your wider knowledge and understanding to the senior examiner.

◆   Marketing is a practical business so examples that illustrate the way that theory relates to practice will demonstrate your broader knowledge and understanding of marketing.

◆   Reports from examiners are published regularly and are available to students. These reveal that there are similar concerns and problems occurring frequently across all subject areas. The most common mistakes are caused by a lack of exam technique and examination practice.

  ◆   **Not answering the question set** – examiners are looking for both relevant content and its application in an appropriate context. You must be able to work flexibly with the material you have studied, answering different questions in different ways, even though the fundamental theory remains the same.

  ◆   **Presentation and style** – These skills are important to a marketing practitioner. The examiners expect work to be presented in a well-written, professional manner. 'Report' style, using subheadings and indented numbering for points, and so on looks much more credible than an essay style. This approach allows you to break the work up, highlight the key points, and structure your answer in a logical way. Take care with your grammar and use of language; small errors can change the sense.

  ◆   **Timing** – Read the instructions carefully, identify what has to be done and how the marks are allocated. Spread your time proportionately to the mark allocation. Allow a few minutes at the end to read through your work.

  ◆   **Failure to develop answers** – This was often a symptom of insufficient time planning and management.

♦ **Failure to structure answers and/or leaving gaps in the treatment of the issues** – Just a few minutes spent quickly 'roughing out' a question plan will provide vital perspective to ensure focus on the specifics of the question, developing planned cover of all the relevant issues. The danger of rushing into the answer without planning is that the development can drift away from the specific focus required. Also some key issues can be overlooked. Thus important gaps are left in the answer.

♦ Unless otherwise stated, all answers are required in report format style. However, lengthy introductions, title pages and contents listings for every question and sub-question are not required. They can waste valuable time. Conversely, focused tables and context developed diagrams are welcomed.

Sample questions

December 2005, Question 3

What management actions can JJ's take to change the organization from a product focused philosophy to a marketing orientation?

'@ Medi Wrap' is to be launched in 12 months time in 'New Territory'. What project management tools and actions would you recommend to ensure a trouble-free launch of this new product?

(Total 25 marks)

December 2004, Question 5

Pinnacle's new website will be launched at a major photographic exhibition in six months time. What project management tools and actions would you recommend to ensure that all necessary activities were undertaken to ensure a trouble-free exhibition launch?

(Total 25 marks)

Bibliography

Adizes, I (2004) *Managing Corporate Lifecycles*, New York: Prentice Hall

Boddy, D. (2002) *Management: An Introduction*, Financial Times/Prentice Hall, 30–32

Butler, T. and Waldroop, J. (2004) Understanding "People" People, Harvard Business Review, June

Christopher, M., Payne, M. and Ballantyne, D. (2001) *Relationship Marketing: Creating Shareholder Value*, Oxford: Butterworth-Heinemann

ESCAP: Guidelines for Development of Railway Marketing Systems and Procedures www.unescap.org/tctd/pubs/marketingtoc.htm

Goleman, Daniel P.(1996) *Emotional Intelligence*, London Bloomsbury

Gronroos, C. (1994) From marketing mix to relationship marketing: Towards a paradigm shift, *Management Decision*, 32 (2), 4–20

Hamel, G. with Breen, B. (2007) *The Future of Management*, Boston MA: Harvard Business School Press

Handy, C. (1976) *Understanding Organizations*, Harmondsworth: Penguin

Handy, C. (1990) *The Empty Raincoat*, Random House Business Books

Handy, C. (1991) *The Age of Unreason*, Random House Business Books

Harrison, R. and Stokes, H. (1992) *Diagnosing Organizational Culture*, San Francisco: Pfeiffer

Handy, C. (1993) *Understanding Organizations*, New York: Oxford University Press

Kohli, A.K., and Jaworski, B.J. (1990) Market Orientation: The Construct, Research Propositions, and Managerial Implications, *Journal of Marketing*, 54 (April), 1–18

Kotler, P and Keller, K.L. (2006), *Marketing Management*, Prentice Hall; 12th edition

Kotler, P., Zaltman, G. (1971) Social marketing: An approach to planned social change, *Journal of Marketing*, 35, 3–12

Kumar, Nirmalya (2002) The path to change, *Financial Times*, 6 December

Levitt, T. (1983) *Marketing Imagination*, The Free Press

McKinsey, Creating leading-edge marketing organizations, www.mckinsey.com/practices/marketing

Mintzberg, H. (1973) *The Nature of Managerial Work*, London: Harper & Row

Parasuraman, A., Zeithaml, V.A. and Berry, L.L. (1988) SERVQUAL: A multiple item scale for measuring consumer perceptions of service quality, *Journal of Retailing*, 64, 13–37

Moorman, C, and Rust, R.T. (1999) The role of marketing, *Journal of Marketing*, 63, 180–197

Peters, T. and Waterman, R.H. (1988) *In Search of Excellence*, New York: Harper & Row

Sedloff Orton, L. (2002) Growing your marketing department into a knowledge management team: Aim to hire assets not overheads, www.llrx.com/features/market.htm

Unit 2

Recruiting the team

Learning objectives

1.1 Describe the functions, roles of marketing managers and typical marketing jobs and the nature of relationships with other functions in organizations operating in a range of different industries and contexts. This objective was also partly covered in Unit 1.

1.3 Identify and explain the key challenges of managing marketing teams in a multinational or multicultural context.

1.4 Explain how you would use the techniques available for selecting, building, developing and motivating marketing teams to improve performance (1.4). This last objective is partly dealt with in this unit and also in Unit 3. In this unit, the focus is more upon selecting the team.

Statement of Marketing Practice

Lc.1 Manage a marketing team.

Lc.2 Maintain relationships with other functions and disciplines within the organization.

Lc.3 Encourage and help others to develop their competencies relevant to a marketing role.

Key definitions

Cultural empathy – An understanding of and a true feeling for a culture.

Cultural environment – Institutions and other forces that affect society's basic values, perceptions, preferences and behaviours.

Cultural universals – Cultural characteristics and attributes that are found in a wide range of cultures: that is, features that transcend national cultures.

Culture – The set of basic values, perceptions, wants and behaviours learned by a member of society from family and other important institutions.

Groupthink – A term to describe one process by which a group can make bad or irrational decisions. In a groupthink situation, each member of the group attempts to conform his or her opinions to what they believe to be the consensus of the group. This results in a situation in which the group ultimately agrees on an action which each member might normally consider to be unwise.

> **ICT** – Information and Communications Technology
>
> **International division** – A form of international marketing organization in which the division handles all of the firm's international activities. Marketing, manufacturing, research, planning and specialist staff are organized into operating units according to geography or product groups, or as an international subsidiary responsible for its own sales and profitability.
>
> **International market** – Buyers in other countries, including consumers, producers, resellers and governments.
>
> **Strategic alliance** – A formal relationship, short of a merger or acquisition, between two companies, formed for the purpose of gaining synergies because in some aspect the two companies complement each other.
>
> **Team selling** – Using teams of people from sales, marketing, production, finance, technical support, and even upper management to service large, complex accounts.

It needs to be borne in mind that in different cultures there may be different expectations about how people should relate to each other in the workplace and certainly different legislation that governs issues such as, for example, the employment relationship, equality and diversity. Most of the examples used throughout this book relate to North America and Europe. When reading the book you should always ask yourself how what is written matches your own experience and working context.

Teams

Introduction

A number of factors are contributing to an increasing emphasis on teams, including the increasing availability and affordability of Information and Communication Technology (ICT) and demands for making work more flexible by reducing its dependence on location. Many organizations have flattened their structures and delegated responsibility in order to cut costs and to utilize the skills of the workforce more effectively. Shifting authority and responsibility down the organization allows teams to take over roles and functions previously performed by management. There are also changes in relationships – among employees, between employees and employers, and between all kinds of organizations and their customers and business partners. Companies that formerly developed products solo are now forming development alliances with suppliers, customers, contractors, consultants and even competitors.

Why teams?

The complexity of most of the processes in an organization places them beyond the control of any one individual, and the only efficient way to tackle process improvement or redesign is through the use of teamwork.

Teamwork has many advantages:

◆ A greater variety of complex issues can be tackled by pooling expertise and resources.

◆ Problems are exposed to a greater diversity of knowledge, skill and experience.

◆ The approach boosts morale and ownership through participative decision-making.

◆ Improvement opportunities that cross departmental or functional boundaries can be more easily addressed.

◆ The recommendations are more likely to be implemented than if they come from an individual.

Employees will not engage in continuous improvement activities without commitment from senior managers, a culture for improvement and an effective mechanism for capturing individual contributions.

Teamwork must be driven by a strategy, have a structure and be implemented thoughtfully and effectively.

When properly managed and developed, teamwork improves processes and produces results quickly and economically through the free exchange of ideas, information, knowledge and data. It is an essential component of a total quality organization, building trust, improving communication and developing a culture of interdependence, rather than one of independence.

People development and teamwork

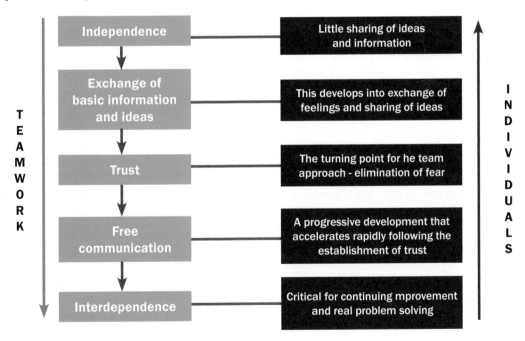

Source: www.businessballs.com/dtiresources/TQM_development_people_teams.pdf

Most teams are created to increase productivity, maximize co-operation and communication, and minimize conflict. Work teams, which are part of larger systems like managerial or production systems, perform a wide array of activities within the organization. Teams often have well-defined boundaries, and norms or rules governing interaction and behaviour.

The internal leader may be a full-time team member. Management may appoint an external leader, who serves as co-ordinator, facilitator or mentor. The leadership role may also be shared by several people, or the leader may perform several functions.

Insight: Four types of leader

There are two main leadership drives:

Dominance – Desire to dominate (manage) other people.

Eminence – Desire to achieve status through competition based on ability.

These two drives can be combined in four ways, a nd each combination creates a different type of leader.

Type	Dominance drive	Status drive
A: Dominant Boss	High	High
B: Ambitious Professional	Low	High
C: Informal Influencer	high	Low
D: Reluctant Leader	low	Low

Type A – Dominant bosses have the desire to dominate plus the desire to achieve status through competitive striving. Included here are business leaders like Bill Gates and Steve Jobs.

Type B – Ambitious professionals have little interest in dominance over others. They are leaders because they possess some technical ability.

Examples: Faceless technocrats running investment banks and science-based firms, or colourful creative people who lead media and arts organizations but have no real interest in managing people.

Extreme A's are often followed by B's because B's are not so pushy.

Type C – Influencers do not want to compete because they fear failure. But their high dominance drive makes them want power. So they gravitate to roles in which they have power without responsibility.

They can be cheerleaders for the boss or rebellious dissidents who sit on the sidelines working the crowd against him.

They only become leaders if there is little risk attached (e.g. in organizations which are run collectively or where the leadership role merely represents a higher power).

Type D – Reluctant leaders prefer a safe, rewarding niche, free from competition. They become leaders when no one else is available or when the leader role confers little status or power.

They can also come to power via natural succession in a family firm but when they do they are usually awful.

Reluctant leadership is also common in bureaucracies in which people automatically inherit the role via rules of seniority.

Source: Recruiting.com www.recruiting.com/recruiting/2004/12/hrfont_colorred_2.html.

Teams differ in many ways, including size, purpose, type of work performed, structure, leadership, influence and decision-making ability.

Types of teams include:

◆ Natural work group

◆ Management

◆ Project improvement

◆ Process redesign or re-engineering

◆ Cross-functional, for example, design and production include people of various skill levels from throughout the organization

◆ New product and service design teams.

More and more work is performed in new ways, so as to exploit the possibilities of co-operation across national boundaries and time zones. Many tasks are too complex for individuals to handle alone and teams are potentially more effective in solving problems and learning more quickly than individuals. When a team works well, it can improve problem-solving, become more creative and generate acceptance, support and commitment. However, teams can also be inefficient, indecisive, frustrating and, ultimately, inferior to what a collection of individuals working on their own can accomplish. Equally, some people are more comfortable working on their own than they are in a group.

Teams can be used as integrating mechanisms that co-ordinate and integrate information across an organization by enabling co-ordination and integration, or as self-contained units (self-managed or autonomous work teams, self-directing teams) that manage aspects of an organization's work.

In knowledge-based organizations both integrating teams and self-contained teams are common and cross-functional project teams are needed to integrate the work of different functions while being as self-contained as possible.

As mentioned previously, a key part of the Marketing Management in Practice unit is working within a team to develop the marketing plan and managing teams implementing the plan by undertaking marketing activities and projects. Unit 5 of this book looks at Project Management in detail but one of the key aspects of project management is the recruitment of a team or teams of people who are able to work together effectively.

Effective product and process development requires the integration of specialized capabilities. This can be achieved, with varying advantages and disadvantages with various team structures.

Clark and Wheelwright (1997) identify four types of project teams:

1   **Functional teams** – Members are grouped by discipline, working under the direction of a functional manager. Primary responsibility for the project passes sequentially from one function to the next. An advantage of this type of organization is that managers control resources and performance in their functional areas, and team members bring specialized expertise to the project. A disadvantage is that a task must be subdivided according to functions and team members may be judged independently of the success or failure of a project.

2   **Lightweight teams** – Like a functional team but with a liaison representative. Members stay in their functional areas but each function designates a liaison person to represent it on, for example, a project co-ordinating team to co-ordinate different function's activities. There is likely to be improved communication and co-ordination compared to a functional team but project leaders may have no real control.

3   **Heavyweight teams** – In these, the project manager has direct access to and responsibility for the work of all those involved in the project, managed by leaders who may have a higher status than the functional managers. An advantage of this type of team is the integration of a project that may require fewer members compared to a more traditional team. However, it may conflict with the functional organization and be seen as an 'elite' group, alienating the rest of the organization.

4   **Autonomous team structure** – this includes teams often called 'tiger teams', in which individuals from different functional area, are formally assigned, dedicated, and co-located to the project team. Tiger teams tend to be very focused but it can be difficult to integrate their 'solutions' into the 'parent' organization.

Tiger teams can be used in various aspects of marketing but are particularly suited to customer-focused initiatives where quick solutions may be needed. The following extract provides an example of its use in the context of Tiger teams.

Insight

Don't give up on the Hubble Space Telescope and its stunning cosmic images just yet. After NASA's reluctant decision to let one of the most productive and well-known astronomical instruments in history die early, scientists are showing that one of the best inspirations is desperation.

Stunned by the decision, 'tiger teams' of scientists and engineers have been appointed to find technological loopholes in the bad news. The search is on for new power-conserving procedures to extend battery life, ways to keep the telescope pointing at targets with as few as two gyroscopes (two of six are already kaput), and, most daring, 'teleoperated' service robots. Sent on unmanned rockets, they would be controlled from the ground like imitation astronauts to replace batteries and gyros and upgrade cameras and detectors.

But a reprieve is what astronomers want most. With one more round of service plus clever conservation, Hubble might operate until 2011 or longer, says Bruce Margon, the telescope institute's science director. That's when, if current plans hold, the even larger James Webb Space Telescope should be ready to pick up Hubble's torch. 'Do we really want to go several years with no space telescope at all?' he asks.

Source: http://www.nasa.gov/home/hqnews/2005/aug/HQ_M05133_tiger_teams.html

Effective project management requires planning and co-ordination. In vertical management, employees are organized along top-down chains of command and may have little opportunity to work with other functional areas. In horizontal management, work is organized across various functional groups that work with each other. This should lead to improved co-ordination and communication among employees and managers. When people are able to work horizontally and vertically there are more opportunities to understand the operations of other functions and how they relate to each other. The vertical aspects of organizations can limit the ability of a project manager to pull together the horizontally integrated teams that are often important for project success. A key characteristic of a team is that the members have a common purpose.

The team ideal

Robbins and Finley (2001) in their provocatively entitled book *Why Teams Don't Work: What Went Wrong and How to Make It Right* maintain that in the 1980s the functional or specialist team worked in its organizational 'silo' in parallel rather than with other teams. These teams included, for example, accounting, finance, advertising and marketing who spoke their own functional language and did not really communicate across their functional boundaries. In contrast, today there is more variety and a cornucopia of different types of teams. For example, there are teams where everyone has the same skills but people perform different tasks, teams where people with different expertise each tackle a different part of a task, functional teams, cross-functional teams, inter-organizational teams and intra-organizational teams. Some teams work together for long periods of time while others form for a week or two then dissolve. There are self-managed teams, leader-led teams and teams where leadership is distributed within the team so that everyone leads. Clearly, what is meant by the concept of a 'team' can vary considerably and cover various organizational arrangements. However, teams are not the answer to all organizational ills and if used inappropriately they can mean that less, rather than more, is achieved.

Insight

The great sin of the age of teaming is to ask teams to do everything. A job done by a team is better than a job done by a single individual. You get that synergy going, you know, all that shared information. The truth is that teams are inherently inferior to individuals, in terms of efficiency. If a single person has sufficient information to complete a task, he or she will run rings around a team assigned the same task. There are no hand-offs to other individuals. No misunderstandings or conflicting cultures. Beware. Teaming can be bad. Sometimes managers prefer teaming because it spreads accountability around, makes blaming more difficult. Or it means hand-picking team members. The saddest thing we hear is 'We were told we had to do everything as a team.' The CEO is all ga-ga about teams, so now unless you do something as a team you're a pariah in your organization. It is team tyranny and people resent it.

Source: Robbins and Finley (2001)

Types of marketing teams

Examples include the following:

Sales teams which can consist of one or a mix of the following:

◆   Field sales people

◆   Sales engineers

◆   Sales technicians

◆   Office sales staff

◆ Sales manager

◆ Export sales force.

Marketing research teams which can consist of one or a mix of the following:

◆ Market analysts

◆ Market researchers

◆ Interviewers.

Product management teams which can consist of one or a mix of the following:

◆ Research and development engineers

◆ Design engineers.

Activity 2.1

Identify key stakeholders and their expectations.

◆ Stakeholders in this exercise are individuals and groups with whom you work to achieve your work objectives. This can include other teams in the organization, for example, support functions such as finance, HR or suppliers.

◆ Who are your key stakeholders and what do you need to do together to produce your product, service, and so on?

◆ What are your key stakeholders' expectations of your team and how do you know?

◆ What is your team's purpose and role in the organization?

◆ What products and/or services do you provide?

◆ What skills and capabilities does your team contribute to customer value?

◆ Who are your customers?

Even if teams are comparatively inefficient, they should be more effective than individuals because they enable the collective talents of people to be brought to bear on issues, problems and situations. They can also ensure that the organization presents a consistent and coherent face internally and externally and that plans are developed to make the best use of organizational resources. There are synergies that can be derived from working together that can produce efficiency and effectiveness. Few people could deny that a marketing campaign is more effective if people in the organization are working together to ensure that it is integrated with schedules for production, operations, sales and merchandising.

All parts of an organization should have a common focus and work together purposefully to pursue the organization's overall objectives. In practice, however, relationships between different parts of an organization can be characterized by rivalry and distrust. This can affect all types and sizes of organization and give rise to what is often referred to euphemistically as 'office politics', or 'the informal and sometimes emotion-driven process of allocating limited resources and working out goals, decisions and actions in an environment of people with different and competing interests and personalities' (Dobson and Dobson, 2000). Sometimes conflict arises from differences in view about what is in the organization's best interests; sometimes it is from trade-offs between what is seen to be best for the organization as a whole against what is best for a particular part of it and sometimes it arises from stereotypes and prejudices about the relative worth of different functional specialisms. In organizations staffed by professionals, the conflict can sometimes occur around who feels that they know best about what is in the interests of the customer. The customer might be a patient, a parent, a client or other service-user but in the tradition of paternalistic public services, the professional may feel that they know much better what is best rather than managers, customers or clients.

The wisdom of cross-functional teams

Don H. Lester, an operations manager for Hoechst, developed criteria for staffing cross-functional new product teams.

◆   What team leadership style and level of expertise is required?

◆   What team member skills and expertise are needed?

◆   What is the level of interest in the particular product concept? Is there a champion? Is there a high level of ownership and commitment?

◆   Motivation – What will motivate individuals to want to take part in the product development project?

◆   Diversity of team members – The greater the diversity, the greater the range of viewpoints represented.

Source: Lester (1998)

The role of the manager in a team

The role of the manager is important in creating, co-ordinating and maintaining the team. This requires an understanding of the specific skills and abilities of team members, and their ways of working. Managers need to understand their staff and use their influence over the way the team works, transforming them from a group of individuals to a team that is able to work together. It is also the manager's responsibility to oversee the assimilation of new recruits into a team.

Most teams are created to increase productivity, maximize co-operation and communication, and minimize conflict. Work teams that are part of larger systems like managerial or production systems, perform a wide array of activities within the organization. The manager may be a full-time team member. Management may appoint an external leader, who serves as co-ordinator, facilitator, mentor, encourager, cheerleader, or consultant, but not as a foreman or supervisor. The management role may also be shared by several people, or the manager may perform several functions. Teams differ in many ways, including size, purpose, type of work performed, structure, leadership, influence and decision-making ability. Figure 2.1 gives an indication of the range of stakeholders with whom a product manager may need to interact, although the extent to which this might be called a meaningful team is questionable. More realistically, it is likely that the product manager and his or her team need to relate these to other teams in the organization and/or, the product manager forms a middle management team with other managers from other functions.

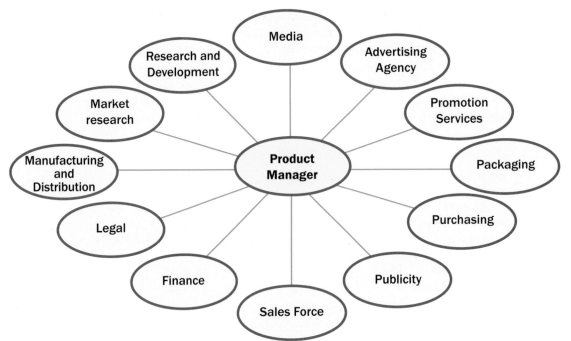

Figure 2.1: The product manager and other stakeholders

Relations between teams in an organization

Managers see teams as a way of accomplishing some or all of the following:

Providing a structure where people with a range of technical skills, functional specialisms and different perspectives can come together, exchange ideas, learn from each other and, ultimately, provide a better service to internal and external stakeholders.

Providing a forum in which issues or problems can be aired and dealt with.

Encouraging acceptance and understanding of a problem and a proposed solution.

Enable people to develop their roles.

Each part of an organization can have an impact on customer satisfaction. If it has a marketing orientation, all departments should focus on the customer or service-user and work together to meet needs, wants and expectations. An organization with a marketing orientation sees the needs of customers and consumers as central to everything and, depending on size, may have something like the following structural characteristics:

Activity	Function
Identifying customer/consumer needs and wants	Marketing research
Developing products to meet customer/consumer needs and wants	R&D and production
Deciding on the value of the product to customers	Pricing (sales and marketing)
Making the product available to customers at the right time and place	Distribution
Informing customers/consumers of the existence of the product and persuading them to buy it	Promotion

However, there are other orientations and there is little agreement on how much influence and authority marketing should have over other departments. Kotler (2003) has identified the differences and conflicts of interest that can exist between different functions in an organization. Left to their own devices, departments can interpret organizational goals from their own viewpoint rather than the interests of the whole organization. There is no suggestion that the following descriptions are typical of all organizations but they do occur in some contexts. They should be thought of as worst-case scenarios.

Sales and marketing

As mentioned above, sometimes sales and marketing are combined in one department, section or job description so as to avoid the damaging splits that can occur when they are separate. Sales and marketing teams should work together creating opportunities for new business, identifying new markets and gathering competitive intelligence. However, they may work quite differently. Sales managers direct the efforts of sales professionals by assigning territories, establishing goals, developing training programmes, and supervising local sales managers and their personnel. Sales teams need immediate information to close sales quickly whereas marketing teams are often focused on longer-term results. Differences in approach between sales and marketing can create barriers to sharing information and make it difficult to close sales.

Sales and marketing

A key aspect of developing and maintaining effective relationships with people in other functions and disciplines within the organization is how sales and marketing work together. This is a critical relationship and can take different forms depending on factors such as the size of the company, number of products and services and its geographical reach. Greater complexity creates greater demands on the co-ordination of activities.

According to IT market analysis firm Aberdeen Group Inc., as much as 80 per cent of marketing expenditures on lead generation are wasted because these efforts are ignored by salespeople. Marketing teams overlook critical input from salespeople regarding customer data and needs. Marketing exists to support sales. A marketing department can develop a good product strategy, but it is up to sales staff to implement it. And when the marketing and sales departments fail to share the right information, the organization suffers.

Salespeople are required to spend the bulk of their time in the field meeting with customers, in the office on the phone, or at the computer. Marketing people are under pressure to solve challenges quickly and creatively while analysing the available information on the competition, the marketplace, the company's products and services, and the target audience. They rarely interact with customers, unless it is through second-party reports from surveys or focus group research. To succeed, marketing people and sales staff both need to be involved in the development of sales and marketing programmes and planning marketing activities – from product launches through promotional campaigns – If the sales force is not involved programmes are likely to fail. Sales staff need to share customer insights as well as candid information on the usability and effectiveness of marketing tools and campaigns.

Source: www.entrepreneur.com

R&D

The drive for successful new products is often hindered by weak working relations between R&D and marketing. This can arise because of different professional and organizational cultures meaning that they operate with different priorities. R&D scientists and technicians may pride themselves more on scientific curiosity and detachment whereas marketing and sales personnel are likely to have a more practical set of concerns and look for products and services with features that can be promoted and sold in the marketplace. In some companies, R&D and marketing share responsibility for market-oriented innovation. R&D staff take responsibility for innovation and product launch, and marketing staff must take responsibility for new sales features and for correctly identifying customer needs and preferences.

Engineering and purchasing

Engineering is responsible for finding practical ways to design new products and production processes. Engineers, who may be focused more on technical quality and manufacturing simplicity, may be in conflict with the marketing function if they are asked for products with slightly different features, adding to manufacturing complexity. Purchasers want to obtain materials and components in the right quantities and quality at the lowest possible cost. They may have a perception of marketers as people who want products with small quantities of many components rather than large quantities with fewer components. They can also be critical of the forecasting inaccuracy of marketing personnel.

Manufacturing and operations

They may see marketers, stereotypically, as people who complain about delays in production, poor quality control and poor customer service. They may also see marketers as providing inaccurate sales forecasts who promise a higher level of service than is reasonable. Marketers are seen as not particularly interested in production problems but focused much more on the problems of customers who need goods and services quickly, who may receive defective merchandise, and who do not receive the service they need. In marketing-driven companies, the company will do all it can to satisfy its customers but this can result in high and fluctuating manufacturing costs. Organizations that have a balanced orientation ensure that manufacturing and marketing jointly determine what is best for the organization. Managing operations in service industries is concerned with service levels, and it is necessary for marketing and operations to work together. Marketing people must fully understand the capabilities and mindset of those delivering the service, and continuously try to improve attitudes and capabilities.

Finance

Financial executives evaluate the profit implications of proposed business activity. Marketing executives ask for substantial budgets for advertising, sales promotions and the sales force, without being able to prove how much this expenditure will contribute to the bottom line. They believe marketers are too often tempted to reduce prices to win orders instead of pricing to make a profit. However, marketers can see finance as conservative, risk-averse and the cause of lost opportunities because of a failure to invest in long-term development.

Insight: Marketing departments coming under greater financial scrutiny

Within the financial services sector, 94 per cent of marketing heads surveyed say they are under greater pressure than ever to demonstrate a return on investment (ROI) for marketing initiatives, but the majority do not have the tools to accurately track marketing spending and measure returns, according to new research.

The findings come from a survey of 50 marketing directors and managers within the UK financial services sector. The research reveals that while marketing departments are today being held more accountable, even keeping track of spending is difficult with 88 per cent of companies forced to rely on spreadsheets and 80 per cent relying on company-wide financial systems.

Accounting

Accountants may not be very keen on the special deals sales people make with customers because these require special accounting procedures. Marketers may dislike the inflexible way that accountants allocate fixed costs to products and services. They would also like accounting to produce special reports on sales and profitability by segments, important customers, individuals and products, channels, territories, order sizes and so on. Marketers may feel that credit standards are too high, and when they do find customers they may not be able to sell to them because of a low credit rating.

Making teams effective

Concerns about working in teams

- ◆ Few companies know how to properly implement a team process. Many managers lack the necessary skills to provide strong leadership in a team environment.

- ◆ Managers too frequently select people in their own image.

- ◆ Managers do not understand the strengths of their team members and do not allocate work appropriately.

- ◆ Members of unbalanced teams often feel that their particular talents and abilities are not being used to the full. Managers do not know how to motivate people because they do not understand individual needs.

- ◆ Groupthink drives out critical judgement, for example illusion of invulnerability, illusion of unanimity, self-censorship.

What are effective teams?

Mike Woodcock identified a number of characteristics in his Team Development Manual, as follows:

Openness and confrontation – Where the team is working well, people can express themselves openly and confront mistakes, confusions or frustrations. Such feedback can be received without recrimination and act as feedback to team members and management.

Support and trust – Trustful working relationships stem from positive orientations to others. In reality there is often too much at stake between people at work (personal rivalry, politics). Concerns such as being helpful, endeavouring to understand the perception and difficulties of others are important for team leaders responsible for giving feedback to members whose actions generate difficulty within the team.

Co-operation and conflict – Helpful competition can stimulate ideas and energy but unhelpful competition and conflicts, hidden agendas and stereotyping of people and problems need to be avoided.

Sound procedures – Effective teams need sound procedures for calling meetings, drawing up agendas, managing meetings, ensuring that follow-up action is implemented. Sound procedures include, for example, chairing skills, briefing, summarizing, questioning and exploration skills. Decision-making arrangements also need to be clear. Should the team vote on issues? Does the chair have the final say?

Appropriate leadership – The team leader has to focus on the task, the team and the needs of individuals, ensuring that the team works effectively and efficiently, and achieves its aims and objectives. The range of styles that a leader or manager can use has been captured by Tannenbaum and Schmidt (1958).

Boss-centred leadership

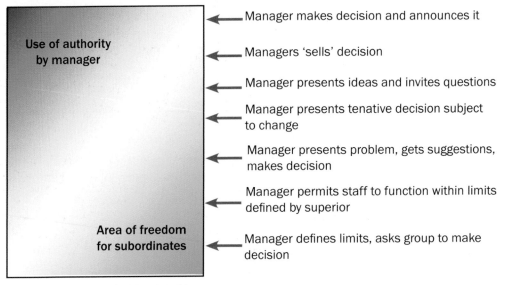

Figure 2.2 : Leadership styles

There is no one best style to adopt, rather it depends on the nature of the context, the type of work tasks undertaken and the people who make up a team and the relative importance of the decision. Styles are also contingent on factors such as timescales for making a decision. Therefore, fitness for purpose means that different approaches might be used according to how this range of factors varies.

◆   **Regular review** – A team regularly reviews where it is going and focuses on issues such as: Are we achieving our objectives? Are we being effective? How well are we working together? How can we improve?

◆ **Individual development** – Members' needs for growth, all-round ability, satisfaction of needs, opportunity and experience need attention.

◆ **Sound inter-group relations** – Effective teams have good relationships with other departments/teams. Each values and respects the other. The respective leaders themselves comprise an effective team. Inter-group processes require shared information and an open approach to problem-solving.

The following case study is an example of the importance of teams.

Case study

RWE npower is an integrated energy company. It is the third largest supplier of electricity, through its npower brand and one of the largest electricity generators.

There are different types of business problems – and different solutions to them.

◆ **Deviation problems** – where targets are not being met. Problem solving in this case is centred on closing the gaps.

◆ **Improvement problems** – where solutions are needed to address how the business can become for example more efficient or more green.

◆ **Open-ended problems** – where conventional solutions will not work. Solutions are generally linked to the idea of 'thinking outside the box' i.e. coming up with new and untried ideas.

Engineers at RWE npower have to handle these problems all the time. In the first two cases, there are often proven techniques and solutions which can be worked out in teams. Teamwork brings together engineers with different skills and experience.

Teamwork is essential for effective decision-making. Groups of engineers with different skills come together to shed light on problems and to come up with improvements. In a team there will be engineers with different technical knowledge and experience. These will include mechanical, electrical and civil engineers, and computer specialists.

Teamwork involves good communication skills, particularly the ability to listen to others' ideas. Being able to identify the root cause of the problem and understand the symptoms is essential. Engineers enjoy solving problems. They like to be creative. Working together allows them to bounce ideas off each other.

Source: http://www.npowermediacentre.com

Activity 2.2

Choose a team in your organization.

What is its function?

What are the key considerations to take into account in building the team?

How would you rate its effectiveness using Woodcock's criteria, above?

What, if any, are the key barriers to effectiveness in your chosen team?

Virtual teams

A virtual team is a group of people who are working together, even though they are not all in the same geographical location. Specifically, teams may be distributed for a variety of reasons:

◆ Organization-wide projects or initiatives

◆ Alliances with different organizations, some of which may be in other countries

◆ Mergers and acquisitions

◆ Emerging markets in different geographic locations

◆ The desire of many people and government organizations for telecommuting

◆ The continuing need for business travel and information and communications technologies available to support this travel

◆ A need to reduce costs

◆ A need to reduce time-to-market.

Types of virtual team

There are essentially four types of virtual team:

1   **Department Virtual Teams** are made up of people who all work for the same department but based in different locations, for example a team of sales representatives working for the same manager but who spend most of their time out of the office or working from home. The team members have common objectives, work under the same day-to-day management and have a detailed understanding of each other's responsibilities and working conditions.

2   **Company Virtual Teams** comprising people who all work for the same company but within different departments and, most likely, locations. For example, a product development team formed from research and development, design, manufacturing, marketing and customer care divisions. Although the team members have an overriding shared goal – to produce a successful new product – they do not report to the same line of management and have different day-to-day roles and responsibilities. They are unlikely to know one another personally but will be used to working within the same corporate culture and have shared working conditions and hours.

3   **Organization Virtual Teams** made up of members who do not all work for the same organization. For example, a marketing team that works in partnership with an external agency responsible for carrying out creative work on their behalf. The team members will most likely have no existing relationship, work under different management and working conditions, have conflicting ideas about what their objectives should be and have no awareness of their colleagues' other responsibilities or big projects.

4   **Multiple Virtual Teams** made up of a mixture of virtual teams. For example a cross-department team, all based in different locations, that also works with an external supplier based in another country. In addition to the issues highlighted above there will be more complex communication issues that will make it a difficult challenge for members of this team to co-ordinate their thoughts and ideas collectively.

Team members use communication technologies such as e-mail, videoconferencing and telephone more often than face-to-face meetings to communicate with each other. Common reasons for forming virtual teams are to integrate expertise from different locations, to save on travel time and travel costs, and to build relationships, shared understanding and shared identities across workplaces or organizations. Virtual teams face both the same challenges as traditional teams, and some unique ones such as those relating to communication technologies and working at a distance. The dispersion of team members can make it difficult to establish a strong team identity, and it can be more of a challenge for the team members to work towards a common goal. Examples of virtual teams include a team of people working at different geographic sites and a project team whose members telecommute.

It is changes in the nature of teams and not the use of technology that creates new challenges for team managers and members. Most 'virtual' teams operate in multiple modes including having face-to-face meetings when possible. Managing a virtual team means managing the whole gamut of communication strategies and project management techniques as well as human and social processes in ways that support the team. Knowledge of group dynamics can help managers to understand what happens when people interact using new media.

Managers need to help virtual teams identify roles in the same way required of all teams. Virtual teams may need technical support and specialists in using different media. For all roles, virtual teams need to spend more time being explicit about mutual expectations for facilitators, managers and members because the patterns of behaviour and dynamics of interaction are unfamiliar.

Virtual teams form and share knowledge on the basis of information pull from individual members, not a centralized push. One goal is to find ways that support the transformation of individuals' personal knowledge into organizational knowledge. This means designing environments where all the individuals have incentives to share what they know.

Managers of virtual teams can support their teams by:

◆ Encouraging members to explore questions that matter including questions about how they are working together.

◆ Supporting the creation of some kind of shared space (the feeling that there is an infrastructure where people are working together).

◆ Facilitating the co-ordination of the technology, work processes and the formal organization.

Insight

Virtual teams are having major problems and managing their progress has been a superlative challenge for most. When it comes down to online collaboration, team co-ordination and management, there are so many human-based variables at play, so many critical components to effective information exchange, workflow distribution and knowledge sharing, that delegating technology to take the full responsibility of the solution can only do so much to improve our collaboration and co-operation efficiency.

Organizations face the need to analyse and comprehend which are the key obstacles to the successful management of effective online collaborative business networks. Virtual collaboration for networked business teams is a complex and challenging activity in which there are major important components to be accounted for. Virtual business teams DO NOT operate like traditional physical teams, as their requirements reflect a whole new way of communicating, working collaboratively, sharing information and mutually supporting other team members.

The new technologies and approaches required to achieve this are completely alien to most of our present organizational culture. And this is why they fail. Co-operative processes are not the automatic results of implementing collaborative, real-time communication technologies, but the result of a carefully designed and systematically maintained virtual team development plan.

www.masternewmedia.org

Seven things virtual teams can do to work better:

1   Have face-to-face meetings with all the members as soon as possible after the team is formed.

2   Find ways of building trust between the team members.

3   Clearly define goals, roles and tasks.

4   Ensure all team members are trained in cultural awareness and interpersonal skills.

5   Encourage informal communication between team members.

6   Set standards for time taken to respond to communications, and acceptable times to call those in different time zones.

7   Leaders of virtual teams need to be proactive in building the team, and should anticipate and resolve misunderstandings and conflicts before they are allowed to develop.

Difficult areas for dispersed teams include co-ordination and collaboration, and dealing with conflict and performance problems when team members cannot be observed directly.

There is a useful online resource on virtual teams at http://www.startwright.com/virtual.htm

Diversity

Managing diversity

The trend towards a global economy is bringing people of different ethnic and cultural backgrounds together. The development of greater intercultural understanding should be an important element in all organizations because of the nature of the societies in which we live, the markets in which organizations operate, and the customers and clients that are served. Organizational culture encompasses the shared values, beliefs, behaviour and background of people, and includes race, gender, sexual orientation, age or disability. Ethnocentricity is the inclination for majority group members to view their beliefs, behaviours and values more positively than those of other minority 'out' groups and to evaluate the latter's beliefs, behaviours and values negatively from the perspective of the majority group. The members of virtual teams often include people from different countries, cultures, disciplines or organizations. Such differences mean that people have different expectations, for example, about how things should be done or said, or how people should behave. This can make it difficult to build and maintain trust and personal relationships between the team members. Bringing the team together for face-to-face meetings can help here, but one of the most important things is to ensure that team members have a good degree of cultural and interpersonal awareness and are prepared to give each other the benefit of the doubt and thus avoid a blame culture.

People of different ethnic backgrounds do not always share the same attitudes, values and norms. The contemporary organizational trend is to acknowledge, accept and value the differences among diverse groups. This raises interesting questions about how best to manage people in a workforce which becomes increasingly diverse.

Insight

The term Latino covers some two dozen nationalities, and includes a variety of cultures, physical types and racial backgrounds. Cuban, Mexican, Puerto Rican, Dominican and other Central and South American groups are included under the Latino umbrella. It is the fastest growing minority in the United States and presents some major challenges to marketers. However, there are also common elements such as strong family values, product loyalty and a concern for product quality. Spanish language TV is the best medium for reaching Latinos, who tend to watch more TV than their American counterparts.

Source: Wynter (1997)

One area that has been researched extensively is the contrast between individualism and collectivism. Compared to individualist cultures, collectivist cultures emphasize the needs of the group, social norms, shared beliefs and co-operation with group members. In general, Asians, Hispanics and Blacks have roots in nations with collectivist traditions, while Anglos have roots in the European tradition of individualism. Groups composed of people from collectivist cultural traditions tend to exhibit more co-operative behaviour than groups of people from individualistic cultural traditions.

Geert Hofstede (2001) conducted perhaps the most comprehensive study of how values in the workplace are influenced by culture. He analysed a large database of employee values scores collected by IBM between 1967 and 1973 covering more than 70 countries, from which he first used the 40 largest only and afterwards extended the analysis to 50 countries and three regions. Subsequent studies validating the earlier results have included commercial airline pilots and students in 23 countries, civil service managers in 14 counties and 'elites' in 19 countries. He developed different axes for measuring cultural factors and found considerable differences from one nation to the next.

Power Distance Index (PDI)

This focuses on the degree of equality, or inequality, between people in the country's society. A high Power Distance ranking indicates that inequalities of power and wealth have been allowed to grow within the society. These societies are more likely to follow a caste system that does not allow significant upward mobility of its citizens. A Low Power Distance ranking indicates the society de-emphasizes the differences between citizen's power and wealth. In these societies equality and opportunity for everyone is stressed.

Individualism (IDV)

This is the degree to which the society reinforces individual or collective achievement and interpersonal relationships. A high ranking indicates that individuality and individual rights are paramount within the society. Individuals in these societies may tend to form a larger number of looser relationships. A low ranking typifies societies of a more collectivist nature with close ties between individuals. These cultures reinforce extended families and collectives where everyone takes responsibility for fellow members of their group.

Masculinity (MAS)

This refers to the degree to which the society reinforces, or does not reinforce, the traditional masculine work role model of achievement, control and power. A high Masculinity ranking indicates the country experiences a high degree of gender differentiation. In these cultures, males dominate a significant portion of the society and power structure, with females being controlled by male domination. A low ranking indicates the country has a low level of differentiation and discrimination between genders. In these cultures, females are treated equally to males in all aspects of the society.

Uncertainty Avoidance Index (UAI)

This focuses on the level of tolerance for uncertainty and ambiguity within the society – that is unstructured situations. A high Uncertainty Avoidance ranking indicates the country has a low tolerance for uncertainty and ambiguity. This creates a rule-oriented society that institutes laws, rules, regulations and controls in order to reduce the amount of uncertainty. A low ranking indicates the country has less concern about ambiguity and uncertainty and has more tolerance for a variety of opinions. This is reflected in a society that is less rule-oriented, more readily accepts change, and takes more and greater risks.

Long-Term Orientation (LTO)

This focuses on the degree the society embraces, or does not embrace, long-term devotion to traditional, forward-thinking values. A high Long-Term Orientation ranking indicates the country prescribes to the values of long-term commitments and respect for tradition. This is thought to support a strong work ethic where long-term rewards are expected as a result of today's hard work. However, business may take longer to develop in this society, particularly for an 'outsider'. A low Long-Term Orientation ranking indicates the country does not reinforce the concept of long-term, traditional orientation. In this culture, change can occur more rapidly as long-term traditions and commitments do not become impediments to change.

Hofstede's data revealed an Anglo culture of management based on high individualism, low to medium power distance between bosses and their subordinates, low to medium uncertainty avoidance and high masculinity. However there are also considerable differences within Anglo cultures. Of the 52 countries in his study, Australians were the most likely to say that leaving staff alone to get the job done was the attribute that made for a good manager. Canada ranked next, while the United States was not far behind. In relationships with suppliers, Europeans are more likely to develop a long-term relationship based upon ideas of partnership, whereas both Americans and Australians perceive contracts with suppliers as 'deals'.

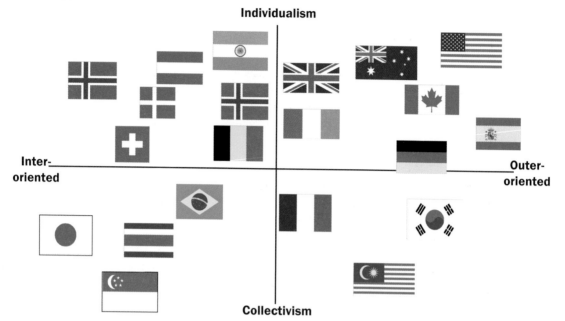

Figure 2.3: How managers see their working lives

International marketing activities are usually organized in three ways: through export departments, international divisions or a global organization

◆   A global strategy looks upon the world as single market.

◆   A multinational strategy treats the world as a portfolio of national opportunities.

◆   A 'global' strategy is based on standardizing some aspects and localizing other aspects of a Company's products and services.

Source: Bartlett and Ghoshal (1989).

Trompenaars and Hamden-Turner's seven-dimensional model

Trompenaars and Hamden Turner developed a model to analyse cultural differences, the 'Seven Dimensions of Culture Model', to show how managing complexity in a heterogeneous environment is a major challenge for today's international managers and corporate leaders as well as a critical component of long-term success. He explains how reconciling cultural differences will lead to competitive advantage.

He worked for the Royal Dutch Shell Group handling operations in nine different countries and has 15 years of research experience. His work discusses the implications for managing or being managed, working together, building relationships, team working, negotiating and communicating with people from other cultures. His basic premise is that an understanding of the underlying values of different cultures leads to greater respect for diverse ways of operating and to the desire and skills for reconciling cultural differences to achieve business performance.

- ◆ **Universalism versus particularism** – Here there is consideration of the rules versus relationships. Does the cultural emphasis on living by the rules – respect for law, and so on – take precedence over personal relationships.

- ◆ **Communitarianism versus individualism** – Consideration of groups versus individuals. Cultures, for a variety of reasons, either tend to value self-orientation or group orientation. This can affect the decision-making process and from a negotiating perspective it is vital to understand the culture.

- ◆ **Neutral versus emotional (affective)** – This reflects the range of emotions that people are able to express openly. This could have a considerable impact upon the way in which products are promoted, and how relationships are established with customers and the organizations in which they operate.

- ◆ **Specific versus diffuse** – This reflects how people will adjust their behaviour in different settings (specific). However, diffuse reflects the consistency of a person's relationships regardless of their situation. This has implications for managing staff, that is 'once the boss, always the boss', as opposed to specific where 'the boss is the boss in work and friend out of work'. This has a number of complexities, particularly for international working relationships.

- ◆ **Achievement versus ascription** – This relates to how status is accorded. Status is achieved via years of experience, service, education and age. In other words the 'respect your elders' scenario.

- ◆ **Sequential time versus synchronic time** – This is essentially the difference between a sequence of events or simultaneous events. It is a question of being able to juggle a lot of balls in respect of time, or needing to operate in a sequence to differentiate activities. This can indicate a lot about an individual's ability to work individually, within a team, on a self-motivated basis, or on a delegated activity basis.

- ◆ **High context and low context** – High context behaviour will have a form of ritual behaviour in everyday life. Priorities, status, and so on will be important. Low context will see little in the way of ritual behaviour and can generally cope with a number of events happening at any one time.

Fons Trompenaars and Charles Hampden Turner (2001) interviewed 15,000 managers in 28 countries to explore the cultural differences between what they called universalist societies and particularist societies. In universalist societies, people follow the rules and assume that the standards they support are the correct ones. Further, they believe that society works better if everyone conforms to them. Particularist societies believe that particular circumstances are more important than general rules, and that people's responses depend on circumstances and on the particular people involved. In universalist countries written contracts are taken seriously. Teams of lawyers are employed to make sure that a contract is correctly drafted, and once signed it must be policed to ensure it is kept. Particularist countries think that the relationship is more important than the contract and that a written contract is not always necessary – the particular people and the particular situation matter more than the universal rules. Different cultures have different ways of coping with life, a different set of responses to the same underlying dilemmas. In Far Eastern cultures, books start 'at the back' and are read from right to left in vertical columns. To Westerners, this seems a reversal of normal practice. Managers need to display cross-cultural competence and reconcile cultural differences. Successful leaders are those who are flexible, sensitive and skilled enough to be able to ride what they call 'the waves of culture'.

Insight

Even in the best of teams, individual agendas can sometimes get in the way of progress. All marketing professionals understand the importance of teamwork, and 'integrated marketing communications' (IMC) is a concept all of us are familiar with by now. It is the rather simple, but surprisingly elusive, concept that organizations should plan all of their communications efforts in tandem so that they not only contribute to the same overall business objectives, but actually reinforce each other. Synergy should make $1 + 1 + 1 = 5$.

1   Synergy occurs only when all parties are working towards the same, clearly articulated marketing objectives.

2   Measure results according to outcome, not output or glitz. Make it clear that results are all that count.

3   Assemble your IMC team before setting strategy. Involve your team during the early stages of strategic planning.

4   Manage competition between partners. Specialists tend to accentuate the advantages of their particular discipline.

5   Beware of sacred cows.

Adapted from GS Insight www.gibbs-soell.com/insight/GS_InsightV6-6Aug98.pdf

Activity 2.3

◆   Do you have experience of working with international organizations, or does your own organization have international divisions? If not, try to find out about the business culture in a very different country from the one in which you work.

◆   What are the key differences in culture between each country that have an impact on working life, for example, are there different approaches to teamwork, team leadership, management style, delegation, making mistakes?

◆   What do you think will be the key differences that would have an impact on the manager's role? There are many aspects of culture to pay attention to, particularly in marketing activities.

The use of language can be a barrier even when the same language is spoken. Unit 1 provided some examples of this but business cultures can vary a lot. Every organization manifests patterns of member behaviours and values which together may be said to form a 'culture'. Organizational effectiveness and decision-making processes are influenced by cultural expression, for example, attitudes and responses of employees and styles of management. Interpreting and understanding organizational culture is an important activity for managers because it affects strategic development, productivity and learning at all levels. Cultural assumptions can both enable and constrain what organizations are able to do. A key role for culture is to differentiate the organization from others and provide sense of identity for its members. A strong culture is one that is internally consistent, is widely shared, and makes it clear what it expects and how it wishes people to behave. Sometimes different disciplines or departments within organizations develop their own subculture which can make it difficult when there is a need for people to work together to achieve the goals of the organization. Understanding what cultural differences exist within organizations is important for achieving a common approach and managing change.

Human resource management

All large organizations have developed HRM departments, and their managers can rely upon the existence of clear personnel policies and back-up through every aspect of concern to personnel management. For many managers, however, there is likely to be little formal support and it is for them to recruit, select and manage. Even for managers with HRM support, there is a need to understand fully the systems and procedures so that they have sufficient understanding to be able to exert control as needed. In this, the relationship with HRM is exactly the same as with any other specialist function.

Recruitment and selection

The process involves clearly defined stages and the use of a systematic approach should ensure that you do not overlook anything important and, significantly, it will reduce the area of subjective judgement where people's biases, prejudices and weaknesses can creep in. This is important for several reasons. First, on grounds of natural justice, there is the obvious point that everyone needs to be treated fairly and equitably. One of the most depressing situations that can arise in organizations is when people are denied opportunities for reasons beyond their personal control such as their age, ethnicity, disability or gender. This may deny the organization the opportunity to appoint the best candidate. Other weaknesses in the recruitment process can mean that weak or unsuitable people may be appointed on superficial criteria. There are also legal, recruitment and poor public relations consequences that can follow if a recruitment process is flawed. Who is the best candidate for a post depends on the nature of the job, the people with whom the person will need to work and interact, and the context in which the work is carried out. It is a matching process between the existing strengths and weaknesses of team members, future requirements of the role, and the qualities and capabilities of the prospective candidates.

Case study: Derbyshire County Council

Derbyshire's 'Putting People First' Change Management Programme had as one of its primary goals to improve access to Council services. The Council also wanted to widen its pool of applicants and improve efficiency in its recruitment practices. It also wanted to make recruitment practices consistent across the organization. Derbyshire knew that 40 per cent of site hits were recruitment-related, however, it had no means of assisting people to use the Internet to actually apply online. There were also a number of requests for job packs but much fewer applications for the jobs. Through surveys as well as feedback received from potential applicants, Derbyshire established that they were missing out on key groups of applicants who were put off by the fact that they could not apply online.

Following the implementation of the project, the website and call centre are now fully integrated within the Council's recruitment process, and citizens now have three ways of applying for jobs; online, by post or by e-mail attachment.

Job adverts are placed directly on the web site, the weekly job sheet is automatically produced and recruitment analysis tools (i.e. who is applying, demographics, what they are applying for, etc.) are being used extensively.

There is now consistent recruitment practice across the Council, and improved management information allows for more effective use of advertising and related expenditure. Applicants can store job applications for future adjustment and submission for other vacancies. Applicants can register what type of jobs they are looking for and an e-mail will automatically alert them when a job that meets their criteria becomes available.

Source: http://www.derbyshire.gov.uk/council/policies_plans/customer_care_charter

Recruiting externally

Businesses could choose to search using the following media:

◆ Advertising in papers, magazines or locally

◆ Employment agencies

◆ Executive 'headhunters'

◆ Job centres

◆ Colleges/universities

◆ Careers fairs.

These are all useful, but there are some disadvantages:

◆ Companies might be overlooking and frustrating talented internal candidates.

◆ External recruitment can be expensive.

Internal recruiting

Internal recruiting has traditionally been done by a manager appointing or promoting people. Some organizations use formal internal advertising to find the best candidate. They will advertise on notice boards, via intranets or newsletters.

Not everyone agrees with formalized internal recruitment:

◆ Employees may think it is an empty exercise, believing decisions are already made.

◆ Some managers anticipate problems in succession planning if they must use open internal markets.

To avoid problems, businesses can bring someone impartial – managers from other departments, someone from HR – into the procedure. Internal recruitment can be efficient because:

◆ The person and the firm know each other.

◆ Savings on commercial advertising rates for recruitment can be made.

Employees are motivated because they can see the possibility of progression.

Whilst there is a cost in building on existing skills internally, this can be more reliable and less expensive than external recruitment. On the down side:

◆   Good people outside could be overlooked.

◆   Unsuccessful internal candidates can feel slighted.

◆   Entirely new skills may need intensive training.

Case study: McDonald's

Recruiting, selecting and training for success

McDonald's employs on a large scale. A typical McDonald's employs about 60 people. Most are hourly-paid. Managers and office staff are paid a salary. For each job there is a job description which describes the duties of the job and a person specification that describes the skills and personal qualities needed for the job.

Hourly-paid workers are recruited through adverts in restaurants, job centres and career fairs. Interviews are planned using the McDonald's interview guide. Candidates are rated on a scale. Jobs are offered to those with higher ratings. The management department recruits managers. They come from two main sources. Over half are promoted hourly-paid workers. Most of the rest have degrees. People can apply on line, via a recruitment hotline or by post. The online process includes a psychometric test. A good first-stage interview is followed by two days on site called 'On the Job Experience'. If the OJE is a success there is a final interview after which it is decided whether or not to appoint. Those who are successful are inducted into the business. The Welcome Meeting gives an outline of the company. It includes the job role and food, hygiene and safety training. Standard policies and methods of doing things are explained. The meeting also covers administration, benefits and training. McDonald's provides for workers to further their careers through a development programme.

McDonald's puts great emphasis on on-the-job training. Staff are given a training card on which to record their achievements. They are expected to check with their managers to ensure progress is properly recorded and that they gain experience in all work areas. New employees are teamed up with a 'buddy', a member of the training team. Job rotation is practised and there are 19 work areas to which staff can be assigned.

Observation and questioning are used to assess staff and two observations must be passed before someone is regarded as 'competent'. Restaurant managers spend a lot of time on a one-to-one basis with new recruits. Managers have training responsibilities and can spend 60 per cent of their time on the floor with the crew. Their own training involves learning everything a crew member needs to know and further classroom work.

Source: http://home.comcast.net/~nelson1397/mcdonaldscase.htm

Advertising and the use of agencies

Advertising is a major marketing activity and marketers use agencies regularly. The concepts of positioning, segmentation and targeting apply just as much to recruitment as to any other form of advertising. The agency's job is to translate your needs into shortlisted candidates. The aim is to design an advert so that only those who have a realistic chance of being successful apply for the position. It is as important for unsuitable candidates to rule themselves out as it is to encourage eligible people to apply. Having a large field of candidates is of little use if many of them would stand little chance of being appointed.

E-recruitment

E-recruitment is becoming a more important tool in the 'war for talent' environment. Research conducted by DEMOS3 looks at the trends that will shape the recruitment industry for years to come. Recommendations included:

◆ Companies should align human resources, public relations and marketing, and be clear on core organizational values .

◆ Companies should find ways to connect with the passive job seeker .

◆ Companies should broker and make use of peer-to-peer relationships .

◆ Companies should use Web 2.0 technologies (such as blogs, web-based communities and hosted services including social-networking sites) to build personalized relationships online.

Creating relationships with potential employees is important, the key way being through employer brand. In order to maximize a brand's potential to attract the right people, it must express core organizational values and messages and be found in the right places.

Broadband

For recruiting purposes, broadband enables the hosting of 'live' employee video profiles and virtual office tours to illustrate life within the organization and create engagement and commitment early in the recruitment process.

Social networking and blogs

A number of organizations have started to make use of recruitment 'blogs' (or online diaries) from employees as part of the information they offer to potential candidates about working for the organization (for example based on the experiences of graduates on a development scheme). This is a potential way to build relationship with would-be candidates - and to feature different areas of a company and its vacancies.

Advantages of using e-recruitment

E-recruitment has the potential to:

◆ Speed up the recruitment cycle and streamline administration.

◆ Allow organizations to make use of IT systems to manage vacancies more effectively and co-ordinate recruitment processes.

◆ Reduce recruitment costs.

◆ Reach a wide pool of applicants.

◆ Reach a niche pool of applicants.

◆ Make internal vacancies widely known across multiple sites and separate divisions.

◆ Provide the image of an up-to-date organization, reinforcing employer branding and giving an indication of organization culture.

◆ Offer access to vacancies 24 hours a day, 7 days a week reaching a global audience.

- Be a cost effective way to build a talent bank for future vacancies.
- Help handle high volume job applications in a consistent way.
- Provide more tailored information to the post and organization, e.g. case histories of the 'day in the life' or self-assessment questionnaire or quiz to assess fit with role.
- Be spontaneous for candidates as ease of use means there is the ability for applications to be instantaneous.

Disadvantages of using e-recruitment

The disadvantages to using e-recruitment include the potential to:

- Limit the applicant audience as the Internet is not the first choice for all job seekers.
- Cause applications overload or inappropriate applications if care isn't taken drafting the job profile/specification.
- Exclude those who do not want to search for a new job online.
- Atract fewer of those unable to fully utilise technology, e.g. certain disabled groups.
- Give rise to allegations of discrimination, in particular the use of limited keywords in CV search tools.
- Make the process impersonal, which may be off-putting for some candidates.
- Impact on the 'cultural fit' dimension of recruitment.
- 'Turn-off' candidates, particularly if the website is badly designed or technical difficulties are encountered.
- Lose out on candidates, especially if your own website is below the search engine ranking of your competitors.
- Provide too little or inappropriate information, for example, corporate recruitment guidelines might not be written in a web-friendly style.

Activity 2.4

What are the recruitment methods used in your organization for:
- Administrative jobs?
- Sales jobs?
- Professional jobs?
- Managerial jobs?

Applications

After the closing date, a long list of possible candidates can be drawn up. From the long list you can use your personnel specification to compile a short-list. It is good practice to respond to all applicants, but some organizations feel they cannot afford it. Applicants are consumers in the marketplace so it is important to create a favourable impression with everyone who applies for a job.

Discrimination

What the law says

There are a number of Acts of Parliament which are relevant to the recruitment of staff. The main provisions are the Sex Discrimination Acts of 1975 and 1986, the Race Relations Act 1976, the Race Relations (Amendment) Act 2000 and the Disability Discrimination Act of 1995. These Acts seek to promote equality of opportunity and to ensure that no person is treated less favourably than another person on the grounds of disability, colour, race, nationality, ethnic or national origins, sex or marital status. The Disability Discrimination Act 1995 gives disabled people the right not to be treated less favourably than others. Special care must be taken in the wording and placing of recruitment advertisements to avoid seeming to prefer one type of person over another. Since 2005, third-party publishers, for example newspapers, have been liable for publishing discriminatory advertisements. The government has introduced legislation to combat age discrimination in employment and vocational training. It covers both employment and vocational training. It includes every member of the workforce, young and old. Employers will have to adopt age positive practices. This means it will no longer be possible to recruit, train, promote or retire people on the basis of age unless it can be objectively justified.

The 2005 legislation covers young and old alike throughout their working lives.

The Sexual Orientation Regulations apply to discrimination on grounds of orientation towards persons of the same sex (lesbians or gays), the opposite sex (heterosexuals) and the same and opposite sex (bisexuals). They cover discrimination on grounds of perceived as well as actual sexual orientation and the sexual orientation of someone with whom the person associates.

As with other forms of discrimination, the new legislation recognizes both direct and indirect discrimination on the grounds of sexual orientation. Since 2005, this definition has been extended to include civil partner employees, i.e. a partner in a same-sex couple who have registered their relationship under the Civil Partnership Act 2004. A person who is in a registered civil partnership of a same-sex couple will be protected from unlawful direct or indirect sexual discrimination on the grounds of being a civil partner.

Insight: Age – a key business issue

In 2005, John Cridland, Deputy Director-General, CBI noted that 'the key business issue within the framework of equality over the next few years will be the introduction of the age discrimination regulations in 2006. The CBI wishes to encourage people to work beyond the age of 65 where there is a business case for doing so. We want to see workable age legislation and will be working as part of the Age Partnership Group to inform employers of their new responsibilities under the regulations.'

You should check there are no hidden age barriers in your selection and promotion processes – for example, aim to place advertisements in publications read by a range of age groups. You should also make sure that redundancy procedures are based on business needs rather than age.

In certain circumstances discrimination may be allowed if it is seen to be a genuine occupational qualification for the job in question.

When interviewing people for a job there are certain questions you should not ask, either directly or indirectly, including whether a candidate is married, in a same-sex civil partnership, or plans to have children. You must not attempt to elicit information about a person's sexual orientation or their religion. Read about the actions you should take to give equal treatment to civil partners in your policies, forms and other material on the ACAS website.

Care should also be taken when asking about a disability. Whilst the Disability Discrimination Act does not prohibit an employer from seeking information about a disability, that information must not be used to discriminate against a disabled person. An employer should only ask such questions if they are relevant to the person's ability to do the job, after a reasonable adjustment, if necessary.

Discrimination

The main forms of discrimination are:

Direct discrimination – that is where a woman is treated less favourably than a man or vice versa, a married person is treated less favourably than a single person or vice versa, or someone is treated less favourably on grounds that they are intending to undergo, are undergoing or have undergone a gender reassignment. Direct discrimination can occur where someone is treated less favourably on the grounds of their sexual orientation.

Indirect discrimination – that is applying a requirement or condition which, although applied equally to all groups, is such that a considerably smaller proportion of a particular racial group, sex or married persons can comply with it and which cannot be shown to be justifiable. Possible examples are unjustifiable age limits which could discriminate against women who have taken time out of employment for child rearing and rules about clothing or uniforms which disproportionately disadvantage a particular racial group.

Both types of discrimination are unlawful irrespective of whether there has been any intention to discriminate.

Disability discrimination – While legislation covering discrimination on grounds of race and sex makes discriminatory conduct unlawful, the Disability Discrimination Act 1995 goes further by requiring employers to make 'reasonable adjustments' to the workplace where that would help to overcome the practical effects of disability. Failure to carry out this legal duty amounts to discrimination unless an employer is able to justify it. People with disabilities who feel that they have been unfairly discriminated against can seek redress through Employment tribunals.

Sexual orientation

The Employment Equality (Sexual Orientation) Regulations 2003 outlawed discrimination in employment and vocational training on grounds of sexual orientation. The law means that it will be unlawful to deny lesbian, gay and bisexual people jobs because of prejudice. The legislation provides protection throughout the employment relationship – during the recruitment process, in the workplace, on dismissal and, in certain circumstances, after the employment has finished. They apply to terms and conditions, pay, promotion, transfers, training and dismissals.

Religion and belief

The Employment Equality (Religion or Belief) Regulations 2003 outlawed discrimination and harassment on grounds of religion or belief in large and small workplaces in England, Scotland and Wales, both in the private and public sectors. They cover all aspects of the employment relationship and outlaw treating people less favourably than others because of their religion or belief.

Equal pay

The Equal Pay Act 1970, as amended by the Equal Pay Regulations, covers all contractual conditions of service, not only pay. It gives both sexes the right to an 'equality clause', which means that if any term in their contract is less favourable than that in a contract of the opposite sex, it must be modified to make it equitable. Aspects covered include:

◆ 'Like work', that is work of the same or a broadly similar nature.

◆ Work rated as equivalent under a non-discriminatory evaluation scheme.

◆ Work of equal value in terms of the demands made, for example, under such headings as effort, skill and decision-making.

Job description

A job description is the focus of any employee's relationship with the employer. In establishing what the job is, the manager provides the foundation for all the stages of recruitment, selection, training and appraisal that follow. The job description describes the tasks and responsibilities which make up the job. As well as being a prerequisite to the recruitment process, it provides a standard against which the performance and development needs of the post-holder can be assessed. It also enables the department to focus on the characteristics of the post rather than those of the previous occupant. Job descriptions have several standard components, provided in greater detail as needed:

◆ **Job title** – Accurate titles reflecting the function and level of the job; modest duties should not have grand titles. 'Engineer' should only describe a qualified engineer.

◆ **Position** – Stating the job title of the person to whom the employee is responsible as well as those who report to the job holder.

◆ **Areas of responsibility** – Stating the overall purpose of the job; the principal role of the job holder and the expected contribution to achieving objectives.

◆ **Main tasks** – Identifying the tasks, grouping together related ones. Includes the objective or purpose of each task but not how it is done.

◆ **Description of tasks** – In short numbered paragraphs, with no more than two sentences per description; gives details of measures of work involved and proportion of time involved for any task; descriptive headings used to group together related tasks.

◆ **Special requirements** – Equipment, tools, special skills.

◆ **Location** – of the job and travelling needed.

◆ **Special circumstances** – Lifting, dangerous or unpleasant conditions, night work, overtime, weekend working.

◆ **Challenging aspects of the job** – This can be useful in attracting applicants.

◆ **What is the overall purpose of the job?** – Describe in one sentence, for example, 'to assist the Head of Department in the efficient running of the departmental office'.

◆ **What are the main tasks of the job?** – Try to use active verbs, for example, 'producing', 'planning', rather than vague terms such as 'deals with', 'handles'.

◆ **What are the main responsibilities involved?** – 'Responsibilities' define the scope of the job, for example for managing staff, materials, money, and so on.

◆ **The key result areas of the job and the standards expected** – These may include such aspects as the degree of precision required and/or the consequences of error.

◆ **With whom does the post-holder work?** – These may include other staff, students, and so on.

◆ **Terms and conditions of the post** – Unsocial hours, necessity to work regular overtime, and any restrictions on periods during which annual leave can be taken, and so on.

The job description provides a basis for drawing up a 'person specification', that is, the skills and experience required to carry out the duties of the job.

The person specification

Purpose – The person specification forms the basis of the recruitment process from the advertisement through to the final interview stage. It describes the skills, aptitudes and experience needed to do the job and should be based on the job description, rather than a subjective view of the sort of person you would like to see filling the job. Generally, person specifications are laid down under standardized headings.

Qualifications and training:

1 **General education** – It may be more appropriate for applicants to have certain levels of literacy or numeracy rather than academic qualifications. If qualifications are stipulated, equivalent qualifications that would be considered must be included.

2 **Specific training** – For example, vocational certificates, professional qualifications and apprenticeship certificates.

Knowledge – This is knowledge without which the job cannot be done, for example, of computer systems. It should not include knowledge that can be imparted in an induction programme.

Experience – Either directly relevant or similar experience in a different environment might be considered. The type, range and depth of experience should be qualified (e.g. staff supervision). Specifying length of experience is usually unhelpful as some people learn more in a shorter time than others will learn in a longer time.

Skills and abilities – This includes such aspects as the ability to communicate effectively, numeracy, analytical skills, attention to detail, and so on. However, these skills must be clearly measurable as part of the selection process.

Special requirements – This should only form part of the specification where it is relevant to the job, for example, a special type of driving licence if fork lift truck driving is to be part of the job, or a need to travel and stay away from home. The required characteristics are then entered against the appropriate heading, and subdivided into essential and desirable categories. The candidate who meets both the essential and desirable criteria will do the job particularly well, but obviously this person may be hard to find. Training and development may be needed in some areas. The person specification should be realistic. Too high an ideal will mean that potentially good candidates are excluded.

The Rodger seven-point plan

This was devised by Alec Rodger (1952), who developed a systematic approach for constructing person specifications. Having defined the demands of the job and evaluated the knowledge-base, skills, personal orientations, predispositions and preferred values, the recruiter identifies the ideal 'qualities' needed. Using the seven headings, the aim is to determine whether the candidate satisfies the essential criteria (factors that should disqualify those who do not possess them). Desirable factors are ones that could be developed through training or development activities but could help in the process of distinguishing one eligible candidate from another – does one present a better profile than another?

1   **Physical make-up:** What does the job demand in the way of general health, physical strength, stamina, eyesight, hearing, speech, appearance, and so on? Legislation to prevent discrimination has stopped most of the specifications for 'attractive', 'young', a nd so on. The increasing number of people with disabilities in the workforce has encouraged many managers to re-evaluate just what physical attributes are necessary for a post.

2   **Attainments:** What general education, technical knowledge, specialized training and relevant experience are required? To avoid becoming too overpowered by qualifications and diplomas, it is more useful to list specific knowledge areas, for example, a marketing research job holder needs a proven knowledge of statistical sampling techniques. Conversely, sometimes there is an unwillingness amongst employers to recognize the value of working hard to achieve formal marketing qualifications when appointing marketing professionals. Questions need to be asked to establish the candidate's experience. Experience indicates knowledge and skill and how these have been used together. Much personal development comes from experience.

3   **General intelligence:** What level of reasoning and learning ability is required? This can be a difficult area to evaluate since it is subjective in nature. For some jobs, the need is for people who prefer to have clearly structured rules and procedures to follow. For other jobs, the need may be for someone who does not mind ambiguity where little is clear-cut and each situation is different.

4   **Special aptitudes:** Aptitudes and abilities are difficult to quantify, but they can be specified as the ability to be creative in generating solutions, to work under pressure, to think strategically, to negotiate contracts, and so on. Once specified, it is possible to devise ways for assessment and evaluation.

5   **Interests**: Are any general interests likely to be relevant to job success?

6   **Disposition:** Does the job require people to get on with people, to be a self-starter, work on their own initiative, to accept responsibility, to work under pressure, to

influence others? What attributes are needed to be able to fit into the culture of the department, section, and so on. Disposition is important when individuals are going to be working as part of a team. An attempt should be made to assess how they might fit in and what contribution they might make. Characteristics such as loyalty and reliability may be more suited to the role of a product manager than to a sales person who needs to be outgoing and independent, self-motivated and confident.

7   **Candidate's circumstances:** What domestic circumstances are relevant? Daily travel from home to work, time spent away from home on business. Is working overtime possible, if needed? However, care needs to be taken when asking such questions and the following are to be avoided – 'Are you married?', 'Do you have children?' 'Are you intending to start a family?' These are not relevant to the selection decision and could be perceived as discriminatory because they are about the person rather than the ability to do the job.

The following advertisement is for a marketing manager working for a leader in online recruitment.

Advertisement for a marketing manager

This is an opportunity to be part of one of the most highly regarded companies in an exciting and fast-moving industry. We are currently looking for a passionate Marketing Manager with heaps of initiative to oversee all marketing activities and communications. You'll be responsible for devising and implementing the company's annual marketing plan and helping to ensure continued growth in our client, user and subscriber numbers.

The Person

You must have:

◆   At least 3–4 years' experience in a similar marketing role.

◆   Extensive experience of planning, buying and monitoring online marketing expenditure, aimed primarily at candidates, including spend with major search engines.

◆   Experience of devising and executing trade marketing campaigns to new and existing clients.

◆   Experience of managing a marketing budget of several hundred thousand pounds.

◆   Ideal, but not essential, are exposure to and understanding of the (a) accountancy and finance sectors, (b) the online recruitment industry and (c) some exposure to search engine optimization.

You must be:

◆   Enthusiastic, with a hands-on approach to marketing.

◆   Self motivated and adaptable with a can-do attitude.

◆   An excellent communicator, with creative, accurate written skills.

◆   Able to act as part of a wider management team, interfacing with all parts of the business especially sales.

Munroe Fraser – 5-point plan

This focuses more upon a candidate's career to date as an indicator of future potential.

1 **Impact on others** – Whether a person's appearance and demeanour are important.

2 **Qualifications and experience** – Skills and knowledge required.

3 **Innate abilities** – How quickly and accurately a person's mind works.

4 **Motivation** – The kind of work that appeals to a person and the amount of effort they are prepared to put into it.

5 **Emotional adjustment** – Capability of working with others.

Activity 2.5

Using one of the sets of headings identified above, draw up a person specification for the Media Relations post below:

1 **Job purpose**

The Media Relations Executive will work in conjunction with the company's senior executives to develop and implement a comprehensive communications strategy. This will require building sound media contacts to ensure positive media coverage for the company's activities.

2 **Tasks**

a Conduct a comprehensive review of media relations, and provide a diagnostic report for the Board of Directors.

b Develop and implement a company media relations strategy.

c Provide a quarterly analysis of media coverage with recommendations to improve coverage.

d Arrange and publicize corporate events and host media representatives.

e Anticipating and responding to events by issuing press releases, giving professional advice and guidance to other company managers.

f Co-ordinate press conferences as necessary.

g Provide in-house training on media relations and skills to company staff according to need.

h Establish robust relationships with key media representatives.

Interviews

In relation to the focus of an interview there are three principal interview models:

◆ **Biographical interview** – exploring the candidate's experiences

◆ **Behavioural interview** – eliciting information about how applicants have behaved in similar situations

◆ **Situational interview** – comprising a series of job-related questions.

Many interviewers (or organizations) prefer to use one technique, but these different models can be useful in different situations and an interview can combine all three aspects.

With regard to the process of interviewing there are, again, various models that can be used, for example panel interviews.

Panel interviews

Panel interviews can provide a better picture of a candidate than a one-on-one interview. There is more chance to think about a candidate's responses because the interviewer is more of an observer than a participant. This increases the validity of the assessment. In most one-on-one interviews, the interviewer is often thinking about what question to ask next, rather than listening to a candidate's answer. Many people hate these sort of interviews and find them a bit of an endurance test. To do well you will need to identify the important figures on the panel and which role each is fulfilling. The chairperson is easy to identify as they will generally make the introductions. You will also need to identify the person whom you will be working for directly – make sure you give them plenty of eye contact. When you are talking to the panel, remember that you are talking to all of them and not just the person who posed a particular question – your answer has to be the correct one for each panel member! If there is one particular panel member who everyone else seems to agree with, you should make sure you impress him or her.

Source: http://www.alec.co.uk/interview/panel.html

The interview room

It is essential that candidates be made to feel relaxed so that a proper assessment of their suitability for the job can be made. In the case of interview panels, care should be taken to ensure that the candidate is not seated too far away from the interviewees so as to feel isolated, nor so close as to be able to read the interviewers' notes.

Planning the interview

For an interview to succeed, it should be conducted in an orderly, empathetic but efficient manner. It is recommended that interviewers should undertake the following preparation:

◆　Compare the candidate's application form with the person specification and pick out the points which need investigating further, for example experience, qualifications, gaps in a career history and inconsistencies.

◆　Once the interview panel has done this, they should then prepare a plan of how the interview is to be conducted to ensure that nothing is omitted.

◆　Questions need to be planned. These should be designed to probe the selection criteria of the person specification, namely a candidate's knowledge, ability and experience. Other questions should be aimed at a more general assessment.

◆　Where a candidate is attending an interview and they have informed you of any disability that they have, which may affect them during the interview process, it is a requirement of the Disability Discrimination Act to carry out 'reasonable' adjustments to ensure they can perform to their maximum potential, for example, if access is a problem for a candidate, the interviews should be held in a room accessible to all.

- Identify key questions pertinent to the job that is asked of all candidates. This ensures that they have been asked equivalent and relevant questions.
- Allocate the subjects to be explored. Each interviewer can cover different areas, for example work experience and training.
- The candidate should have an opportunity to ask questions and interviewers should be prepared for the more obvious ones, such as hours of work and annual leave.

Objectives for an interview

Interviewers should be clear on the objectives of the interview:

- To find out whether a candidate is suitable for the job advertised
- To find out whether the job and the department/organization are suitable for a candidate's needs (an aspect which is often overlooked)
- To fairly select the most suitable candidate.

Conducting the interview

The interviewer should control the focus of the interview:

- Introduce the members of the panel. Start the interview slowly, to allow the candidate to relax.
- Explain the structure of the interview and what it is trying to achieve.
- Give an overview of the context of and brief background for advertising the job.
- Put the candidate at their ease and begin your questioning by identifying areas that are familiar, for example his/her present job, before working through to the candidate's thoughts on the job for which he/she has applied.

Questioning

Encourage the candidate to speak freely, by asking open-ended questions such as 'tell us what you think about …?' or 'how do you deal with …?' Closed questions do not encourage the candidate to express his/her opinions in his/her own way.

Open-ended questions start with: 'how', 'what', 'why', 'when' or 'where'.

Behavioural questions are a good way of exploring what candidates have actually done in areas relevant to the job, for example:

'Give us an example from your last job when you had to persuade others to adopt a particular course of action.'

Hypothetical questions, for example 'what would you do if?', should be used with care.

- Allow the candidate time to think of his/her answers.
- Summarize if you need to clarify ambiguous answers and to keep the interview on course.
- Listen closely to what is being said and how it is expressed; as by observing keenly, an interviewer can pick up clues that will enable him/her to explore an issue in more depth.
- Be aware of your own biases for or against certain types of dress, appearance, and so on as this could impair your judgement on the candidate's ability to do the job.

◆　　Make sure the candidate is aware of any special requirements of the job and that these are acceptable.

◆　　Allow time for the candidate to ask questions and invite him/her to do so.

◆　　Take brief notes which will let you return to a point later and to deliberate at the end.

◆　　To make comparative judgements of candidates, you must be able to remember the key points that each candidate made.

Finishing the interview

Once the interviewers have obtained all they need from the interview, they should check that the candidate has no further questions and then signify the end of the interview. They should then:

Tell the candidate when he/she can expect to know the outcome.

Check the candidate's expenses are covered, if appropriate.

Thank the candidate for attending the interview and see him/her out.

Key points

Remove as much stress from the interview as possible.

Ask open-ended questions.

Ascertain all relevant facts, and probe ambiguous or vague answers.

Listen to what the candidate has to say.

Provide information relevant to the job.

Provide opportunities for the candidate to ask questions.

Tell the candidate when they can expect to know the outcome of the interview.

The interview assessment

When a succession of candidates are seen over a period, it is essential to record accurate views on each immediately after each part of the process. Never allow interviewers to rely on memory.

The interview assessment allows each of your defined categories to be rated and a justification noted. This greatly facilitates the discussions that must take place at the end of the session as the shortlist is constructed or the successful applicant is identified. Do not allow any sharing of views about candidates until after individual assessments have been recorded in writing.

Debriefing

Arrange a debriefing to:

Shortlist or reject candidates.

Make improvements to the recruitment and selection procedures.

If possible, provide advice to the unsuccessful candidates – this is good for public relations and is used routinely in the public sector.

Other aspects of interviews

The following examples of different selection techniques are not mutually exclusive and can be used in different combinations with each other.

Second interviews or follow-up interviews

Employers invite those applicants they are seriously considering as an employee following a screening or initial interview. These are generally conducted by middle or senior management, together or separately. Applicants can expect more in-depth questions, and the employer will be expecting a greater level of preparation on the part of the candidate.

One-on-one interviews

Candidates are interviewed by one person. These interviews tend to be more informal; however, it depends on the employer's style. The interviewer will often have a series of prepared questions, but may have some flexibility in their choices.

Group interviews

Employers may bring several candidates together in a group situation to solve a problem. These may be aimed at testing your ability to work in a team environment or other interpersonal or problem-solving skills. It is difficult to prepare for this type of interview except to remember what is being tested and demonstrate team member or leadership skills.

Presentations

Asking candidates to make an oral presentation about a relevant topic can measure both their presentational and analytical skills.

Report writing

Candidates can be asked to write something on or before the interview day. This could test writing skills, subject knowledge or both.

Simulation exercises

An interpersonal exercise with a particular agenda and objectives, to observe how the candidates perform in a typical work situation, such as a manager faced with an industrial relations issue.

Group discussions

Typically, all candidates are put together to deal with a particular problem, and are observed and evaluated doing so, such as a planning meeting on next year's appeal.

Psychometrics

These tend to measure current or potential skills levels, or personality profiling, which shows work styles and preferences and can be used to assess how well candidates will fit in to the organization. Psychometric testing describes a range of exercises used by employers to find out about an individual's aptitude or personality. They usually form part of an overall selection process.

Ability tests may consist of one or more of numerical, verbal reasoning, spatial awareness and diagrammatical reasoning. Those used depend on the type of role for which someone is being assessed. Verbal and numerical tests are used in selecting graduates for a wide range of jobs including most business and management functions. Diagrammatic tests are used mainly for computing/IT jobs. The earlier in the selection procedure candidates are asked to sit a test, the more important the results are likely to be to the outcome. Employers who use tests only at second interview stage are likely to look upon the results as one of the number of criteria to be used in the selection process.

Case study: The recruitment process at Apple

In marketing, you have the unique opportunity to work on revolutionary products from concept to launch with the best creative minds in the industry. Working with the most creative people in the business on breakthrough products is as satisfying as it is challenging. Our marketing department is comprised of the best and brightest, and we're always looking for stand-out talent to add to our team.

The Marketing division spans a variety of different disciplines including: Developer Relations, Events, Graphic Design, Marketing Communications, Product Marketing, Public Relations, Research and Analysis, Worldwide Markets.

Take a look at our website at www.apple.com. Explore the site and get to know our products. If you're a Software Engineer, make sure to visit our Developer site. Interested in Sales? Learn how our customers are using our products in creative ways in the Education, Pro, and Business sections. Make sure you take the time to explore the website, it will tell you a lot of what you need to know about Apple and our customers.

Try our products in person at one of our retail stores or resellers. Listen to music on an iPod. Ask questions of one of the Mac Specialists. When you're at home, download our iTunes software to your Mac or PC and check out the iTunes Music Store. It's important that you familiarize yourself with our products to see what makes Apple unique. Once you're in the interview, relax and be yourself. The interview process is designed for us to make sure that we're a good fit for each other, which means that you should ask questions of us in addition to answering the questions that we ask you. Come prepared to discuss a variety of topics, not just your past experiences and accomplishments. And don't forget, we don't have a dress code, so wear clothes that make you comfortable.

http://www.apple.com/jobs/marketing/interview.html

Numerical critical reasoning

Numerical critical reasoning tests look at how well you can reason with numbers and understand information presented in a numerical form. In this sort of test you are presented with information followed by a number of questions. Your task is to select the right response from a range of possible responses.

Typical behaviour

Employers often want to assess aspects of personality, and in particular the way in which you work in a team situation. One way of doing this is to complete a 'self-report' questionnaire. This asks about the sort of role you tend to take when working in a team or group.

1   If it is not at all like you

2   If it is a bit like you

3   In between

4   Quite a lot like you

5   Very like you.

Sample statements

1   I like to talk about new ways of doing things   1 2 3 4 5

2   I am good at spotting mistakes   1 2 3 4 5

3   I prefer to work with people I know well   1 2 3 4 5

4   I make sure people know what to do   1 2 3 4 5

5   I often use tried-and-tested methods   1 2 3 4 5

6   I can be very forceful when I need to be   1 2 3 4 5

Assessment centre approach

One of the advantages of assessment centres is that it allows key job behaviours to be directly observed and measured. An assessment centre is a programme that organizes a range of tests for a group of candidates. The rationale for the approach is that multiple assessment techniques are more valid and reliable compared to single-method approaches such as interviews and personality questionnaires. The following dimensions are often assessed in assessment centres:

◆   Planning and organizing

◆   Leadership

◆   Analytical

◆   Problem-solving

◆   Sensitivity

◆   Decision-making

◆   Creativity

◆   Sociability

◆   Management control and delegating.

Assessors have to demonstrate the capability to observe and record the behaviour of candidates. Video is frequently used to aid assessors in gathering behavioural information. Assessors also need to be able to integrate information from various exercises, to discuss the ratings with fellow assessors and to be able to compare candidate performance.

Drawbacks of selection interviews

There is some doubt that an interview is the most appropriate mechanism for assessing candidates' suitability with accuracy, witness:

◆   First impressions are often lasting impressions; decisions tend to be made early on in the interview.

◆   Interviewers may prefer candidates who are like themselves, which may lead to discrimination.

◆ There is a danger of the interviewer only hearing information which supports pre-conceptions or first impressions.

◆ Interviewers can get jaded and confused if too many interviews are held in one day – early interviews get forgotten and later ones are less effective.

Activity 2.6

How have those who have interviewed you performed in their role?

What would you have done differently?

What was good/bad about the best/worst interview you've ever had?

Summary

Teams differ in many ways, including size, purpose, type of work performed, structure, leadership, influence and decision-making ability. It is important to recognize that teamworking is not the best solution in every situation, and teams are not always more effective and efficient than individuals working to solve a problem. However, in many business situations, the ability to work in teams is valuable and teams can accomplish more than individuals who plough their own furrow. Criteria for an effective team were identified. An effective team has cohesion and a common purpose. Recruitment and selection guided by a personnel specification and proper preparation for interviews is of key importance. There are a wide range of selection procedures that can be used depending on the nature of the job and its importance to the organization. Recruitment and selection can be expensive but so can appointing the wrong person to a post.

Do's and don'ts for successful selection interviewing:

◆ **Do** prepare thoroughly.

◆ **Do** check the organization's policies.

◆ **Do** watch for inconsistencies between verbal and non-verbal behaviour.

◆ **Don't** make decisions based on a gut reaction.

◆ **Don't** break your schedule.

◆ **Don't** allow interruptions.

◆ **Don't** talk too much.

Working with diversity is an important skill for managers and team members, and they need to have good cultural and interpersonal awareness. The differences amongst individuals and groups should be acknowledged, accepted and valued. Working with people in different countries raises particular issues of cultural awareness.

Further study

Read Boddy, D. (2005) *Management: An Introduction*, Harlow: Pearson Education, Chapter 4, 'The international context of management' and Chapter 15, 'Teams'.

Hints and tips

It is always good to demonstrate your broader knowledge of marketing. So try to include examples from the marketing press, textbooks, journals and the Internet to support your answers. This is one way to demonstrate your knowledge and understanding to the Senior Examiner. Marketing is a highly practical activity and using examples to illustrate theory in practice is important. However, do make sure that your examples are relevant to the question in hand. Many questions do not explicitly ask for examples, but, where it is appropriate, do use them.

Bibliography

Achrol, R. and Kotler, P. (1999) Marketing in the network economy, *Journal of Marketing*, 62, 146–163

Adler, L. (2002) *Hire with Your Head*, New York: Wiley

Ashton, C. (1998) *Strategic considerations in facilitative evaluation approaches*, The Action Evaluation Project (Available from www.aepro.org/inprint/conference/ashton.html)

Bartlett, C.A. and Ghoshal, S. (1989) *Managing Across Borders*, Cambridge, MA: Harvard Business School

Chartered Institute of Personnel and Development (2005) *People management and technology: progress and potential*, London: CIPD. Available at http://www.cipd.co.uk/surveys

Chartered Institute of Personnel and Development (2006) *Recruitment, Retention and Turnover Survey Report 2006*, London: CIPD. Available at http://www.cipd.co.uk/surveys

Clark, K.B. and Wheelwright, S.C. (1995), *The Product Development Challenge: Competing through Speed, Quality, and Creativity*, Boston, MA: Harvard Business School Publishing

Cronlly-Dillon, M. (2007) Face up to rules on researching recruits online, *People Management*, 13 (21), 20

Department of Indian and Northern Affairs Canada (2003) http://www.ainc-inac.gc.ca These ideas are adapted from the Department of Indian and Northern Affairs' website

Department of Indian Affairs (2001) http://www.nqi.ca

Dobson, D. and Dobson, M. (2000) *Enlightened Office Politics*, New York: AMACOM

Doke, D. (2007) Opening up the future, *Recruiter,* 2 May, 14-16.

Earley, P.C. (1993) 'East meets west meets mid east: Further explorations of collectivist and individualist work groups', Academy of Management, 36 (2) 319–48

Fraser, John Munro (1978) Employment Interviewing, MacDonald and Evans, 5th edition

Hamel, G., Doz, W.L. and Prahalad, C.K. (1991) 'Collaborate with your competitors and win', *Harvard Business Review*, 67 (1), 133–39

Hofstede, G. (2001) *Culture's Consequences, Comparing Values, Behaviors, Institutions, and Organizations Across Nations*, Thousand Oaks, CA: Sage

Hofstede, G. (2004) *Cultures and Organizations: Software of the Mind* (London: McGraw-Hill, 2004); New York: McGraw-Hill, 1997). 3rd edition

Katzenbach, J.R. and Smith, D.K. (1993) *The Wisdom of Teams*, MA: Harvard Business School

Kotler, P. (2003) *Marketing Management*, New York: Prentice Hall 11th edition

Lester, Don H. (1998) 'Critical success factors for new product development', *Research Technology Management*, January–February, 36–43

Maclaurin, I. (1999) 'Strategic direction', *Human Resource Management International Digest*, July/August

Pettigrew, A. and Whipp, R. (1991) *Managing Change for Competitive Success*, Oxford: Basil Blackwell

Rankin, N. (2005) 'Online recruitment in the UK: 10 years older and wiser', *IRS Employment Review*, No 822, 29 April, 42-48.

Robbins, H.A., Finley, M. (2001) *The New Why Teams Don't Work: What Goes Wrong and How to Put it Right*, San Francisco: Berrett Kohler

Rodger, A. (1952) The seven-point plan, London: National Institute of Industrial Psychology

Tannenbaum, R. and Schmidt, W.H. (1958) How to choose a leadership pattern, *Harvard Business Review*, No. March-April, pp 95-101

Trompenaars, F., Hampden Turner, C. (2001) *21 Leaders for the 21st Century: How Innovative Leaders Manage in the Digital Age*, London: Wiley & Sons. (The best known book from the authors is *Riding the Waves of Culture* (1997), Nicholas Brealey Publishing.)

Wertheim, E.G. (2000) *Surviving the group project: A note on working in teams*, http:// www.cba.neu.edu, accessed 20 April

Wilcox, D. (1994) 'The guide to effective participation', *Partnership* (Available at www.partnerships.org.uk/guide/index.htm.) Brighton.

Woodcock, M. (1989) *Team Development Manual*, Gower Publishing , 2nd Edition

Woodcock, M (1979) *Team Development Manual*, Aldershot: Ashgate

Wynter, Leon E. (1997) 'Business and race: Hispanic buying habits become more diverse', *Wall Street Journal*, 8 January, B1

Virtual Teams – Beneficial or Detrimental? http://www.leadingvirtually.com/?p=32

Unit 3
Developing the team

Study guide

Teams – Differ in many ways, including size, purpose and type of work performed, structure, leadership, influence and decision-making ability.

Types of teams include:

1   Natural work group

2   Management

3   Project improvement

4   Process redesign or re-engineering

5   Cross-functional, that is, design and production include people of various skill levels from throughout the organization

6   New product and service design teams.

Stages of team development

In the 1960s, psychologist B.W. Tuckman developed this model and suggested that there are four team development stages that teams have to go through in order to be productive (Tuckman, 1965). Some teams may go through the four stages fairly rapidly and move from forming through to performing in a relatively short space of time. A lot depends on the composition of the team, the capabilities of the individuals, the tasks at hand, and the team management and leadership.

Forming

Polite but not yet trusting. Formalities are maintained and members are treated as strangers. This can be a stressful phase when new teams come together. Everyone is a bit wary of everyone else, particularly if they do not know anyone and particularly if the manager is new. At this stage, each individual tends to want to establish his or her personal identity within the group.

Storming

Testing others. Members start to communicate their feelings but probably do not yet view themselves as part of the team. Most groups go through a conflict stage when initial consensus on purposes, leadership, norms of behaviour and work is challenged and re-established. No matter how clear the team was in relation to the goals, roles and rules during the forming stage, it is often the case that individual interpretations of these are somewhat different in reality. At this stage, personal agendas are revealed and a certain amount of interpersonal hostility is generated. If successfully handled, this period of storming leads to a new and more realistic setting of objectives, procedures and norms. This stage can be important for testing the norms of trust in the group.

Norming

Valuing other types. People feel part of the team and realize that they can achieve work if they accept other viewpoints. Norming is characterized by acceptance. The group needs to establish norms and practices. When and how it should work, how it should take decisions, what type of behaviour, what level of work, and what degree of openness, trust and confidence is appropriate. Whereas in the storming stage, people were apt to rebel very quickly; this is not the case now and if someone has a grievance, complaint or suggestion then the proper processes are used. Goals are understood and roles are clarified. The rules and regulations are being adhered to and people are working together positively. Relationships become stronger as people are more aware of each other.

Performing

Flexibility from trust. The team works in an open and trusting atmosphere where flexibility is the key, and hierarchy is of little importance. Not every team makes it to this stage. Many get stuck at norming and although everything appears normal, there is a lack of momentum and motivation towards achieving all the important team goals. At the performing stage, team members are focused on team goals and are aware of the strengths and weaknesses of the team. Only when the three previous stages have been successfully completed, will the group be at full maturity and be able to be fully and sensibly productive.

Some kind of performance will be achieved at all stages of the development but it is likely to be impeded by the other processes of growth and by individual agendas.

Tuckman's 5th Stage Adjourning

Bruce Tuckman refined his theory around 1975 and added a fifth stage to the Forming Storming Norming Performing model – he called it Adjourning, which is also referred to as Deforming and Mourning. Adjourning is arguably more of an adjunct to the original four stage model rather than an extension – it views the group from a perspective beyond the purpose of the first four stages. The Adjourning phase is certainly very relevant to the people in the group and their well-being, but not to the main task of managing and developing a team, which is clearly central to the original four stages.

Characteristics of Adjourning

◆ A team that has reached the Adjourning stage will:

◆ The team has achieved its purpose and is ready to move on to new things.

◆ Team members feel good about what they have achieved.

How to address the Adjourning Stage:

◆ Recognize and be sensitive to team member's vulnerability in this stage.

◆ Members may feel threatened by the change.

◆ Tuckman, Bruce W. (1975) *Measuring Educational Outcomes*, Harcourt Brace Jovanovitch, New York.

Roles in a team

Based on research with over 200 teams conducting management business games at the Administrative Staff College, Henley, in the United Kingdom, Belbin (1996,a) identified nine team types. People usually have a mix of roles and will have dominant and sub-dominant roles.

Belbin team type	Contributes	Allowable weaknesses
Co-ordinator	❖ Mature ❖ Confident ❖ Clarifies goals ❖ Focuses on the team ❖ Delegates well	❖ Can often be seen as manipulative. ❖ Off-loads personal work
Shaper	Challenging ❖ Thrives on pressure ❖ Has drive and courage to overcome obstacles	❖ Prone to provocation ❖ Offends people's feeling
Plant	❖ Creative ❖ Imaginative ❖ Solves difficult problems	❖ Ignores incidentals ❖ Not a good communicator

cont...

Continued

Belbin team type	Contributes	Allowable weaknesses
Resource Investigator	• Extrovert • Enthusiastic • Communicative • Develops contacts	❖ Over-optimistic ❖ Loses interest very quickly
Company Worker	❖ Disciplined ❖ Reliable ❖ Turns ideas into practical actions ❖ Efficient	❖ Inflexible ❖ Slow to respond to new ideas
Monitor Evaluator	❖ Sees all options ❖ Strategic ❖ Judges accurately	❖ Lacks drive and ability to inspire others
Team Worker	❖ Co-operative ❖ Listens ❖ Diplomatic ❖ Averts	❖ Indecisive in crunch situations
Completer/ Finisher	❖ Delivers in time ❖ Anxious ❖ Searches our errors	❖ Inclines to worry unduly ❖ Reluctant to delegate
Specialist	❖ Single-minded ❖ Dedicated ❖ Self-starting	❖ Contributes only on a narrow front ❖ Dwells on technicalities

Co-ordinator

The co-ordinator is a person-oriented leader. This person is trusting, accepting, dominant, and is committed to team goals and objectives. The co-ordinator is someone tolerant enough to always listen to others, but strong enough to reject their advice. This is a person who calls meetings, keeps people on track and pays attention to group processes. For example, the co-ordinator makes sure that everyone is involved and notices when someone is upset. Some of the things that successful co-ordinators try to do are as follows:

◆ Focus team on task

◆ Engage participation from all members

◆ Protect individuals from personal attack

◆ Suggest alternative procedures when the team is stalled

◆ Summarize and clarify the team's decisions.

Shaper

The shaper is a task-focused leader who has a high motivation to achieve and for whom winning is the name of the game. The shaper is committed to achieving ends and will 'shape' others into achieving the aims of the team. He or she will challenge, argue or disagree and will display aggression in the pursuit of goal achievement. According to Belbin, two or three shapers in a group can lead to conflict and in-fighting.

Plant

The plant is a specialist idea maker characterized by high IQ and introversion, while also being dominant and original. The plant tends to take radical approaches to team functioning and problems. Plants are more concerned with major issues than with details.

Weaknesses are a tendency to disregard practical details and to be argumentative.

Resource investigator

The resource investigator is the executive who is never in his room, and if he is, he is on the telephone. The resource investigator is someone who explores opportunities and develops contacts. Resource investigators are good negotiators who probe others for information, and support and pick up other's ideas and develop them. They are characterized by sociability and enthusiasm, and are good at liaison work and exploring resources outside the group.

Weaknesses are a tendency to lose interest after initial fascination with an idea, and they are not usually the source of original ideas.

Company worker/implementer

Implementers are aware of external obligations, and are disciplined, conscientious and have a good self-image. They tend to be tough-minded and practical, trusting and tolerant, respecting established traditions. They are characterized by low anxiety and tend to work for the team in a practical, realistic way. Implementers figure prominently in positions of responsibility in larger organizations. They tend to do the jobs that others do not want to do, and do them well: for example, disciplining employees. Implementers are conservative, inflexible and slow to respond to new possibilities.

Monitor evaluator

According to the model, this is a judicious, prudent, intelligent person with a low need to achieve. Monitor evaluators contribute particularly at times of crucial decision-making because they are capable of evaluating competing proposals. The monitor evaluator is not deflected by emotional arguments, is serious-minded, tends to be slow in coming to a decision because of a need to think things over and takes pride in never being wrong.

Weaknesses are that they may appear dry and boring or even overcritical. They are not good at inspiring others. Those in high-level appointments are often monitor evaluators.

Team worker

Team workers make helpful interventions to avert potential friction and enable difficult characters within the team to use their skills to positive ends. They tend to keep team spirit up and allow other members to contribute effectively. Their diplomatic skills together with their sense of humour are assets to a team. They tend to have skills in listening, coping with awkward people and to be sociable, sensitive and people-oriented.

They can be indecisive in moments of crisis and reluctant to do things that might hurt others.

Completer/finisher

The completer/finisher dots the i's and crosses the t's. He or she gives attention to detail, aims to complete and to do so thoroughly. They make steady effort and are consistent in their work. They are not so interested in the glamour of spectacular success.

Weaknesses, according to Belbin, are that they tend to be overanxious, and have difficulty letting go and delegating work.

Specialist

The specialist provides knowledge and technical skills within the team. They may be introverted and anxious but tend to be self-starting, dedicated and committed.

Significance of Belbin team roles

Where there is an uneven spread of roles in a group there may be problems in addressing the task allocated. Team members need to be aware of their main team role, know their second-best role and see if these can complement the other group members' roles. In this way, an effective team can be constructed. A person's team role may alter over time and he or she may play different roles in different teams.

There is a tendency in top teams for too many 'shapers' and 'plants' with few if any 'completer/finishers'. This means that everyone likes to talk, wants their own ideas to be accepted by all and relies on others to take the follow-through actions. Another role that is often lacking in top teams is that of 'monitor/evaluator' – this person may be perceived as trying to prevent things from happening by introducing balance and reality into the discussions.

Specific teams

Knowing the predominant Belbin roles of your team may provide an explanation as to why a particular team does not work well. Where there is a role that is not fulfilled at all in the team, then either the leader will need to ask someone to take on the role, or it needs to be covered by the team members.

Leadership and management of teams

Not all leaders are managers and not all managers are leaders. However, managers can be leaders and vice versa. Leadership is derived from an Anglo-Saxon word meaning the road or path ahead. Managing comes from a Latin word 'manus', meaning hand, and is more associated with handling a system or machine of some kind.

As indicated above, some managers will do some of the same things that leaders do and vice versa. It is more a question of the balance of activities that comprise a job, and the expectation is that leaders would spend more time focusing on the strategic direction of the organization. However, there are many different theories about leadership and in the 1980s, a new paradigm emerged called 'transformational leadership' as opposed to 'transactional leadership'. The relative instability and unpredictability of the environment has given rise to this new conception, and there is a premium on leadership to ensure that an organization can adapt to and be successful in a world of constant change. The transformational leader motivates and inspires staff and ensures that staff understand the vision for the future of the organization.

Five characteristics of leadership

◆　Challenging the process – encouraging others to develop new ideas and judicious risk taking.

◆　Inspiring a shared vision about the future.

◆　Enabling others to act – encouraging collaboration, co-operation, building teams and empowering others.

♦ Modelling the way – planning and reviewing progress and taking corrective action in a way that gains the respect of others; being clear about values and acting in a manner consistent with them.

♦ Recognizing and celebrating others' achievements.

Source: Kouzes and Posner (2002)

Team leadership

John Adair's (1988) Action-Centred Leadership model is based on three parts:

1 Defining the task

2 Managing the team or group

3 Managing individuals.

People need to be briefed properly about the objectives that need to be achieved, what needs to be done, why, how and when. The extent to which all of this needs to be spelled out by the leader or manager will depend on the people involved, the work context and the nature of any particular task. In a situation where there is an expectation that tasks will be delegated, there is no need to go into great detail about how something should be done because this will be the responsibility of the person carrying out the task. The purpose of the business is to deliver something of value to people. The leader is responsible for ensuring that the marketing task determines what that value is, and then organizes work in the most effective and efficient way to deliver it (see Figure 3.1).

Figure 3.1 What a leader has to do. *Source:* Adair (1988)

Core functions of leadership

Adair sets out the core functions of leadership that are central to the Action-Centred Leadership model (see Figure 3.2):

♦ **Planning** – Seeking information, defining and allocating tasks, setting aims, initiating, briefing, setting standards.

♦ **Controlling** – Maintaining standards, ensuring progress, ongoing decision-making.

♦ **Supporting** – Individuals' contributions, encouraging team spirit, reconciling, morale.

♦ **Informing** – Clarifying tasks and plans, updating, receiving feedback and interpreting.

♦ **Evaluating** – Feasibility of ideas, performance, enabling self-assessment.

The Action-Centred Leadership model, therefore, does not stand alone, it must be part of an integrated approach to managing and leading. There should be a strong emphasis on applying these principles through training.

Adair's Leadership checklist

	Key Functions	Task	Team	Individual
C O M M U N I C A T I O N	Define objectives	Clarify task Obtain information Identify resources and constraints	Assemble team Give reasons why Define accountability	Involve each person Gain acceptance
	Plan and Decide	Consider options Establish priorities Plan time	Consult Encourage ideas Agree standards	Listen Asess abilities Delegate Agree targets
	Organize	Establish control Brief plan Obtain feedback	Structure Answer questions Prepare and train	Check understanding Counsel Enthuse
	Control and support	Maintain standards Report progress Adjust plan if necessary Set personal example	Co-ordinate Maintain external co-operation Relieve tension	Guide and encourage Recognize effort Discipline
	Review	Evaluate results against objectives Consider action	Recognize team's success Learn from setbacks	Appraise performance Identify further training needs Aid personal growth

Figure 3.2 Adair's leadership checklist

Generic role definition for team leaders (Armstrong, 1996)

Purpose of role – To lead teams in order to attain team goals and further the achievement of the organization's objectives.

Key result areas:

◆ Agree targets and standards with team members which support the achievement of the organization's objectives.

◆ Plan with team members work schedules and resource requirements which will ensure that team targets will be reached, indeed exceeded.

◆ Agree performance measures and quality assurance processes with team members.

◆ Co-ordinate the work of the team to ensure that team goals are achieved.

◆ Ensure that the team members collectively monitor the team's performance in terms of achieving output, speed of response, and quality targets and standards.

◆ Agree with team members any corrective action required to ensure that team goals are achieved.

◆ Conduct team reviews of performance to agree improvement plans.

◆ Conduct individual reviews of performance to agree areas for improvement and personal development plans.

◆ Recommend appropriate team performance rewards and individual rewards related to the acquisition and effective use of skills and capabilities.

Capabilities:

◆ Builds effective team relationships, ensuring that team members are committed to the common purpose.

◆ Encourages self-direction amongst team members but provides guidance and clear direction as required.

◆ Shares information with team members.

◆ Trusts team members to get on with things – not continually checking.

◆ Treats team members fairly and consistently.

◆ Supports and guides team members to make the best use of their capabilities.

◆ Encourages self-development by example.

◆ Actively offers constructive feedback to team members, and positively seeks and is open to constructive feedback from them.

◆ Contributes to the development of team members, encouraging the acquisition of additional skills and providing opportunities for them to be used effectively.

Tannenbaum and Schmidt (1958) leadership continuum

1   **The manager decides and announces the decision.** The manager review options in light of aims, issues, priorities, timescales and so on, then decides the actions and informs the team of the decision. The manager will probably have considered how the team will react, but the team plays no active part in making the decision.

2   **The manager decides and then 'sells' the decision to the group.** The manager makes the decision as above, and then explains reasons to the team, particularly the positive benefits that the team will enjoy from it. In so doing the manager is seen by the team to recognize their importance, and to have some concern for the team.

3   **The manager presents the decision with background ideas and invites questions.** The manager presents the decision along with some of the background which led to it. The team is invited to ask questions and discuss with the manager the rationale behind the decision, which enables the team to understand and accept or agree with the decision more easily than in 1 and 2 above. This more participative and involving approach enables the team to appreciate the issues and reasons for the decision, and the implications of all the options. This will have a more motivational approach than 1 or 2 because of the higher level of team involvement and discussion.

4   **The manager suggests a provisional decision and invites discussion about it.** The manager discusses and reviews the provisional decision with the team on the basis that the manager will take on board the views and then finally decide. This enables the team to have some real influence over the shape of the manager's final decision. This also acknowledges that the team has something to contribute to the decision-making process, which is more involving and therefore motivating than the previous level.

5   **The manager presents the situation or problem, gets suggestions, then decides.** The manager presents the situation, and maybe some options, to the team. The team is encouraged and expected to offer ideas and additional options, and discuss implications of each possible course of action. The manager then decides which option to take.

6   **The manager explains the situation defines the parameters and asks the team to decide.** At this level the manager has effectively delegated responsibility for the decision to the team, albeit within the manager's stated limits. The manager may or may not choose to be a part of the team which decides. While this level appears to gives a huge responsibility to the team, the manager can control the risk and outcomes to an extent, according to the constraints that he stipulates. This level is more motivational than any previous, and requires a mature team for any serious situation or problem.

7   **The manager allows the team to identify the problem, develop the options, and decide on the action, within the manager's authority limits.** The team is given responsibility for identifying and analysing the situation or problem; the process for resolving it; developing and assessing options; evaluating implications; and then deciding on and implementing a course of action. The manager also states in advance that he/she will support the decision and help the team implement it.

Managing team behaviour

Avoid self-serving behaviour that has nothing to do with the team performing. For example:

◆   **Attention getting** – Nobody seems interested in what I have to say.

◆   **Aggression** – Don't care what you say, you're wrong.

◆   **Withdrawal** – We're getting nowhere, why don't we each work on the problem by ourselves.

Managing team behaviour requires skill and a clear understanding of what is required. Again good communication skills can significantly improve team behaviour. Communication skills that help encourage team members to focus on the task include the following:

◆   **Initiating** – Where shall we start?

◆   **Clarifying** – Isn't Jo suggesting that ...?

◆   **Direction** – Don't you think we should be moving the discussion along?

◆   **Information seeking** – Don't you have some sales figures on ...?

◆   **Information giving** – The latest marketing research report shows ...

A team leader is accountable for the effective functioning of the team. The leader monitors team performance and takes action to improve team effectiveness. Teams tend to perform best when responsibilities are shared and leadership tasks are distributed among members.

Evaluation of team performance

Developing a process plan for the way a team will work together can provide a useful reference point to evaluate how well a team is doing. A team's process plan should describe how the team will approach its work, including how the team will resolve conflict. Controlling politics is critical to team decision-making because internal politics produce poor team performance and restrict information flow within the team. Techniques for controlling internal politics include the following:

◆ Conduct open and frank discussions

◆ Fully share information

◆ Make meetings open to all members.

When a team approach to work is in place, the focus of performance management is on the accomplishments of the team as well as the individual's contributions to them. Team effectiveness is improved when both team and individual performance are recognized as significant and factored into the performance management process. Team performance standards refer to skills which make employees effective team members as well as the standards expected of individuals. Performance management of a self-directed work team may be undertaken by the team itself but this can vary from organization to organization, or department to department. The organization should provide guidelines and a framework for that performance management, but within this, the team may be responsible and accountable for its own performance. A self-directed work team may be able to describe its own jobs, set its own standards, give feedback to its own members about work performance and team skills, appraise itself and identify and support the training and development needs of its members. However, this is likely to be a rare occurrence because of the greater demands of accountability that have developed in the past couple of decades.

The ability to provide effective observation and feedback is important because it is through observation that areas for improvement can be identified and the team made aware of them. Whether the team is self-directed and managing its own performance, or team members that report to one or more line managers, teams will benefit from observation and feedback. If the team as a whole has a formal reporting relationship with a line manager, he or she will be concerned with observing and giving feedback about the work-related behaviour and outputs of the team as a whole, as well as that of individual team members. If team members report to different line managers, or if the line manager is not present when the team does its work, he or she will need to establish procedures and relationships for learning about the work the team is doing and how it is working together. This could involve receiving input from the team leader, team members and customers of the team.

Performance standards and statistical data relating to the achievement of objectives and targets help in providing 'objective' feedback. However, statistics never speak for themselves and should only be used as the platform for a discussion as to why targets have or have not been reached. There may be a host of extraneous and unforeseen factors that have influenced the attainment of targets. For example, no one could have predicted what would happen to the airline industry in 2001 when the Twin Towers were attacked in New York. Another source of feedback for teams is customers. This feedback may come in a variety of forms: surveys, feedback cards, suggestion boxes, in-person interviews, telephone interviews and focus groups.

When the basis for appraisal is the performance of individual team members, the incentive to work effectively with other team members may be missing. Because of this, some organizations appraise team performance and not individual performance but this can undermine a sense of individual responsibility. Some organizations appraise both team performance and individual performance. The main issues regarding the performance management of teams relate to the variety of reporting relationships and degree of independent responsibility that teams may exercise, as well as the need to reinforce team values and efforts without undermining individual responsibility. Typically, a line manager will be involved in some or all of the following activities:

◆ Allocating work to teams and individuals

◆ Agreeing objectives and work plans with teams and individuals

◆ Assessing the performance of teams and individuals

◆ Providing feedback to teams and individuals on their performance

◆ Dealing with poor performance in a team

◆ Supporting team members who have problems affecting their performance

◆ Implementing disciplinary and grievance procedures

◆ Dismissing team members whose performance is unsatisfactory.

Constructive feedback

Feedback is a way of learning more about ourselves and the effect our behaviour has on others. Constructive feedback increases self-awareness, offers options and encourages development.

Start with the positive

Most people need encouragement and to be told when they are doing something well. If the positive is identified at the beginning, negative points are more likely to be acted upon.

Be specific

Generalized comments are not very helpful. Try to be specific about particular examples of behaviour that are not acceptable. Try to identify what a person did well or behaviour that can be praised.

Refer to behaviour that can be changed

Give feedback about something that the person can change.

Offer alternatives

If you give negative feedback, suggest what the person could have done differently. Turn the negative into a positive suggestion.

Be descriptive rather than evaluative

Tell the person what you saw or heard and the effect it had on you rather than merely saying that something was good, bad, and so on. Explain fully.

Own the feedback

All that anyone is entitled to give is their own experience, of that person, at a particular time. Comments such as 'you always ...' or 'you are ...' as if they are agreed statements about what a person is like are not productive. It is important that we take responsibility for the feedback that we offer.

Leave the receiver with a choice

Feedback which demands change may meet with resistance. Skilled feedback offers people information about themselves in a way which leaves them with the choice about whether to act on it or not. It can help to examine the consequences of any decision to change or not to change.

Keep the individual motivated to give their best.

Insight: The 12-minute interview

A regular meeting with an employee to talk one-on-one about issues, problems and progress in work and the workplace.

Why should it be used? – To make sure that employees have direct contact with the team leader. Talking to staff regularly encourages each employee to contribute to the team effort. If time is invested, it will help to avoid losing touch with people when it is a busy time.

How can this tool help? – One of the concerns of front-line staff is a lack of direct contact with their supervisor or manager. This tool helps to build meeting time into the daily routine.

How does it work? – Create a rotating schedule so that, for example, every day at a particular time the team leader meets with a different member of staff.

Doing – Ensure that 12 minutes at the set hour. Do not try to control the session; what is important will come up.

Follow-up – Once the 12-minute interview becomes part of workplace culture, it will enable better and more planned use of time. Staff will keep note of questions, problems and issues that can be addressed during their regular interview and only ask for special meetings for more urgent or complex matters.

Allocating responsibilities

In order to allocate work to teams and individuals, the manager needs to decide with the team how to distribute tasks and responsibilities. This means ensuring that the allocation makes best use of team members' abilities, and provides opportunities for them to learn and develop in their roles. The manager needs to make it clear what is expected of them. Where resources are limited, a manager may have to prioritize objectives or reallocate resources while minimizing the disruption this may cause.

Objectives and work plans

In order to agree objectives and work plans with teams and individuals, they need to be SMART, that is, specific, measurable, realistic, time-bound and consistent with the organization's overall objectives and policies. Ways of working need to be explained, and there is a need to update objectives and work plans in the light of progress and changes. In order to assess the performance of teams and individuals, the manager needs to make it clear why performance is monitored and assessed. Individuals and teams need to be encouraged to evaluate their own performance wherever possible.

Motivation

One of the best-known theories is McClelland's motivational theory (McClelland et al., 1953) which is based on three types of motivational need that are found to varying degrees in all workers and managers.

Achievement motivation – The person seeks attainment of realistic but challenging goals, and advancement in the job. There is a strong need for feedback about achievement and progress, and a need for a sense of accomplishment.

Authority/power motivation – The person needs to be influential and effective to make an impact. There is a strong need to lead and for their ideas to prevail. There is also motivation and need towards increasing personal status and prestige.

Affiliation motivation – The person has a need for friendly relationships and is motivated towards interaction with other people. The affiliation driver produces motivation, and needs to be liked and held in popular regard. These people are team players.

Most people possess and exhibit a combination of these characteristics. Some people exhibit a strong bias to a particular motivational need, and this affects their behaviour and working/managing style. McClelland felt that people with a strong 'achievement motivation' made the best leaders although there was a tendency to demand too much of their staff in the belief that they too are highly achievement-focused and results-driven.

McClelland suggested that for achievement-motivated people:

◆ Achievement is more important than material or financial reward.

◆ Achieving the aim or task gives greater personal satisfaction than receiving praise or recognition.

◆ Financial reward is regarded as a measurement of success, not an end in itself.

◆ Security is not the prime motivator, nor is status.

◆ Feedback is essential, because it enables measurement of success, not for reasons of praise or recognition (the implication here is that feedback must be reliable, quantifiable and factual).

◆ Achievement-motivated people constantly seek improvements and ways of doing things better.

◆ Achievement-motivated people will logically favour jobs and responsibilities that naturally satisfy their needs, that is, offer flexibility and opportunity to set and achieve goals, for example, sales and business management, and entrepreneurial roles.

McGregor XY Theory

In 1960, Douglas McGregor advanced the idea that managers had a major part in motivating staff. He divided managers into two categories – Theory X managers who believe that their staff are lazy and will do as little as they can get away with; and Theory Y managers who believe that their people really want to do their best in their work. Theory X managers believe that staff will do things if they are given explicit instructions and plenty of stick if they do not do what they are supposed to. Theory Y managers believe their people work their best when empowered to make appropriate decisions.

Achievement-motivated people tend towards X-Theory style, due to their high task focus.

Theory X assumptions:

1   People inherently dislike work.

2   People must be coerced or controlled to do work to achieve objectives.

3   People prefer to be directed.

Theory Y assumptions:

1   People view work as being a natural activity.

2   People will exercise self-direction and control towards achieving objectives to which they are committed.

3   People learn to accept and seek responsibility.

Since McGregor, Theory Z has been advanced by William Ouchi (1981). This states that employees crave responsibility and opportunities for growth all the time. It is strongly influenced by Japanese management styles.

Activity 3.1

Think about jobs you have had. What do you think the assumptions of your boss were. What impact did those assumptions have on performance and morale?

Can you generalize about organizations you familiar with? Can you detect patterns of management that reflect either X or Y assumptions?

Hertzberg motivators and hygiene factors

Hertzberg et al (1959) constructed a two-dimensional paradigm of factors affecting people's attitudes about work. He concluded that such factors as company policy, supervision, inter-personal relations, working conditions and salary are hygiene factors rather than motivators. According to the theory, the absence of hygiene factors can create job dissatisfaction, but their presence does not motivate or create satisfaction. In contrast, motivators are elements that enriched a person's job; he found five factors in particular that were strong determinants of job satisfaction: achievement, recognition, the work itself, responsibility and advancement. These motivators (satisfiers) were associated with long-term positive effects in job performance while the hygiene factors (dissatisfiers) consistently produced only short-term changes in job attitudes and performance, which quickly fell back to its previous level.

Satisfiers describe a person's relationship with what he or she does, many related to the tasks being performed. Dissatisfiers, on the other hand, have to do with a person's relationship to the context or environment in which he or she performs the job. The satisfiers relate to what a person does while the dissatisfiers relate to the situation in which the person does what he or she does. A manager may not be able to easily influence all the hygiene factors of a person's job but he or she can have a big influence on many of the motivators.

Motivator factors that increase job satisfaction:

◆ Achievement

◆ Recognition

◆ Work itself

◆ Responsibility

◆ Advancement

◆ Growth.

Hygiene factors – absence of 'good' factors can create job dissatisfaction:

◆ Company policy

◆ Working conditions

◆ Salary

◆ Peer relationships

◆ Security.

Source: Frederick Hertzberg, *Work and the Nature of Man* (1966).

Equity theory

Adams' (1965) Equity Theory is based on the principle that individuals want a fair balance between the inputs, or what they give to their job, and the outputs, or what they get from it. Employees develop a view of what is fair by comparing their own situation with other people who they regard as 'referents'. Typical inputs might be effort, loyalty, hard work, commitment and skill. Typical outputs are obvious ones such as pay and expenses and also more intangible ones such as recognition, praise, responsibility, sense of achievement and so on.

If people feel that their inputs outweigh the outputs then they may become demotivated. In this situation, some people switch off and do the minimum that they can, or even become disruptive. Others aim to seek to improve the outputs by making pay claims or looking for other work. The key aspect of the theory is that extrinsic rewards such as level of pay are neither motivating nor demotivating in themselves. Rather it is how fair we perceive them to be when we compare ourselves with significant others, that is, people who we feel should be paid less than or about the same as ourselves, or people whom we expect to be paid more than us.

If we feel that inputs are fairly and adequately rewarded by outputs (the fairness benchmark being subjectively perceived from market norms and other comparable references) then we are happy in our work and motivated to continue inputting at the same level.

The work of Edgar Schein

Schein is a major contemporary writer in the field of organization theory. His focus is on the way that an organization's culture can aid or hinder its effectiveness. In Schein's view there is a need for leaders to understand and analyse organizational cultures and how the dynamics of groups can help develop strategies for changing that culture. He argues that too little attention has been given to the ways in which groups within an organization develop their own cultures that affect their functioning in forms that are difficult for an 'outsider' to detect. Therefore, unless we begin to unveil and analyse cultures, we cannot really understand what happens within an organization, why things happen in the way they do, and why leaders act in the ways they do.

For Schein, culture is the deeper level; basic, shared assumptions that operate unconsciously and that are largely taken for granted by an organization's members. These are learned responses to the problems that the organization and its members face. These are a result of the group's efforts to survive in its external environment (and the pressures it receives from it), and resolve its problems of internal integration. Understanding the dynamics of groups can help develop strategies for changing an organization's culture.

One of the key issues facing all organizations is the extent to which each part of it develops its own culture and, if so, how that relates to the wider organization. An organization founded on competing sections where loyalty is to a section or team rather than the organization as a whole is usually a very dysfunctional one or else it is working in a context where it is not held accountable for what it does and there is little scrutiny. The relevance for marketing lies in the cultures that might be associated with different parts of an organization and how easy or difficult it is to get the necessary co-operation and 'buy-in' for strategies and decisions.

Insight

The measurement of both marketing culture and behaviour provides the opportunity to gain more insight into the overall market focus of organizations. Understanding the market orientation and marketing culture of all staff within organizations, to ascertain to what extent other members of an organization support or create barriers to the successful implementation of the marketing concept is a useful exercise. A small-scale study in a library service in Victoria, Australia, found that whilst all areas within the organization were apparently committed to marketing, there were various interpretations of what was meant by marketing marketing and how it should be implemented.

Source: Harrison and Shaw (2004).

Teamwork

Creating a culture of teamwork

The actions needed to make teamwork happen are:

◆ Leaders need to communicate the clear expectation that teamwork and collaboration are expected. No one completely owns a work area or process all by him or herself. People who own work processes and positions are open and receptive to ideas and input from others.

- Leaders and managers model teamwork in their interaction with each other and the rest of the organization. They maintain teamwork even when things are going wrong, and the temptation is to slip back into former behaviour.

- Teamwork is rewarded and recognized. The lone ranger, even if he or she is an excellent producer, is valued less than the person who achieves results with others. Compensation, bonuses and rewards depend on collaborative practices as much as individual contribution and achievement.

- The performance management system needs to emphasize and value teamwork. Often 360-degree feedback is integral to the system; this feedback from colleagues, direct reports and managers can have a powerful impact on work behaviours.

- Teams need to be formed to solve real work issues and to improve real work processes. Provide training in systematic methods so that the team expends its energy on the project, not on how to work together to approach it.

- Hold department meetings to review projects and progress, to obtain broad input, and to co-ordinate shared work processes. If group members are not getting along, examine the work processes they mutually own. The problem may not be the personalities of the people. Rather it may be the fact that they often have not agreed on how they will deliver a product or a service or the steps required to get something done.

- Celebrate group successes publicly.

- A team leader should be focused on achieving the task, building and maintaining the team and developing the individual.

Are there situations in which teamwork can be detrimental?

YES! If the group is not primarily interdependent, then teamwork can be detrimental to the effectiveness of the group. For instance, team-building programmes for salespeople will usually be counterproductive. Salespeople are typically independent and self-motivating. Therefore, team-building activities will be seen by the group as a waste of time. More effective for a group that is not interdependent would be communication training, leadership training, or other forms of personal development.

If the group is interdependent, but doesn't realize that the actions of the individual affect the group, then teambuilding activities will also meet with resistance. This may occur in an organization where departments are autonomous. Department heads may begin to see themselves in competition with other heads for resources including budgets, capital, and personnel. Before implementing teambuilding activities with this type of group, spend some time helping them realize how interdependent they really are.

Building and maintaining the team

Individuals are often required to move between working with many different groups of people in their working lives. Most teams are created to increase productivity, maximize co-operation and communication, and minimize conflict. Work teams, which are part of larger systems like managerial or production systems, perform a wide array of activities within the organization. Teams usually have well-defined physical and task boundaries, matching technical systems, and norms or rules governing interaction and behaviour. The internal leader may be a full-time team member. Management may appoint an external leader, who serves as co-ordinator, facilitator, mentor, encourager, cheerleader or consultant. The leadership role may also be shared by several people, or the leader may perform several functions. There are two critical elements to effective team building: a connection between all members of the team, and a shared understanding between the leadership and each team member.

Cross-functional teams consist of people from many parts of an organization. Organizations tend to have flatter structures and functional departments may not be well-defined. The rise of self-directed teams reflects these trends. Cross-functional teams require a wide range of information to reach their decisions. They need to draw on information from all parts of an organization's information base. This includes information from all functional departments. Cross-functional teams require information from all levels of management. Technical, financial, marketing, and all other types of information must come in a form that all members of a cross-functional team can understand.

The Six Deadly Sins of Team Building (Bacal, 2002)

If the need for team development is recognized, there are some pitfalls to avoid.

1   **Lack of a model** – It is not uncommon for people leading a team-building process to focus on a single aspect of team functioning. Often the emphasis will be on communication practices, to the exclusion of other elements that are critical to team success and effectiveness. A one-dimensional team-building process may increase frustration, and destroy the credibility of the process.

2   **Lack of diagnosis** – Each team is different. Each team has distinct strengths and weaknesses, and team building must build on these specific strengths and address weaknesses. Without knowing these strengths and weaknesses, the team-building leader runs the risk of using a process that will be irrelevant.

3   Short-term intervention – It is not uncommon for a manager to arrange for a team-building day, without developing a longer-term strategy for team development. At best, a single day on its own will result in a brief motivational surge that quickly fades. At worst, the day will bring to light issues that cannot be solved during that day, and are left to fester.

4   **No evaluation of progress** – It is common for team-building efforts to take for granted that things are improving without putting in place a mechanism for regular evaluation of team functioning. The team-building leader must be able to identify barriers so that the team can work to eliminate them.

5   **Leadership detachment** – Management sometimes enters into team building in a somewhat detached way. The detached manager treats it as something that will help others change, so that the team will function more effectively. However, team effectiveness cannot be improved unless the manager is willing to look at his or her contributions to the team. Management usually has to change too.

6   **Doing it all internally** – Team-building generally will not succeed unless conflicts and problems can be brought into the open and dealt with properly. Poorly functioning teams are characterized by a climate of blame, defensiveness and a lack of ability to deal with conflict. Poor teams lack the ability to improve themselves.

Whether you are leading team-building activities, or hiring someone, it is important that you stay away from these six deadly sins.

Insight: The stand-up

This is a tool to help create a group identity and a sense of shared purpose. It is a regular, standing-up, 15-minute team session, to make sure that everyone is aware of all the important things in your workplace that affect you and your work.

How can it help?

It helps to address the 'Why am I never told?' syndrome. The stand-up is an easy way to make sure that everyone is up-to-date. There is no time for long descriptions of the progress of each person's work.

How does it work?

It requires a shared understanding among the members of your group about what this 'anti-meeting' should accomplish and how it works.

Planning

There is no chairperson and no agenda but only items that concern the whole group are raised. Meetings occur regularly in a central location where everyone has room to stand.

Doing

Keep it simple, optimistic, focused and fun. It is better to say nothing than to talk about something of no concern to the group. Talkers learn to listen and listeners have an opportunity to talk.

Conflict in organizations

Conflict is inevitable but it can be minimized, diverted and/or resolved. Workplace conflict can lower morale and productivity, increase turnover and employee burnout, and add greatly to sick pay costs. Some conflicts are good and some not so good. Conflict occurs naturally when people interact, and teams, organizations and even individuals can grow as a result of the new ideas and the new ways of thinking that can emerge through conflict. However, conflict can also be destructive for individuals and for organizations. Organizational change can require members of an organization to work together in new ways and under new rules. Competition can exacerbate personality conflicts and the complexities of communication can make it more difficult for culturally, economically and socially diverse workers to resolve the issues and problems they encounter on the job.

Lankard Brown (1998)

Different people have different ways of dealing with situations but in general, human beings share certain characteristics that are very similar – even across gender, racial, and socio-economic lines.

◆   People tend to like it when people agree with them.

◆   People tend to not like it when people disagree with them.

◆   People tend to like other people who agree with them.

◆   People tend to dislike other people who disagree with them.

◆ People who are good at resolving conflicts look for some point of agreement and use good people skills to get others to see a different point of view.

Conflict occurs when individuals or groups do not obtain what they need or want and are seeking to look after their own self-interests. Sometimes the individual is not aware of the need and unconsciously starts to act out. Other times, the individual is very aware of what he or she wants and actively works at achieving the goal.

Conflict is destructive when it:

◆ Takes attention away from other important activities

◆ Undermines morale or self-concept

◆ Polarizes people and groups, reducing co-operation

◆ Increases or sharpens difference.

Conflict is constructive when it:

◆ Results in clarification of important problems and issues

◆ Results in solutions to problems

◆ Involves people in resolving issues important to them

◆ Causes authentic communication

◆ Helps release emotion, anxiety, and stress

◆ Builds co-operation among people through learning more about each other

◆ Makes people join in resolving the conflict

◆ Helps individuals develop understanding and skills.

Some strategies for dealing with conflict

1   **Non-verbal alert** – Non-verbal behaviour can be an early warning sign of conflict. Ask people to verbalize their feelings wherever possible.

2   **Team development phase** – See the Tuckman forming, storming, norming, performing model (p. 88). Sometimes conflict is predictable because that is what happens at one particular phase of group development.

3   **Resort to authority** – This means bringing in someone using a legitimate power base (and perhaps other power bases) to lay down the law. This may be necessary if team members are playing destructive roles.

4   **Planning** – Techniques such as task scheduling, timelines and project diaries and meetings may provide an authoritative and neutral way of sequencing tasks to be performed by different individuals or subgroups, thus reducing potential for conflict.

5   **Use communication skills more effectively** – Sometimes it is best to utilize what you know about good communication skills. Try to control destructive role-playing. Acknowledge individuals by praising their input.

6   **Conflict management techniques:**

   ◆ Collaborating: win/win

   ◆ Compromising: win some/lose some

   ◆ Accommodating: lose/win

◆ Competing: win/lose

◆ Avoiding: no winners/no losers.

Collaborating

I win, you win.

Fundamental premise – Teamwork and co-operation help everyone achieve their goals while also maintaining relationships.

Strategic philosophy – Working through differences will lead to creative solutions that will satisfy both the parties' concerns.

When to use:

◆ When there is a high level of trust

◆ When you don't want to have full responsibility

◆ When you want others to also have 'ownership' of solutions

◆ When the people involved are willing to change their thinking as more information is found and new options are suggested.

◆ When you need to work through animosity and hard feelings.

Drawbacks:

◆ Takes lots of time and energy

◆ Some may take advantage of other people's trust and openness.

Compromising

You bend, I bend.

Fundamental premise – Winning something while losing a little is OK.

Strategic philosophy – Both ends are placed against the middle in an attempt to serve the 'common good' while ensuring each person can maintain something of their original position.

When to use:

◆ When people of equal status are equally committed to goals

◆ When time can be saved by reaching intermediate settlements on individual parts of complex issues

◆ When goals are moderately important.

Drawbacks:

◆ Important values and long-term objectives can be derailed in the process

◆ May not work if initial demands are too great

◆ Can create cynicism, especially if there is no commitment to honour the compromise solutions.

Accommodating

I lose, you win.

Fundamental premise – Working towards a common purpose is more important than any of the peripheral issues.

Strategic philosophy – Appease others by downplaying conflict, thus protecting the relationship.

When to use:

◆ When the issue is not as important to you as it is to the other person

◆ When you know you can't win

◆ When it's not the right time

◆ When harmony is extremely important

◆ When what the parties have in common is much more important than their differences.

Drawbacks:

◆ One's own ideas don't get attention

◆ Credibility and influence can be lost.

Competing

I win, you lose.

Fundamental premise – Associates 'winning' a conflict with competition.

Strategic philosophy – When goals are extremely important, one must sometimes use power to win.

When to use:

◆ When you know you are right

◆ When you need a quick decision

◆ When a strong personality is trying to steamroller you

◆ When you need to stand up for your rights.

Drawbacks:

◆ Can escalate conflict

◆ Losers may retaliate.

Avoiding

No winners, no losers.

Fundamental premise – This isn't the right time or place to address this issue.

Strategic philosophy – Avoids conflict by withdrawing, sidestepping or postponing.

When to use:

◆ When the conflict is small and relationships are at stake

◆ When more important issues are pressing and you don't have time to deal with this

◆ When you see no chance of getting your concerns met

◆ When you are too emotionally involved and others around you can solve the conflict more successfully

◆ When more information is needed.

Drawbacks:

◆ Important decisions may be made by default

◆   Postponing sometimes makes matters worse.

Source: Culbert (2002)

Insight: Managing conflict between teams

Teams don't have to like each other to work together, but they do need to respect and value each other's existence. Find common goals and work out a compromise. Ultimately, the groups share a common goal: Both want the company to succeed. If both teams contribute to the same product, having a successful product launch is a shared goal. Even though product developers may not write ad copy, they must still support marketing's goals if they want employment this time next year. Product developers do have strengths they can offer. They may be good at building systems or analysing problems. Have each team identify the strengths they have that they can offer across the company.

After celebrating their own strengths, have the teams brainstorm the strengths of some of the other teams and design a request they might make of another team. Keep each team focused on the strengths of other teams. Have the teams keep their own written record of this part of the strengths conversation, especially the strengths they discover in other teams. If they put it in writing themselves and share it, it will have much more psychological power than a one-time discussion.

Bring the groups together. Frame the meeting as a joint exploration of how you can, as a group, move past conflict and reach the shared goals that the groups have already owned individually.

Adapted from: Managing conflict between teams, by Steven Robbins, 16 June 2003, www.entrepreneur.com

Groupthink

Groupthink is a concept that was identified by Irving Janis, referring to faulty decision-making in a group. Groups experiencing groupthink do not consider all alternatives, and they desire unanimity at the expense of quality decisions. Janis listed seven symptoms that show that consensus seeking has led the group astray. The first two stem from overconfidence in the group's prowess. The next pair reflect the tunnel vision members use to view the problem. The final three are signs of strong conformity pressure within the group.

◆   Incomplete survey of alternatives

◆   Incomplete survey of objectives

◆   Failure to examine risks of preferred choice

◆   Failure to reappraise initially rejected alternatives

◆   Poor information search

◆   Selective bias in processing information at hand

◆   Failure to work out contingency plans.

Case study: An illustration of groupthink

Report of the presidential commission on the space shuttle Challenger disaster

Illusion of invulnerability – Despite the launch pad fire that killed three astronauts in 1967 and the close call of Apollo 13, the American space programme had never experienced an in-flight fatality. When engineers raised the possibility of catastrophic O-ring blow-by, NASA manager George Hardy nonchalantly pointed out that this risk was 'true of every other flight we have had'. Janis summarizes this attitude as 'everything is going to work out all right because we are a special group'.

Belief in inherent morality of the group – Under the sway of groupthink, members automatically assume the rightness of their cause. At the hearing, engineer Brian Russell noted that NASA managers had shifted the moral rules under which they operated: 'I had the distinct feeling that we were in the position of having to prove that it was unsafe instead of the other way around.'

Collective rationalization – Despite the written policy that the O-ring seal was a critical failure point without back-up, NASA manager George Hardy testified that 'we were counting on the secondary O-ring to be the sealing O-ring under the worst case conditions'. Apparently, this was a shared misconception. NASA manager Lawrence Mulloy confirmed that 'no one in the meeting questioned the fact that the secondary seal was capable and in position to seal during the early part of the ignition transient'.

Out-group stereotypes – Although there is no direct evidence that NASA officials looked down on Thiokol engineers, Mulloy was caustic about their recommendation to postpone the launch until the temperature rose to 53 degrees. He reportedly asked whether they expected NASA to wait until April to launch the shuttle.

Self-censorship – We now know that Thiokol engineer George McDonald wanted to postpone the flight. But instead of clearly stating 'I recommend we don't launch below 53 degrees', he offered an equivocal opinion. He suggested that 'lower temperatures are in the direction of badness for both O-rings ...' What did he think they should do? From his tempered words, it's hard to tell.

Illusion of unanimity – NASA managers perpetuated the fiction that everyone was fully in accord with the launch recommendation. They admitted to the presidential commission that they didn't report Thiokol's on-again/off-again hesitancy with their superiors. As often happens in such cases, the flight readiness review team interpreted silence as agreement.

Direct pressure on dissenters – Thiokol engineers felt pressure from two directions to reverse their 'no-go' recommendation. NASA managers had already postponed the launch three times and were fearful that the American public would regard the agency as inept. Similarly, the company's management was fearful of losing future NASA contracts. When they went offline for their group meeting, Thiokol's senior vice president urged Roger Lund, vice president of engineering, to 'take off his engineering hat and put on his management hat'.

Self-appointed mindguards – 'Mindguards' protect a leader from assault by troublesome ideas. NASA managers insulated Jesse Moore from the debate over the integrity of the rocket booster seals. Even though Roger Boisjoly was Thiokol's expert on O-rings, he later bemoaned that he 'was not even asked to participate in giving input to the final decision charts'. Conflict within groups or teams can often lead to bad decision-making and problem-solving, rash decisions, inadequate consideration of alternative solutions and poor perception of what is happening in a given situation.

Source: Griffin (2002)

Another related phenomenon is the Abilene Paradox which describes a situation when a group of people act in a way that none of them wants but no one intervenes to stop what is occurring. Sometimes people feel uncomfortable acting in a manner contrary to the trend of the group. Sometimes the theory is used to help explain poor business decisions and groups are urged to ask themselves – 'Are we going to Abilene?' to make sure that the decision is what the group members want or whether it is a result of groupthink.

Insight: The Abilene Paradox

In 1988, *The Abilene Paradox and other Meditations on Management* was published by Jerry B. Harvey. The essence of the Paradox is that the limits of a particular situation force a group of people to act in a way that is directly the opposite of their actual preferences. It occurs when groups continue with activities that no group member wants but no one is willing to raise any objections.

A family is playing dominoes when the father-in-law suggests that they take a trip to Abilene (53 miles away) for dinner. The wife says, 'it's a great idea'. The husband has reservations because it is a long drive but thinking he must be out of step he says, 'Sounds good to me. I just hope your mother wants to go.' The mother-in-law then says, 'Of course I want to go.'

The drive is hot, dusty, and long and the cafeteria food is bad. They arrive back home four hours later, exhausted. One of them dishonestly says, 'It was a great trip, wasn't it.' The mother-in-law says that actually she would rather have stayed home, but went along since the other three were so enthusiastic. The husband says, 'I wasn't delighted to be doing what we were doing. I only went to satisfy the rest of you.' The wife says, 'I just went along to keep you happy.' The father-in-law then says that he only suggested it because he thought the others might be bored.

The group sits back, wondering how they managed to take a trip which none of them wanted. They each would have preferred to sit comfortably, but did not admit to it.

Learning in teams

Team learning is essential for organizational learning. Learning between teams, and the structures for this shared learning, is how organizational learning builds. Different people learn in different ways and therefore a training programme that suits one type of person might not suit another. Training should contain a variety of activities so that everyone finds something that is suitable for them. One of the best-known approaches to learning styles is the work of David Kolb through his 'Learning Styles Inventory'. Peter Honey and Alan Mumford published The Learning Styles Questionnaire (1982) which extended Kolb's work.

Developing the team

Activity 3.2

Here is an activity for evaluating your team. Circle the number that is appropriate for your team. What are your priorities for development? – You could also ask a trusted colleague to complete a form like this about you so that you can compare your responses with his or her perceptions. If there were large gaps in perception you might want to pursue this further to understand why your perceptions are different.

Evaluate your team development

Rating team development

How do you feel about your team's progress? (Circle rating).

1. Team's purpose
   I'm uncertain   1 2 3 4 5   I'm clear

2. Team membership
   I'm out   1 2 3 4 5   I'm in

3. Communications
   Very guarded   1 2 3 4 5   Very open

4. Team goals
   Set from above   1 2 3 4 5   Emerged through team interaction

5. Use of team member's skills
   Poor use   1 2 3 4 5   Good use

6. Support
   Little help for individuals   1 2 3 4 5   High level of support for individuals

7. Conflict
   Difficult issues are avoided   1 2 3 4 5   Problems are discussed openly and directly

8. Influence on decisions
   By few members   1 2 3 4 5   By all members

9. Risk taking
   Not encouraged   1 2 3 4 5   Encouraged and supported

10. Working on relationships with others
    Little effort   1 2 3 4 5   High level of effort

11. Distribution of leadership
    Limited   1 2 3 4 5   Shared

12. Useful feedback
    Very little   1 2 3 4 5   Considerable

Insight: Learning and development

Developing our people is one of our most important goals. Essentially, if we do not have the right people, with the right skills and capabilities, at the right time and in the right places, our business will suffer. After all, Serco only has two kinds of product: its processes and its people.

We are committed to developing our people – and we encourage them to learn and grow throughout their careers. In a business as diverse as ours, it is vital that we can share more widely the best practice developed in one market or region. That is why we are using the latest technology to give everyone access to the same information and resources.

We are always being joined by new people as we phase-in new contracts – so we have devised ways of helping them assimilate our values and adopt the Serco culture. Because we have a diverse portfolio of contracts, our training and development processes are designed to produce staff who are versatile, flexible and inventive.

As Serco becomes increasingly global, distance learning is likely to become more important. We are currently investing in solutions that will enable us to deploy and track learning in geographically diverse locations – enabling us to reach all our people, everywhere. Combined with powerful diagnostic tools, including performance appraisal and development centres, this will ensure we deliver learning solutions that meet today's business needs – and help us anticipate future needs.

Source: SERCO: Our World, December 2005

Induction and training

Every organization should have an induction programme that provides all the information that new employees and others need, and are able to assimilate, without being overwhelming or diverting them from the essential process of integration into a team. All new employees need some form of introduction to the organization and the job. A well-planned system of induction provides regular training and/or development sessions. For example, large department stores have a continuing programme of induction with a new course starting every week and special provision for part-time workers. This leaves individual managers in the position of receiving staff who have at least received training that is specific to their job. Some training, such as health and safety awareness, should be given to all employees.

In larger organizations line managers may take responsibility for monitoring and encouraging each individual at their place of work and for off-the-job training. However, there may be a specialist training and development section that is usually part of the Human Resources Department.

Trends in induction

Changing content

◆ Fewer 'chalk and talk' sessions and more multimedia presentations, or active learning tasks (e.g. giving inductees a questionnaire where completion involves talking to people outside the normal scope).

- Moving away from being purely about the practicalities of an organization to discussing culture and values. For example, an online induction and e-learning programme has been developed to introduce the culture for new HR staff in the NHS, and Tesco also uses e-learning for its annual 40 000 new recruits.

- Involving a wide range of personnel in the programme development to ensure that the content continues to match the organization profile; out-of-date or badly produced material is depressing.

- More awareness of socialization issues and using induction sessions for cross-function team building.

Procedures

- More written procedures to provide evidence of induction programme, for example for Investors in People, ISO 9000.

Evaluation

- Holding post-induction reviews, either formally or informally.

- Using statistics (e.g. on early leavers) to monitor the effectiveness of the induction process.

Insight

Without a good induction new employees get off to a bad start and never really understand the organization itself or their role in it. This may lead to:

- Poor integration into the team
- Low morale, particularly for the new employee
- Loss of productivity
- Failure to work to their highest potential.

In extreme cases, the new employee leaves, either through resignation or dismissal; the results of our most recent recruitment and retention survey showed that 19 per cent of leavers had less than six months' service. Early leaving results in:

- Additional cost for recruiting a replacement
- Wasted time for the inductor
- Lowering of morale for the remaining staff
- Detriment to the leaver's employment record
- Having to repeat the unproductive learning curve of the leaver
- Damage to the company's reputation.

Source: Chartered Institute of Personnel and Development (2006) Recruitment, retention and labour turnover survey 2006. London: CIPD. Available at: www.cipd.co.uk/surveys

Example of an induction checklist

It is important to keep a checklist of the areas of induction training received, ideally countersigned by the individual. This helps to ensure all employees receive all the information they need. This checklist can be a vital source of reference later in employment – for example to check if an employee has been briefed on policies, or to produce evidence of training in the event of a health and safety inspection.

Pre-employment	Joining instructions; proof of the right to work in the UK (if not already done during recruitment); conditions of employment; company literature
Health and safety	Emergency exits, evacuation procedures; first aid facilities; health and safety policy; accident reporting; protective clothing; specific hazards; policy on smoking
Organization	Site map – canteen, first aid post and so on; telephone and computer systems; organization chart – global chart; departmental/company products and services; security pass; car park pass; security procedures; Official Secrets Act, Data Protection Act, Freedom of Information Act
Terms and conditions	Absence/sickness procedure; working time, including hours, flexi-time and so on; arrangements for breaks, holidays/special leave; probation period; performance management system; discipline procedure; grievance procedure; Internet and e-mail policy
Financial	Pay – payment date and method; tax and NI benefits; pension/stakeholder pensions; expenses and expense claims
Training	Agree training plan, training opportunities and in-house courses; CPD and Personal Development Plan career management
Culture and values	Background; mission statement; quality systems; customer care policy

Source: Chartered Institute of Personnel and Development (2006)

All new employees should receive an individual induction programme that reflects their specific needs. A typical allocation of induction tasks would be as follows:

◆ **Line manager/supervisor:** explain the departmental organization, the requirements of the job, the purpose and operation of any probationary period and the appraisal system.

◆ **HR:** cover the housekeeping aspects for a new starter (possibly on arrival, certainly on Day 1) such as completing employee forms, taking bank details, explaining the induction programme.

◆ **Safety officer:** explain health and safety issues.

◆ **Section supervisor or a nominated colleague:** provide an escorted tour of the department and introduce fellow workers; then give day-to-day guidance in local procedures for the first couple of weeks.

◆ **Senior manager(s) and/or HR:** give an overview of the organization, its history, products and services, quality system and culture.

◆ Training officer (or line manager): describe available training services, then help to develop a personalized training plan. Provide details of other sources of information during induction such as the company intranet or interactive learning facilities.

◆ **Company representatives from trades unions, sports and social clubs and so on:** give details of membership and its benefits.

◆ **Mentor or 'buddy':** sometimes inductees are allocated a colleague, not their line manager or anyone from personnel, to help speed up the settling-in period.

The benefits of training and development

◆ **Improved motivation** – Individuals see their skills base extending and their promotion prospects being enhanced.

◆ **Lower turnover** – Opportunities for self-improvement, leads to people staying longer in one employment.

◆ **Higher levels of performance** – Trained and motivated staff are more likely to give of their best, which, in the end, justifies the training budget.

Insight

The Polestar Group is the United Kingdom's leading commercial printer and the fourth largest in the world. The Group aims to be the most innovative and profitable printers in Europe. This means that its staff need to be trained to use the latest high-tech digital equipment. Polestar's employees experience training at work that includes the following: induction training – training in new ways of working, technology and software multiskilling – employees are trained to do several different interrelated jobs learning management, organizational and leadership skills developing skills through a wide range of personal enhancement programmes.

Skilled print workers are in short supply, and the average age of the workforce is high. Polestar has developed a training programme called 'Printdynamics' which is designed to both attract and retain good workers. It is an interactive CD-Rom and online training package that offers comprehensive coverage of the print industry. It guides the trainee through the different print processes. Ensuring that employees are multiskilled leads to increased job satisfaction and flexibility. Ongoing training often results in improved productivity by eliminating waste and avoiding delays.

Source: http://www.technicalmarketingltd.com/VNO/Polestar/presspack.html

On-the-Job training (OJT)

Although people's learning styles differ, learning theory suggests that most people learn and retain more through doing and practising activities. OJT is the most common form of training in organizations. To be effective it needs to:

◆ Be properly planned and specified in advance

◆ Take place at trainees' normal work positions

◆ Be accepted that there will be 'downtime' when little is being produced by the people carrying out the training.

It is often carried out with a line manager or other experienced staff but often they will not have received any training in this role so the quality can be variable. OJT is not always the best approach to developing broader transferable skills but it is good for job-specific skills. Training that takes place at or near the job can be more easily tailored to meet specific needs and arranged at convenient times. The involvement of colleagues, supervisors or managers in OJT can also help to build a strong team spirit. OJT is often associated with the development of new employees, but it can also be used to update and widen the skills of existing employees.

Off-the-Job training and development

A key issue is making sure that the event matches up to the values the organization is trying to promote and the expectations of the staff who are taking part in the training. One aspect of this is the venue and, for example, if the intention is to focus on customer care it is important that the participants are treated as well as customers. Everything about the training needs to model the behaviour it is trying to promote.

Online training and education

Online training can be used as a supplement to face-to-face encounters. In some instances, instructors can supplement their material by placing related material on the Web. Some uses include the following:

◆   Aspects of induction training which are routine and technical such as health and safety procedures.

◆   Business training on procedures used to protect information within the company.

◆   Teaching the use of common business applications, such as Microsoft Office.

Managers need to understand their own learning style preferences and those of the people they manage. Responses to e-learning may be according to learning style preference. E-learning is more likely to deliver knowledge-type learning, rather than skills development. It may not be the most suitable answer to a particular individual's learning needs.

Case study: Travis Perkins

Introduction

To succeed, businesses need to monitor the changing business environment and respond accordingly. They also must ensure that the workforce is developed so that it can respond to changing requirements and provide good customer service. Quality customer service is a complex process that leads to competitive advantage. Travis Perkins was formed in 1988. The two businesses that merged had histories stretching back 200 years. It is one of the United Kingdom's biggest distributors of building materials. It uses customer service as a basis for growth. It trades under a number of brand names that have helped to establish its reputation with customers.

Growth

Many organizations from benefit economies of scale when they grow sufficiently large.

These may be internal – such as discounts through bulk buying or using techniques and equipment unavailable to smaller firms, or external – such as access to a skilled labour force, specialist trade associations and being close to specialist suppliers. Travis Perkin's business strategy has been successfully based on growth and it aims to continue to grow.

Business culture

Every business has a particular way of reaching its objectives and its own way of working embodied in its culture. Travis Perkin's culture is based on the assertion that quality of service is paramount. Good service and reliability is particularly important in the building trade when contractors may be fined for late completion.

Training

Travis Perkins continuously improves its workforce. After being inducted, employees go through customer service training. Their performance is continually reviewed and they receive training from managers. There is also skills training to develop effectiveness, ICT, customer care and accounting. In 2003 Travis Perkins launched Excel, a programme for all employees, aimed at continuously improving services to customers. It links training processes to the need to provide high quality customer care. The business has also set up a Development Zone where employees can book sessions to complete training courses.

Management Training

This includes programmes developed in-house for trainees and middle managers. Outside providers run courses for senior managers. Programmes vary according to need. For example, high performance managers can develop a tool kit for performance to help them to analyse, manage, delegate and work in teams.

Conclusion

Travis Perkins recognizes that it is its employees and their understanding of quality customer service that makes the organization distinct. Good training is vital.

Evaluation of training

Most management and employee training is only assessed by the individuals involved in the process and much of the feedback is taken from questionnaires. Although many organizations have developed strategies for developing managers, the evaluation of their training and development is often ineffective. Over a decade ago, research undertaken in the United Kingdom entitled 'Training in Britain: A Study of Funding, Activity and Attitudes' revealed that 85 per cent of UK employers made no attempt to assess the benefits gained from undertaking training. The reasons for this are as follows:

◆ Difficulty in quantifying the effects.

◆ Difficulty in disentangling the effect of a number of variables which might affect performance.

◆ Cost of evaluation that could outweigh the value of the benefit achieved.

◆ Sensitivity of the trainers who are keen to ensure that their training is shown to have had a positive effect.

The ultimate goal of training and development is to effect change in an individual's knowledge, understanding, skills and behaviours. However, for practical reasons of time and resources, often it only focuses on knowledge and to a lesser extent on understanding.

A model of effective evaluation: Joyce and Showers (1980) model

The model has five components:

1   The presentation of theory or the description of a new skill or behaviour deemed useful or desirable.

2   Demonstration or modelling of the new strategy or skill. This could be achieved by observing someone.

3   Initial practice in a protected or simulated setting – most often in a workshop session. The individual or the group participates, trying out the new skill.

4   Providing structured and open-ended feedback about performance.

5   Coaching. As the new idea or skill is being applied and tried in a real setting, follow-up help with implementation is given to the participant.

When participants were given only the first component, a description of the new skill, 10 per cent could transfer or use the skill in the workplace. When the second component, demonstration of the skill, was included, 2–3 per cent more persons could perform the skill in the classroom. When practice, the third component, was added, 2–3 per cent more transfer occurred; similarly, when the fourth component, feedback, was included, another 2–3 per cent transfer occurred. Thus, four components resulted in 16–19 persons out of 100 being able to perform the new skill in the classroom. However, when coaching, the fifth component, was part of the staff development process, up to 95 per cent of the participants transferred the skill into their actual practice. The coaching component was a critical one in effecting a change in the skills of an exceedingly large number of persons.

Coaching

Coaching is a learning opportunity and individual learning preferences need to be considered as part of this. To be an effective coach, the team leader needs to build trusting relationships. Focused listening is one of the most important skills for establishing these.

There are three levels of understanding and skill required for effective coaching:

◆   Recognizing managerial situations as opportunities

◆   Creating an effective learning process

◆   Establishing an acceptable helping relationship.

Organizational benefits of coaching

◆   To improve individual performance – to expand an individual's range of skills, knowledge and insight in order to help them do the job better

◆   To provide a supportive working environment

◆   To value people

◆ To improve communication

◆ To promote effective teams

◆ To ensure appropriate allocation of tasks and projects

◆ To develop managerial skills, for example, to improve the skills of team leaders

◆ To expand the range of skills, knowledge and insight of someone in order to enhance their prospects for a different job

◆ To develop people for more senior jobs

◆ To increase organizational effectiveness and efficiency

◆ To enable best use of resources.

Benefits of coaching to the individual

◆ Support for individual learning needs – tackling the tasks and the issues that concern people in their day-to-day job

◆ On-the-job development for both coach and individual – it can be a learning experience for both participants in the opportunity to reflect on skills, knowledge and behaviour

◆ Increased motivation

◆ Improved capability at work

◆ Potential to support career development.

Activity 3.3

Tick any items where you feel you have a need for coaching. Put them in order of priority for you. Next to your priorities, write the names of people in your organization who might help you with these activities. Work out a strategy for approaching the people concerned.

Coaching checklist

1 Providing guidance and support

2 Helping to get the 'big picture' in the organization

3 Helping with networking/making contacts

4 Interpreting organizational politics

5 Translating organizational jargon

6 Being a sounding-board for action plans

7 Appraising/reviewing performance

8 Providing day-to-day advice on problems

9 Listening and questioning

10 Being a resource person – able to point to opportunities/learning resources

11 Evaluating progress.

Mentoring

Mentoring can be provided in various ways but its aim is to develop people and organizational effectiveness.

Management development

Torrington and Hall (2005) show that management training and management development can be differentiated in four important ways:

1   Management development is a broader concept. It is more concerned with developing the whole person rather than emphasizing the learning of narrowly defined skills.

2   Management development emphasizes the contribution of both formal and informal work experiences.

3   The concept of management development places a greater responsibility on managers to develop themselves than is placed on most employees to train themselves.

4   Although in training generally there is always a need to be concerned with the future, this is especially emphasized in management development. Managers are developed as much for jobs they will be doing, as for jobs that they are doing. Both the managers and the organization benefit from this approach.

Case study: K Shoes

K Shoes first implemented teams in 1990, and 45 per cent of the employees are in teams of 5–8 people. Their responsibilities include: managing team resources based on marketplace demand for styles of shoes, understanding the business and marketplace issues and their impact on demand, and the handling of materials and equipment budgeting. Other responsibilities are controlling team profit and loss, identifying team training needs, and conducting cross-training and problem-solving during non-production time. They are also involved in the training and compensation of teams, member selection, performance evaluation and the impact of teams on the organization.

The primary benefits of undertaking a management development programme for the individual is the modification of their management style, technical or professional skills, while the primary benefits for the organization of such a programme focus on its ability to act as a catalyst in transforming the organization by providing the skills and knowledge to manage innovation and change (Doyle, 2000). These benefits are complementary in developing both the individual and the organization. A significant trend in management development in the 1990s has been the move away from case-based programmes to problem-solving, focusing on real-life issues.

◆   The individual participating must see the issue involved as important.

◆   It must involve some analysis.

◆   It must involve some aspect of creativity.

◆   There must be practical application of the suggested improvement.

Goals of management development

Given that there is some uncertainty about what successful managers actually do, it is difficult to establish clear goals for management development. In general, however:

◆ Management development will focus on the abilities to do, rather than on pure knowledge.

◆ Management development will focus on the needs of individuals and tailor 'developmental opportunities for each'.

◆ Individuals will be expected as a matter of course to take the initiative in their own self-development.

Team reward

Team reward aims to reinforce behaviour which leads to effective teamwork. It encourages group endeavour rather than individual performance. Most team reward systems emphasize team pay rather than non-financial rewards. However, teams may respond to all types of reward from pay, bonuses and public recognition. An advantage is that team pay can encourage co-operative work and behaviour, and develop self-managed and directed teams.

Team pay works best if teams stand alone with agreed targets and are composed of people whose work is interdependent. For it to work well, everybody must understand and accept the targets and the reward must be linked clearly to effort and achievement.

Teams may be able to plan and implement their own improvement programmes if they receive feedback and meet regularly to discuss performance. Team reward is a way for organizations to demonstrate that they value teams and individuals who perform well, and that high levels of performance are important. The quality of teamwork depends on

◆ Culture

◆ Structure and operating processes

◆ Values

◆ Performance management

◆ Management style

◆ Employee development programmes.

Discipline

A disciplinary interview can be thought of as having three stages:

1 **Establishing the gap** – Future performance is the main concern, so any discussion about present behaviour should be focused on changes that are needed for the future and how to achieve them. It is important to be specific about concerns and to provide evidence or examples of how there is a gap between present behaviour and what is required.

2 **Exploring the reasons for a gap** – It is important to allow the person subject to a disciplinary interview to explain the circumstances and to put forward their point of

view about the gap. This may uncover problems or issues that the manager is un-aware of but will need to be dealt with in some way, for example, suggesting that they seek advice and guidance or specialist help.

3   **Eliminating the gap** – There will need to be agreement to a plan of action that may involve training. Arrangements for keeping the situation under review will need to be agreed, and the person should be aware of how and when their performance is go-ing to be monitored. The aim is to help facilitate an improvement in performance.

Summary

Members of a team can contribute to it in two distinct roles: their professional or technical role (production, sales, etc.) and their team role. The effectiveness of the team will depend on the extent to which its members correctly recognize and adjust themselves to the relative strengths within the team. Each team needs a balance of team roles and the optimum balance will depend on the tasks that the team needs to perform and its objectives. Personal attributes fit some roles well but limit the ability to succeed in other roles.

Further study

Read Boddy, D. (2002) *Management: An Introduction*, Harlow: Pearson Education, Chapter 13, 'Motivation' and Chapter 15, 'Teams'.

Hints and tips

◆   If you are asked to interpret some information, it usually means that you need to ex-plain the meaning of it, making it clear that you understand the data provided. This is a likely scenario if undertaking Marketing Management in Practice. This exam will contain data that needs interpreting.

◆   You will need to have an appreciation of the theories and processes applicable to selection, recruitment, appointment and induction of new personnel into an organi-zation. Specific development should reflect the nature of any particular position that is the focus of the recruitment and the context of the organization.

◆   Lengthy description is not necessary. Focused used of theory in the particular case study context is important.

Sample questions

June 2006, Question 4

If the International Conference is to be successful, it will require the formation and development of a multi-disciplinary and multi-cultural team from a number of different organizations.

a. What are the issues that need to be considered when forming a team from different organizations which is multi-disciplinary and multi-cultural?

(15 marks)

b   How might a successful team be developed for the Conference?

(10 marks)

(Total 25 Marks)

June 2005, Question 1b

What issues and actions do '@ Wrap' management need to consider in the selection, appointment and induction of a brand manager to develop the export potential of all the '@ Wrap' products including '@ Medi Wrap'?

(20 Marks)

December 2004, Question 1b

What issues and actions do Pinnacle Pictures' management need to consider in the selection, appointment and induction of a webmaster into the organization?

(20 Marks)

Bibliography

Adair, J. (1988) *Team Leadership*, London: Pan

Adams, J. S. (1965). Inequity in social exchange. In L. Berkowitz (ed.), *Advances in experimental social psychology*. New York: Academic Press

Armstrong, M. (1996) *A Handbook of Personnel Management Practice*, London: Kogan Page

Bacal, R. (2002) The six deadly sins of team building, http://www.work911.com/articles/teambuidingsins.html

Belbin, R., Meredith (1996a) *Management Teams: Why they Succeed or Fail*, Oxford: Butterworth-Heinemann

Belbin, R., Meredith (1996b) *Team Roles at Work*, Oxford: Butterworth-Heinemann

Bennis, Warren, G. (1994) *On Becoming a Leader*, New York: Perseus, 2nd edition

Boddy, D. (2005) *Management. An Introduction*. 3rd Edition. Harlow: Pearson Education

Culbert, H. (2002) Conflict management strategies and styles: Improving group dynamics, http://home.snu.edu/

Doyle, P. (2000) *Value-based Marketing: Marketing Strategies for Corporate Growth and Shareholder Value*, Chichester: Wiley

Griffin, Em. (2006) *A First Look at Communication Theory*, New York: McGraw-Hill

Harrison, P. J. and Shaw, R. N. (2004) 'Intra-organizational marketing culture and market orientation: a case study of the implementation of the marketing concept in a public library', *Library Management*, 25 , (8/9) 391–98

Harvey, J.B. (1988) *The Abilene Paradox and other Meditations on Management*, Jossey-Bass Inc

Herzberg, F., Mausner, B., Capwell, D. and Smyderman, B. (1959) *The Motivation to Work*, New York: Wiley

Hertzberg, F (1966) *Work and the Nature of Man*, TY Crowell Co

H.M.S.O. (1989) Training in Britain: A Study of Funding, Activity, and Attitudes: The Main Report

Joyce B. and Showers B. (1980) Improving Inservice Training: The Messages of Research, *Educational Leadership,* 37, 5: 379–385.

Kolb, D. (1985). *Learning style inventory*. Boston, MA: McBer and Company.

Kouzes, J.M. and Posner, B.Z. (2002) *The Leadership Challenge*, San Fransisco: Jossey Bass, 3rd edition

Lankard Brown, Bettina (1998) Conflict management, http://ericave.org/docs/conflict.html

McClelland, D., Atkinson, J.M., Clark, R.A. and Lowell, E.C. (1953) *The Achievement Motive*, New York: Appleton Century Crofts

McGregor, D. (1960) *The Human Side of Enterprise*, New York: McGraw-Hill

Ouchi, William G. (1981), *Theory Z*, Reading, MA: Addison-Wesley,

Ott Daniel, J. (1999) http://www.egsa.org

Report of the Presidential Commission on the Space Shuttle Challenger Accident, http://science.ksc.nasa.gov/shuttle/missions/51-l/docs/rogers-commission/

Schein, E. (2004) *Organisational Culture and Leadership*, San Fransisco: Jossey Bass; 3rd Edition

Schein, Edgar H. (1996) Three Cultures of Management: The Key to Organizational Learning, *MIT Sloan Management Review* (Available at http://sloanreview.mit.edu/smr/issue/1996/fall/1)

Tannenbaum, R., Schmidt, W.H. (1958) How to choose a leadership pattern, *Harvard Business Review*, No. March-April, pp 95-101

Torrington, D and Hall, L (2002) *Human Resource Management*, London, Prentice Hall, 5th Edition

Tuckman, B.W. (1965) Developmental sequences in small groups, Psychological Bulletin, 63 384–99. (Tuckman later revised his model to include a fifth stage but this is not as well known as his four-stage model. See Tuckman, B.W. and Jensen, M.A.C. (1977) 'Stages of small group development revisited', *Groups and Organization Studies*, 2, 419–27.)

Unit 4
Managing change

Introduction

Organizations face change all the time, driven by internal and/or external influences. Most changes in organizations are minor and incremental. A few changes are major and involve completely new ways of operating. Managing change means taking active control of change because many problems are those of adaptation, that is they require of the organization only that it adjusts to an ever-changing set of circumstances. Factors from outside the business include technological developments, changing market conditions such as exchange rate movements, supplier price increases and demand from customers for new services and legislation such as the working time regulations and the minimum wage. Factors from inside the business include personnel changes, such as key employees leaving and new senior appointments. New management processes such as customer service initiatives are also a source of change, and there are constant pressures to improve efficiency in both the public and private sectors.

Factors driving change

The macro-environment

This includes all factors that can influence an organization, but that are out of their direct control. A company does not generally influence any laws (although it is accepted that they could lobby or be part of a trade organization). It is continuously changing, and the company needs to be flexible to adapt. There may be aggressive competition and rivalry in a market.

The PEST analysis is a useful tool for understanding market growth or decline. A PEST analysis is a business measurement tool. PEST is an acronym for Political, Economic, Social and Technological factors, which are used to assess the market for a business or organizational unit.

The PEST analysis headings are a framework for reviewing a situation, and can be used to review a strategy or position, direction of a company, a marketing proposition, or idea.

PEST is useful before SWOT because it helps to identify SWOT factors. There is overlap between PEST and SWOT, in that similar factors would appear in each. PEST assesses a market, including competitors, from the standpoint of a particular proposition or a business. SWOT is an assessment of a business or a proposition, whether your own or a competitor's. PEST becomes more useful and relevant the larger and more complex the business or proposition, but even for a very small local businesses a PEST analysis can still throw up significant issues that might otherwise be missed. The four dimensions of PEST vary in significance depending on the type of business, for example, social factors are more obviously relevant to consumer businesses or a B2B business close to the consumer-end of the supply chain.

Political

◆ Ecological/environmental issues
◆ Current legislation home market
◆ Future legislation
◆ European/international legislation
◆ Regulatory bodies and processes
◆ Government policies
◆ Government term and change
◆ Trading policies
◆ Funding, grants and initiatives
◆ Home market lobbying/pressure groups
◆ International pressure group.

Economic

◆ Home economy situation
◆ Home economy trends
◆ Overseas economies and trends
◆ General taxation issues
◆ Taxation specific to product/services
◆ Seasonality/weather issues
◆ Market and trade cycles
◆ Specific industry factors
◆ Market routes and distribution trends
◆ Customer/end-user drivers
◆ Interest and exchange rates.

Social

◆ Lifestyle trends
◆ Demographics

◆   Consumer attitudes and opinions

◆   Media views

◆   Law changes affecting social factors

◆   Brand, company, technology image

◆   Consumer buying patterns

◆   Fashion and role models

◆   Major events and influences

◆   Buying access and trends

◆   Ethnic/religious factors

◆   Advertising and publicity.

Technological

◆   Competing technology development

◆   Research funding

◆   Associated/dependent technologies

◆   Replacement technology/solutions

◆   Maturity of technology

◆   Manufacturing maturity and capacity

◆   Information and communications

◆   Consumer buying mechanisms/technology

◆   Technology legislation

◆   Innovation potential

◆   Technology access, licensing, patents

◆   Intellectual property issues.

Globalization

Globalization is helping to remove restrictions on where people can go, what they can buy, where they can invest, and what they can read, hear or see. Economic integration is driven by two forces: advances in technology and decisions to liberalize trade. Globalization means that there is always the threat of substitute products and new entrants. The wider environment is also ever changing, and the marketer needs to take account of changes in culture, politics, economics and technology.

However, there are unanswered questions concerning those people who lose out economically, socially and culturally. Globalization has had a mixed press and the growth in availability of Fair Trade products signals greater interest in the ethics of trade. Critics argue that globalization has led to rising global inequality and exploitation of the poor by transnational companies.

Supporters of globalization argue that the number of people in extreme poverty – living on less than a dollar a day – fell from about 30 per cent of the world population in 1980 to 20 per cent in 1997, according to the World Bank. They also argue that the relatively rapid growth of China and India has led to an improved income distribution, not a deterioration.

A series of corporate scandals that began with the collapse of Enron has caused a crisis of legitimacy and the business of wealth creation has been tarnished. At Enron, this took the form of generating phony profits, whilst at WorldCom, accountants turned operating expenses into capital assets.

Insight: The myth of the global company

Doubt has been cast on the idea that globalization means uniformity and the disappearance of local brands and flavour. Redding identifies six different business systems that currently dominate the world's economy:

1   The large multi-divisional, multinational firm found in Britain and the USA.

2   The continental European large-scale business, such as Volkswagen and Nestlé.

3   The European industrial 'cluster', such as the textile firms of Emilia-Romagna.

4   The Japanese keiretsu, the networks of interlinked firms still predominant in the world's second-largest economy.

5   The Korean chaebol, unique combinations of government and family firms, such as Samsung and LG.

6   The Chinese private company – the 'clans' of vertically integrated small firms that work so well in what is now 'the workshop of the world'.

Using the criteria of 50 per cent of business in their home territory with more than 20 per cent in each of the other two out of three major regions: America, Asia and Europe there are only nine companies that are truly global: IBM, Sony, Philips Electronics, Nokia, Intel, Canon, Coca-Cola, Flextronics and LVMH, the French luxury-goods business.

Source: Redding (2006)

The micro-environment

This environment influences the organization directly. It includes suppliers, consumers and customers, and other local stakeholders. Micro-environment describes the relationship between organizations and the driving forces that control this relationship. It may be more of a local relationship, and the organization may be able to exert its influence. Some external influences like globalization affect all organizations, directly or indirectly, whilst other influences may be more specific to particular sectors.

Stakeholder theory

Instrumental approaches towards stakeholder theory hold that organizations see their stakeholders as part of an environment that must be managed in order to assure returns to shareholders. Attention to stakeholder concerns may help to avoid decisions that might prompt stakeholders to undercut or thwart its objectives. Stakeholder management is a means to the end which may have nothing to do with the welfare of stakeholders in general but rather advance the interests of only one stakeholder group – its shareholders and the maximization of the financial returns to them. One variant of the strategic stakeholder management approach is the direct effects model where managers' attitudes and actions

How confident you are about your estimate

◆ Fully confident

◆ Reasonably confident (some missing information, perhaps)

◆ An informed guess

◆ Wild guess.

Your best estimate of the influence of the stakeholder

◆ High; this person or group has power of veto, formally or informally.

◆ Medium; you could probably achieve your goals against this person's or group's opposition, but not easily.

◆ Low; this person can do little to influence the outcomes of your intended actions.

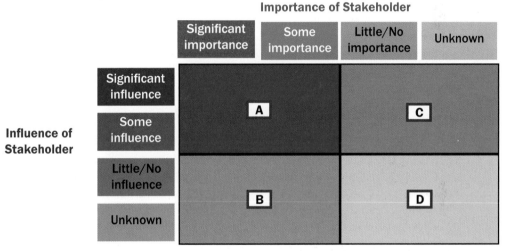

Boxes A, B and C are the key stakeholders of the project. The implications of each box is summarized below:

Box A – These are stakeholders appearing to have a high degree of influence on the project, who are also of high importance for its success. This implies that the implementing organization will need to construct good working relationships with these stakeholders, to ensure an effective coalition of support for the project. Examples might be the senior officials and politicians or trade unions.

Box B – These are stakeholders of high importance to the success of the project, but with low influence. This implies that they will require special initiatives if their interests are to be protected. An example may be traditionally marginalized groups (e.g. indigenous people, youth, seniors), who might be beneficiaries of a new service, but who have little 'voice' in its development.

Box C – These are stakeholders with high influence, who can therefore affect the project outcomes, but whose interests are not necessarily aligned with the overall goals of the project. They might be financial administrators, who can exercise considerable discretion over funding disbursements. This conclusion implies that these stakeholders may be a source of significant risk, and they will need careful monitoring and management.

Box D – The stakeholders in this box, with low influence on, or importance to the project objectives, may require limited monitoring or evaluation, but are of low priority.

Plan strategies

Plan your strategies for approaching and involving each person or group. It usually takes the form of obtaining more information, or of involving the stakeholder in the planning for the change. Highly influential people need to be involved in some way, or their influence needs to be neutralized. The people or groups who require the most attention are those who are influential and opposed to change.

The internal environment of the organization

The internal environment factors can include, for example, personnel changes or new management processes or demands to improve efficiency. They are sometimes ascertained by applying what is called the 'Five Ms' which are (Wo) Men, Money, Machinery, Materials and Markets. The internal environment is as important for managing change as the external. Change is likely to be needed when, for example, the organization is responding to newly identified markets, or taking up the cost-saving opportunities offered by new technologies. Successful organizations are those that are effective at managing cultural change. However, many do not recognize the need for it.

Insight: Today's world of work in the UK

Ten years ago corporations were preparing for a revolution in the way in which their managers worked. This was to be brought on by three things: a flattening of the hierarchies; the fear of losing talented women, which would make companies willing to offer part-time work; and technology, which would mean most work could as easily be done from Starbucks as from the office. Under these new working conditions, people would work where and when they liked. Teams would be virtual and offices flexible. Ten years on, the evidence of revolution has been patchy, its results at best, mixed. Flexible ways of working, hot-desking and virtual teams will be in retreat.

Here are some of the other things that are on the way out:

Work–life balance. The phrase created false expectations among workers, and encouraged companies to be disingenuous about what they wanted (which was really for everyone to work as hard as possible). Indeed, the increasing talk of work–life balance has gone hand in hand with more work and less life. The term will start to sicken and die.

Working from home. The Internet made this possible but it didn't work well. Those at home got disconnected from what was happening, while those at work suspected those at home of skiving, and teams failed to gel.

Part-time working. There may still be some of this in certain jobs, but in competitive professions and in management it will be full-time or nothing.

Instead, there is one big thing we will see more of: long hours. To succeed in high-flying jobs in competitive global markets will increasingly take dedication and talent and time. If you aren't prepared to do your job extremely well, there will be someone in India or China, if not in the next-door office, more than happy to do it for you. This new work environment will be even harsher, but it will also be simpler and rather less filled with guff.

Adapted from: Kellaway (2006)

Implications for marketing

Some of the implications have been discussed in other units, for example being sensitive to cultural differences when working in a multinational environment and the impact of information and communications technology on approaches to marketing. Marketing management is the process of planning and executing the conception, pricing, promotion and distribution of goods, services and ideas, to create exchanges with target groups that satisfy customer and organizational objectives. The emphasis is shifting from transaction-oriented marketing to relationship marketing, and organizations need to retain customer loyalty through continually satisfying their needs in a superior way.

Marketing teams must implement processes that co-ordinate all marketing and sales activities and achieve the level of data access, collection and sharing that is critical to consistent messaging, lead tracking, sales conversion and ongoing marketing intelligence. With the availability of websites, e-mail and mobile devices, and the introduction of high-powered packages for targeting customers, marketing should be easier than ever. However, the increase in marketing contact causes prospects to feel overloaded, reducing response rates and the value of marketing effort. Lack of co-ordination further erodes marketing effectiveness.

Marketers need to know when to:

◆ Cultivate large markets or niche markets

◆ Launch new brands or extend existing brand names

◆ Push or pull products through distribution

◆ Protect the domestic market or penetrate aggressively into foreign markets

◆ Add more benefits to the offer or reduce the price

◆ Expand or contract budgets for sales force, advertising and other marketing tools.

The change problem

At the heart of change management lies the change problem. It might be large or small in scope and scale, and it might focus on individuals or groups, on one or more divisions, the entire organization, or on one or more aspects of its environment. Problems may be formulated in terms of 'how', 'what' and 'why' questions. Which formulation is used depends on where in the organization the person posing the question or formulating the problem is situated, and where the organization is situated in its own life cycle.

For a **C**hange programme (C) to be successful and sustainable, there must be:

◆ A compelling **R**eason for change (R)

◆ A clear **V**ision of the future (V)

◆ And a coherent **P**lan for getting there (P)

$$R + V + P = \text{Sustainable Change}$$

When all these elements are not in place, different scenarios can be envisaged:

$$R + V = \text{Leap of Faith}$$

No coherent plan means that the outcomes are precarious:

$$R + P = \text{Tower of Babel}$$

According to the book of Genesis, the Tower of Babel was built by a united humanity to reach the heavens. To prevent the project from succeeding, God confused their languages so that each spoke a different one. They could no longer communicate with one another and the work could not proceed. After that time, people moved away to different parts of Earth.

V + P = Doomed Crusade

Without having a compelling reason to change it is difficult to gain 'buy in' from the various stakeholders.

Insight: Why change agendas often fail

◆ Complacency

◆ Failing to create teams with enough power to lead the change

◆ Underestimating the power of vision

◆ Failing to communicate the vision

◆ Allowing obstacles, real or imagined to block the vision

◆ Failing to create short-term gains

◆ Declaring victory too soon

◆ Neglecting to embed the changes in the culture

◆ Failure to consult.

Adapted from: Kotler (1996)

As a way of preventing these mistakes, Kotler created the following eight-change-phases model to be followed in the exact sequence:

1 Establish a sense of urgency by broadcasting a dramatic message of crisis or opportunity across your organization.

2 Create a coalition comprising top leaders and others with power to lead the effort.

3 Develop a clear vision – to direct the effort.

4 Share the vision – through multiple vehicles.

5 Empower people to clear obstacles and act on the vision.

6 Secure short-term wins to build momentum.

7 Consolidate and keep moving – use early successes to change systems and policies undermining the vision.

8 Anchor the change – institutionalize new approaches.

Change programmes benefit from a 'champion' to galvanize the plan and the action. Select a team with a mix of competences not necessarily all at senior levels. Develop an outline of what the organization will look like at the end of the change programme. Others need to be persuaded of the need for change. Relate this need to organizational objectives linked to a vision of where the organization will be if change is successful. Persuading people of the need for change can be difficult and it may be useful to bring a facilitator from the outside to act as a catalyst. Changes are best owned by the people implementing them, so it is more effective to encourage people to identify the change factors themselves. In any organization, there will be forces driving and forces restraining change. Try to reinforce the drivers and lessen the restraining forces, through education. Communicate continuously with stakeholders – employees, customers, suppliers and owners.

Checklist

Is an assessment of what the customer wants at the heart of your change strategy?

Do you have relevant measures to indicate your efficiency and effectiveness?

Do you have a realistic ass essment of staff morale?

Making change

Case study: The US Mint

The US Mint needed an enterprise resource planning (ERP) system that would let our business units get at all the customer information hidden in our systems. And we had just 12 months to get it up and running. Three years into the process, we kept running into the wall of our systems. Even though the customer data was there, only a few people had access to it. The biggest challenge was to convince them to sacrifice some of their most talented people to the project. If I could do it all over again, I'd spend more money educating the organization on what life was going to be like after the implementation. We invested a lot in training, but we probably should have spent twice as much time and money. To other executives, I would say, the most critical thing is to start with a business requirement. What does your business lack that such a solution will provide? If the business requirement doesn't justify the pain, don't do it.

Adapted from: Philip Diehl, Making Change: HEADFIRST.

Because change causes fear, e.g. a sense of loss of the familiar, it takes time for employees to understand and commit themselves to it in a meaningful way. Some writers (Bacal, 2000) argue that people tend to go through stages in their attempts to cope with change.

Stage 1: Denial

One way that people cope with change is to deny that it is happening, or that it will continue or last. People tend to avoid dealing with the fear and uncertainty of prospective change because they are hoping they would not have to adapt. This stage is difficult because it is hard to involve people in planning for the future. Moving out of the denial stage occurs when they see tangible evidence that things are different.

Stage 2: Anger and resistance

When it is no longer feasible to deny that something is happening or has already happened, people may move into a state of anger, accompanied by forms of resistance. Leadership is needed to help people work through this and on to the next stage. If leadership is poor, anger and resentment may last indefinitely.

Stage 3: Exploration and acceptance

This is the stage where people are beginning to develop a better understanding of the change and are more willing to explore further, and to accept it. They are more willing to participate in the process.

Stage 4: Commitment

This is the stage where people are willing to work towards making it succeed. They have adapted sufficiently to make it work. While some changes, for example downsizing, may never be accepted, eventually people do commit themselves to making the organization effective within the constraints arising from the change. The change process can take some time to stabilize.

This insight highlights some of the problems that people leading change may face.

Insight

New or different ideas often run into trouble before they reach fruition. However, change leaders need to help teams overcome blocks to change.

Forecasts fall short – A plan is needed but it is difficult to predict timing and cost. Change leaders need to accept departures from plans.

Expect the unexpected – A new path is unlikely to run straight and every change brings unanticipated consequences. Change leaders need to respond, to make adjustments and to make their case.

Momentum slows – You do not have solutions to problems, and the team is discouraged and enmeshed in conflict. Critics emerge. Even if a coalition has been built and key stakeholders are involved, you will be challenged. When the impact of change becomes clear, those threatened by it will formulate objections. This is when change leaders need to respond, remove obstacles and pu h forward. Actual progress will produce more believers than doubters.

Adapted from Kanter (1999)

Change management: the skill requirements

Managing the kinds of changes encountered by and instituted within organizations requires an unusually broad and finely honed set of skills, chief among which are the following:

Political skills

Organizations are first and foremost social systems. Without people there can be no organization. Organizations are intensely political. Change agents need to understand it.

Analytical skills

A rational, well-argued analysis can be ignored and even suppressed but not successfully contested and, in most cases, should be successful. If not, the political issues have not been properly addressed.

Case study: The AEGON Group

The AEGON Group has 27,000 employees and over 25 million customers worldwide. In 1994 AEGON bought a large stake in Scottish Equitable. As most of the acquired companies kept their existing identities, awareness of AEGON in the UK remained relatively low. AEGON realized that such low levels of awareness could have an impact on its ability to achie ve its ambitions.

Reasons for change

If consumers are to invest in a product long term, they need to know more about the organization they are dealing with. They need to recognise the brand and understand more about the brand values that it represents.

How to move forward?

AEGON underwent a discovery phase. The purpose of this was to find out what it had to do to meet the goal of building 'the best long-term savings and protection business in the UK'. This time of discovery focused on three key questions:

1   What do we stand for in the UK?

2   What do we want to stand for in the UK?

3   What should we be doing about it?

Brand audit

To answer these questions AEGON undertook a brand audit. This looked at two aspects:

◆   The company internally

◆   How the organization was positioned externally.

The audit showed that AEGON was solidly placed within the market. Its staff were known for their innovation and clarity of communication. The external audit also helped to discover where AEGON was positioned in relation to its competitors. People were aware of AEGON but there was evidence that people were confused about the breadth of what AEGON did because it traded under a number of different company brands.

With limited awareness of AEGON in the UK, it was important to explain what it had to offer and at the heart of this strategy was the need to:

a   Simplify financial services and provide more customer focus. It was important that consumers understood more precisely what they were buying, as well as the benefits and services they received

b   Develop the workforce. The objective was to develop the skills needed within the business to help it change.

c   Create a more distinct presence within the marketplace. This involved refreshing the AEGON brand in a way that made it more distinctive from its competitors and more attractive to customers.

A behaviour framework

To help embed this culture, AEGON developed a behaviour framework designed to influence how people at all levels within the organization could work and make decisions.

These behaviours emphasise the values of the organization. The eight behaviours are:

- Think customer
- Embrace change
- Encourage excellence
- Act with integrity
- Decisive action
- Work together
- Learn and grow
- Relate and communicate.

Implementing the change

Before the change consumers were confused about who AEGON was, what it did and how it fitted together. The audit had shown that global scale was important but so was local expertise. In the past, the AEGON brand had not been heavily promoted alongside Scottish Equitable or the other brands that it traded under. The brand strategy helped to reposition the brand within the industry.

Impact of the change

The organization has become more focused on the customer. The emphasis is on making information clearer for the customer to understand and the company easier to do business with. However, AEGON had to develop the brand and its reputation. It did this is a number of ways:

- External promotional campaigns emphasized the relationship between Scottish Equitable and AEGON. This helped to reinforce the local knowledge and the global power of AEGON in the UK.

- The CEO talked to the media about the need for change. The refreshing of the brand internally and externally resulted in strong positive feedback.

- AEGON launched new products.

*Source:*http://www.crmadvocate.com/casestudy/protagona/aegon_98.pdf

Planning for a change programme

- Ensure that there is a receptive climate towards the proposed change.

- Identify a champion or a team of champions that will help to promote change and oversee its implementation.

- Audit team capabilities and competences and identify any gaps that may need to be filled through training and development.

- Market the change to the target audience.

- Develop the plan, including a budget.

- Try to anticipate arguments against change, and identify positive responses to them.

Case study: Marketing libraries

Before we can effectively market our libraries to our customers, we have to market within to library staff. Each member of staff markets the library with every single interaction they have with customers. Friendly staff can often make up for shortcomings elsewhere in the service. Staff are also the most potentially damaging part of the marketing equation. Customers do not always notice good service, but they invariably notice and remember poor service, which is often a consequence of limited interpersonal skills. If employees do not care about their company, they will in the end contribute to its demise. Even if you don't have the time, staff, or budget for a formal, full-blown marketing plan, you can make progress on internal marketing.

Step 1: Staff buy-in

Get staff involved, energized, and feeling ownership for your library. Your staff members have a personal stake in your library, and therefore in this process. Every customer interaction is a marketing moment.

Step 2: Mission statement

Do you have a mission statement? Does it explicitly support the mission of your organization? The needs of your customers? Link the work of individual staff members to your mission. Post your mission statement prominently in your library; use it on documents such as fax cover sheets, e-mail, business cards and so on.

Step 3: Image/Brand

A brand is the emotional connection you have with your customers.

Your library's image is created by the collective actions of the library staff.

What expectations do you want to create for your customers?

How will you deliver on those expectations?

Step 4: Identity

Create an identity for your library – Place your identity stamp on intranet banner ads, library brochures and publications, presentations, e-mail signatures, and partner intranet sites.

Step 5: Key customer messages

Identify the key messages you want to communicate to your customers, for example I know the library has an intranet site; I can easily navigate the library's site; I know the library staff can provide consulting and analysis for my projects.

Step 6: Vision

Do you have a vision of where your library is going? What it will look like in two years? In the real world, you need to have a clear picture of your vision – and then communicate that vision to your staff.

What will success look like? – library staff will understand that they are selling or hurting your library during every interaction with customers? – feel increased personal ownership for your library? – know how your mission supports your organization's goals?

In conclusion, every customer interaction is a marketing moment. All staff must know, support, and be able to articulate your library's mission, vision, and key customer messages.

Adapted from: Internal marketing: inside job, Laura Zick, Library and Information Services, Lilly University, Eli Lilly and Company (www.sla.org)

Preparing for change

◆ Current attitude of staff?

◆ How big a change is needed?

◆ Who are the 'influencers'?

◆ How big is resistance likely to be?

Internal marketing

Internal marketing is an important 'implementation' tool. It aids communication and helps to overcome resistance to change. It informs and involves staff in new initiatives and strategies. Internal marketing has a structure similar to external marketing. The main differences are that the customers are the employees.

The marketer's skills are traditionally associated with the interface between organization and customer/consumer. But management also have a need to communicate with those within the organization – and those stakeholders associated with it. It is unlikely that an organization will be truly successful unless these buy in to management plans. There needs to be a common focus, and goals need to be understood and accepted. The prime marketing skills are communication – marketers are the specialists in identifying target audiences, assessing needs and in managing communications plans. Applying these skills internally means that a consumer-centred approach, with the employees identified as the consumers, needs to be adopted.

Internal marketing is an ongoing process whereby an organization aligns, motivates and empowers employees at all functions and levels to deliver a consistent and positive customer experience that helps achieve business objectives.

You should be able to demonstrate that you are able to use marketing communications techniques for an internal marketing plan to support the management of change within an organization. The basis of internal marketing is focusing on the relationship that exists between the organization and its employees. One of the success factors for the implementation of the marketing plan is to treat internal staff as if they are customers who all need the same consideration and attention as external customers. The aim of internal marketing is to develop a unified sense of purpose among employees. It plays an important role in ensuring that the organization is marketing- and customer-focused. Internal marketing is based on a communications programme, and there are a number of steps that an organization can take in order to achieve internal synergy and employee co-operation:

◆ Creating an internal awareness of the corporate aims, objectives and overall mission

◆ Determining the expectations of the internal customer

- Communication to internal customers

- Changes in tasks and activities

- Internal monitoring and control.

It is as important to segment the market internally, as it is segmented externally. A key aim of the marketing plan should be the successful motivation and retention of the internal customer so that the organization can meet the needs of the external market.

Internal marketing aids communication and can help to overcome resistance to change. It can be used to help inform and involve staff in new initiatives and strategies.

The Internet can help to foster the sharing of information but an extranet, that is a computer network that provides communication across selected organizations, enables sharing in a more controlled and secure manner. Often, companies use extranets as part of a search for better ways to communicate with their channel members and reduce costs. Because the extranet is interactive and easily accessible, it has the potential to transform the way channel members communicate with each other. For example, it can make information sharing and communication frequency more timely than the same information obtained from more traditional methods of communication.

Internal relationship marketing techniques

Internal marketing projects can be considered in four phases:

1   **Understanding the nature of the internal market:** An assessment phase that aims to find out the attitudes and beliefs of employees and managers towards each other, the company, customers and marketing mix components.

2   **Communicating with staff:** A review of communications activities and their effectiveness, including a 'mapping' of communications channels.

3   **Developing the plan:** Devising strategies for meeting the objectives of the internal marketing campaign.

4   **Evaluation:** Evaluating the success of the plan according to the set objectives.

Internal marketing can contribute to helping organizations achieve good relationships with their external customers. The key success factors of internal marketing success are:

- Create an internal awareness of the corporate aims, objectives and overall mission.

- Determine the expectations of the internal customer.

- Communicate to internal customers.

- Provide appropriate human and financial resources to underpin the implementation of the marketing strategy.

- Provide training in order that employees have the appropriate skills and competences to undertake the task at hand.

- Implement a change in tasks and activities appropriate to the objectives of the organization.

- Provide a structure whereby cross-functional integrated teams across business units can work together, in order to aid communication of business activity relating to the achievement of corporate goals.

- Provide the systems and processes that enable successful delivery of services and products, enabling employees to successfully implement them and achieve organizational success.

- Maximize the opportunity for customer interaction through effective management of service levels, for example response times, reply processes.

- Internal monitoring and control.

For internal marketing to be successfully implemented, a planned approach is essential to allow evaluation and measurement of the successful execution of a plan. The plan could be designed with the following headings:

- Internal vision
- Aims and objectives
- Internal marketing strategy
- Segmentation, targeting and positioning
- Marketing programme (to include all elements of the marketing mix)
- Implementation.

Planning for internal marketing

Internal marketing requires a similar kind of approach to that used in external marketing. An internal marketing audit is needed to discover who comprises the target audiences and to identify their needs. Channels of communication, both formal and informal, need to be identified. The same kind of questions that are used in any marketing audit can be used. Payback will be in terms of commitment rather than cash. Objectives should be SMART but couched in terms of changed behaviour rather than increases in market share and so on.

Strategy

Establishing a strategy for change will require a long-term view to be taken. What is the long-term need, and what are the short-term issues? Within the long-term strategic goal(s) will be the short-term need to introduce new products, to change operating procedures and so on. New product introduction may not be seen as an internal issue but internal staff need to know about, and be familiar with, new products before the outside world is notified. (One can be sure the telephone calls will start within hours of a launch. Internal staff must not respond 'Is that one of our products? I didn't know.')

Targets

Just as in marketing communications, there is need to identify target audiences. These will range from internal groupings such as individuals, sections, departments, and so on to include those 'exterior' stakeholders such as the organization's shareholders, bankers, lawyers, agencies, consultancies and so on. An internal marketing communications plan can be far more complex than one used to promote a product. The target audiences are more diverse.

Promotion

Two-way communication means that the target audience members should be able to have some input into proposed change. Internal communication media includes meetings, newsletters and noticeboards, but there is a need to achieve impact. Change has to be marketed effectively, and training and development offers a good opportunity to do this.

Price

Faced with 'selling' an idea or proposal to senior managers, the same process should be adopted but the needs of the management team and the stakeholders must be considered, and benefits such as raised profitability quantified and communicated. The price to an internal audience is measured in terms of inconvenience, extra work, coping with unfamiliarity and so on. The question 'Why bother?' must be answered, and answered well.

Product

The product consists of market strategies and the marketing plan. Therefore, the 'product' needs to be 'sold' in terms of values, attitudes and behaviour to employees so that they can buy into it.

Place

For the internal marketer, place can be interpreted as when and where a change will be introduced. For example, it may be better to introduce a new computer system in the off-season rather than at peak times.

Promotion – As has been said above, promote the benefits to those in each target audience.

Process – All aspects of the change need to be thought through carefully, piloted, evaluated, modified and re-piloted. It should ease the burden of adapting to change and, if possible, should simplify an employee's task. The introductory process, similarly, should be timetabled and then managed so that what is announced actually happens when and how it should.

Participants – All involved, from top management to junior staff, must follow the same procedures. If a senior manager does not comply it is unlikely that others will bother.

Managing the implementation of internal marketing

◆ Set objectives for internal marketing, for example to persuade 100 staff to join a new Performance-Related Pay (PRP) scheme.

◆ Tactics would include an internal application of the marketing mix, and could include staff forums, presentations, an intranet, away days, videos, personal visits by company directors or newsletters.

◆ Evaluation would consider the take up of PRP against your objectives, attendees at away days, visits to an intranet page and so on.

Internal marketing involves selling marketing plans to key internal staff or employees. Piercey and Morgan's (1997) model of internal marketing indicates the implications for the marketing mix.

Price – this relates to the benefit to the employee of taking this marketing planning information on board. It relates to the personal psychological cost of adopting different key values, and changing the way jobs are done. Often it requires asking managers to step outside their comfort zones with new methods of operation.

Place/Distribution – this concerns the physical and socio-technical venues at which organizations will have to deliver the product and its communications – that is where employees should be targeted, for example, the Internet and staff canteens.

Promotion/Communication – this is the most tangible aspect of internal marketing – communication media and the messages used to inform and persuade employees. There will be work on the attitudes of the key personnel in the internal marketplace and two-way methodology must be employed.

Service quality is influenced by employees because of the inseparability of services production and consumption in relation to the provider, that is staff. Good communication, motivation and training are central to service quality, and this is influenced by internal marketing.

Internal marketing and change

Internal marketing is like 'change management'. First, internal customers need to be identified. As with external customers, they will have their own buyer behaviour, or way of 'buying into' the changes which you are charged to implement. As Jobber (1995) explains, three different segments, namely 'supporters', 'neutral', and finally 'opposers', can be targeted. Each segment requires a slightly different internal marketing mix to achieve the internal marketing objectives.

For example, if the change was that a company was to relocate closer to its market, 'supporters' could be targeted with information about lower property prices; 'neutral' internal customers could be targeted with incentives such as better rewards. With 'opposers', a choice would need to be made between inaction or forcing acceptance of change. It depends on a calculation of what the impact would be between these two courses of action.

Critical incidents

Critical incidents can also be used to improve service quality. For a critical incident report to be useful, at least three pieces of information must be collected:

1   A description of the situation that led to the incident

2   The actions of the focal person in the incident and

3   The results or outcomes of the incident.

Source: (Jobber, 2006)

How to plan for a change programme

The approach needs to be properly considered before starting the implementation. The climate needs to be accepting of change.

Appoint a change agent, or champion for change that will help to ease changes through.

◆   Audit the skills and capabilities of the team. Train and develop as necessary.

◆   The change must be correctly marketed to your target audience.

◆   Decide upon the plan.

◆   Work out a realistic budget and keep to it.

◆   Try to anticipate the arguments against change.

◆   Ensure that there is a receptive climate towards the proposed change.

- ◆ Identify a champion or a team of champions that will help to promote change and oversee its implementation.

- ◆ Audit team capabilities and competences and identify any gaps that may need to be filled through training and development.

- ◆ Market the change to the target audience.

- ◆ Develop the plan, including a budget.

- ◆ Try to anticipate arguments against change, and identify positive responses to them.

- ◆ Never plan alone:

  - ◆ Planning alone = 'stratagems and wiles'
  - ◆ Planning in a small group = a conspiracy
  - ◆ Planning openly = building a team

- ◆ Deal with resistance early: your plan will be better and you can't be attacked later:

  - ◆ 'Gotcha': Someone complains that you haven't taken into account some aspect of life.
  - ◆ Response: 'Everyone was invited to comment on our plans – if you had a problem you should have said so...'
  - ◆ 'Told you so': Someone has raised an objection about some aspect of the plan.
  - ◆ Response: 'Yes you raised this issue and we considered it and agreed to do something else: you should have ...'

Activity 4.1

Think of an individual you would like to mobilize at senior level.

What intervention could you make to bring this person on side?

Think of one stakeholder group you would like to mobilize.

How can you best reach this group to get your message across with the right level of impact?

Employees are the company. Particularly in the services sectors, they represent the culture, the brand and the customer experience with the company. Employees are the best form of marketing during change. If people don't feel good about the change, customers will quickly know it.

Segment the benefits of the change. What factors are beneficial to employees, shareholders, customers and other stakeholders? Use these benefits to create key messages about the changes to be marketed to the appropriate audience.

Be truthful and genuine. It only takes one example of misdirection or dishonesty to create employee distrust of management's messages. Spin is spin, and people generally know when they are being spun. Be willing to show that a particular change isn't necessarily 'good' for everyone.

Change requires strongly embracing the future and a quick release of the past. Keep the organization's 'eyes' looking forward. Keep it thinking about what the customer wants. Those who have worked at the company for a long time tend to pull the company back into issues of tradition. Customers care little about the past. What will you do for them today or tomorrow?

Focus communications around the people who will remain after any staffing cuts or changes.

Deal with 'survivor syndrome', that is the phenomenon of those who keep their jobs feeling guilty that they have kept their jobs while many lose theirs.

Summary

Change is a natural part of the environment, but is seldom popular and is often re-sisted. Change, as a process, can and should be managed. It is as much subject to management planning and control as any other process. All change should be taken seriously, and planned and implemented with care. Major changes include a switch from a product/sales to a marketing/customer approach, and from a domestic to an in-ternational orientation. Internal marketing is of crucial importance in securing change and is best handled from a corporate level, possibly with marketers seconded for the purpose. Change always requires a price to be paid in human terms.

Hints and tips

Marketing, with its outward focus, is in the vanguard of change in an organization. Candi-dates need to have an understanding of change management theory or contexts. Winning marketing is about driving change, to face new market opportunities and threats. Market-ers are agents of change.

Sample question

June 2005, Question 4

© The Chartered Institute of Marketing, 2005

@ Wrap

An entrepreneur who perceived a market opportunity for a novel product '@ Wrap' founded the company in the UK. The product consists of high quality cling film (thin, transparent, plastic material, often used for wrapping food to keep it fresh) wound onto a cardboard core. The innovation came from the design of a plastic handle. This allows the easy application of the film, which can then be 'cut' without the use of any knife or other tools.

The product was originally developed from devices used to wrap and secure products stacked onto full-size pallets thus ensuring products remained in place in transit. The 100 mm wide '@ Wrap' product provides this type of convenience for smaller applica-tions securing, protecting and wrapping products. The advantages are:

Consumers had perceived the value of the product when watching their goods being wrapped at the checkout and now many retailers (e.g. DIY and office supplies stores) now stock the product for consumer sale after frequent requests from customers. This is opening up a substantial opportunity for the company in the consumer market. A continual flow of letters and e-mails from satisfied customers pointed to new applications for the product.

The company has expanded rapidly from an initial small group to over 50 people. It has just moved into new premises in an industrial estate in the UK that now offers room for even further expansion. This has given some organizational problems, as the entrepreneurial owner has been used to keeping control of all activities; with increasing size and range of activities, the company is moving to a more structured approach with delegation of responsibilities.

A limited export business has started following promotion of the product at an international trade exhibition in the UK. A new agent has been recruited in a selected 'New Territory', and a consultant appointed to advise on product registration issues.

'New Territory' may be taken to be any country of your own selection except the UK.

- Quick and easy-to-use
- Economic in use compared to other systems
- No separate knife or cutter needed (safety feature)
- No adhesive residue on packaging or merchandise
- No damage to other packaging (e.g. boxes)
- Retains label and merchandise visibility
- Used by major wholesalers and retailers nationwide

The above data has been based on a fictitious situation drawing on a variety of events and does not reflect management practices of any particular organization.

Your role

You have been appointed in the new position of marketing manager to bring a professional approach to marketing activities and, in particular, develop new business opportunities including export markets.

Question

'@ Wrap' is growing at a very fast rate.

a.   What change management issues confront '@ Wrap?'

(10 Marks)

b.   How might '@ Wrap' address these 'management of change' issues?

(15 Marks)

(Total 25 marks)

Website: www.cim.co.uk

Bibliography

Bacal, R. (2000) Understanding the cycle of change and how people react to it, www.work911. com/articles.htm

Bedford Consulting Group, www.bedfordgroupconsulting.com (June, 2002)

Firth, D. (2003) 10 rules of change, *People Management*, 6 March

Grove, A.S. (1999) Managing segment zero, *Leader to Leader*, 11, Winter

Jobber, D. (2006) *Principles and Practicing of Marketing*, McGraw-Hill 5th Edition

Kanter, Rosabeth Moss (1999) Enduring skills of change leaders, *Leader to Leader*, 13, Summer, 15–22,

Kanter, R.M. (1999) http://drucker.org/leaderbook/L2L/summer99/kanter.html

Kellaway, L. (2006) Work–life imbalance, The World in 2007, www.economist.com

Kotler, J. P. (1996) *Leading Change*, Boston MA: Harvard Business School Press

Piercy, N.F., Morgan, N. (1991), "Internal marketing – the missing half of the marketing program", *Long Range Planning*, Vol. 24 No.2, pp.82-93.

Redding, G. (2006) The few true multinationals: The myth of the global company, *World Business*, April (Gordon Redding is Director of the Euro-Asia Centre, INSEAD.), Vol 1, 1

Whittington, P.R. and Mayer, M. (2002) *Organising for Success*, London: CIPD

Unit 5
Project management

Learning objectives

2.1 Describe the main stages of a project and the roles of people involved at each.

2.2 Describe the main characteristics of successful and less successful projects and identify the main reasons for success or failure.

2.3 Explain the importance of, and techniques for, establishing the project's scope, definition and goals.

2.4 Use the main techniques available for planning, scheduling, resourcing and controlling activities on a project.

2.5 Explain the importance of preparing budgets and techniques for controlling progress throughout a project to ensure it is completed on time and within budget.

2.6 Explain the main techniques for evaluating the effectiveness of a project on its completion .

Statements of marketing practice

Jc.1 Plan marketing projects and prepare budgets.

Jc.2 Manage and report on delivery against plan and objectives.

Kc.1 Define measurements appropriate to the plan or business case and ensure they are undertaken.

Kc.2 Evaluate activities and identify improvements usin g measurement data.

Key definitions

Business case – Used to define the information that justifies the setting up, continuation or termination of the project. It answers the question 'Why should this project be undertaken?' It can be updated at key points throughout the project.

Critical path – The series of tasks that must be completed on time for a project to finish on schedule. Each task on the critical path is a critical task; any delay to it would delay the project's schedule.

Critical path analysis – A method for scheduling when tasks will happen. Comprising a forward pass and a backward pass, it determines how quickly and how slowly the tasks can be accomplished.

Customer – Used to represent the person or group who has commissioned the work and will be benefiting from the end results.

Gantt chart – A graphical representation of the project's current schedule. It will often contain bars for normal tasks, summary tasks, milestone tasks and slack values. Gantt charts are also referred to as bar charts as they depict task bars against a timescale.

Hard project management tools – Hard approaches to project management require measurable, solid and visible outcomes as represented in numbers, figure, charts, etc. For some organizations the only factor to evaluate is the 'bottom line', i.e. whether a project as made a profit or not.

Soft project management tools – Soft approaches use techniques that are not so easily quantifiable. For example, questions such as: 'was the experience useful?'; 'what skills and attitudes have changed?'; 'has the change in behaviour had a positive result?' The success of a project depends on the ability to develop a team of members who will be actively engaged in the process, will work collaboratively to take ownership of the project, and will see it to a successful outcome. This can be described as the soft or human side of project management and is fundamental for seeing a project to completion. Tools that would be used in this revolve around team building and development.

PERT analysis – A simple form of quantitative risk analysis that can be applied to a schedule to help estimate the duration of a task. After the entry of optimistic, pessimistic and expected durations for each of the tasks, Microsoft Project, for example, will calculate a weighted average of the three durations, and determine a single duration estimate for each task. Gantt charts can display the results of critical path analysis taking all tasks at their optimistic, pessimistic and expected values. In Microsoft Project, a button on the analysis toolbar provides access to PERT commands.

Product, deliverable or outcome – Used to describe everything that the project has to create or change, physical or otherwise. Results of projects can vary from physical items such as buildings to intangible things such as culture change.

Programme – This is a collection of projects that together achieve a beneficial change for an organization.

Project definition – What a project will deliver and how it will be judged.

Project objectives – Three basic objectives that a project must meet to ensure its successful conclusion:

1   Time objective
2   Cost objective
3   Quality objective.

Project objectives are often a contractual agreement between the project manager, the project's sponsor and the project's stakeholders.

Project resources – Work, time and cost are resources of the project that are consumed in its execution. For example, doing some work will take some time and incur some cost, as its accomplishment adds to meeting the project's overall objectives.

Supplier – The group that is providing specialist resources and skills to the project, or goods and services, to create the outcome required by the customer and user(s).

User – The person or group who will use or operate the final product. In some situations, the customer and the user may be the same group of people.

Insight

The Project Management Body of Knowledge (PMBOK) Guide is an internationally recognized standard that provides the fundamentals of project management as they apply to a wide range of projects. The Guide is process-based, meaning it describes work as being accomplished by processes. This approach is consistent with other management standards such as ISO 9000. Processes overlap and interact throughout a project or its various phases. Processes are described in terms of:

◆ Inputs (documents, plans, designs, etc.)

◆ Tools and Techniques (mechanisms applied to inputs)

◆ Outputs (documents, products, etc.)

The Guide recognizes 44 processes that fall into five basic process groups and nine knowledge areas that are typical of almost all projects.

The five process groups are:

◆ Initiating,

◆ Planning,

◆ Executing,

◆ Controlling and monitoring,

◆ Closing.

The nine knowledge areas are:

◆ Project integration management

◆ Project scope management

◆ Project time management

◆ Project cost management

◆ Project quality management

◆ Project human resource management

◆ Project communications management

◆ Project risk management

◆ Project procurement management

Source: Whitty, S.J. and Schulz, M.F. (2006). THE PM BOK CODE. *20th IPMA World Congress on Project Management*, 1, 466-72

Introduction

Some of the underpinning knowledge for this is covered in other modules and units, and a key part is contained in the Unit 7– Developing and implementing marketing plans. When studying the Marketing Management in Practice module, CIM recommends that two-thirds of the sessions should be allocated to a significant practical project involving the formulation and implementation of an operational marketing plan. This should cover the management of information, communications and human resources. The emphasis should be the application of this theory within a marketing team.

A typical project will consist of:

◆ Planning the project to be undertaken to meet the brief given.

◆ Undertaking the task. This will involve collecting and analysing information and developing a marketing plan.

◆ Planning, scheduling and resourcing marketing activities within the plan, identifying and overcoming problems during implementation.

◆ Measuring and evaluating the outcomes.

◆ Reflecting on the performance of the team and the individuals in it.

The basic approach to project management should be the same regardless of the type of project or sector in which the project is carried out. Services marketing professionals, in particular, are facing greater complexity in managing programmes and projects. Typical marketing programmes within large IT services organizations involve teamwork with different functional areas such as research and development, training, manufacturing, communication, as well as with business partners. Global marketing organizations require managing collaboration across numerous cultures and time zones.

What is a project?

The application of knowledge, skills, tools and techniques to a broad range of activities. Project management knowledge and practices are best described in terms of their component processes, for example initiating, planning, executing, controlling and closing.

Key roles in the project process

Sponsor

The person who WANTS the change AND has the POWER to legitimize it.

Advocate

Someone who thinks the change is a good idea. Generally helpful but not to be confused with a sponsor.

Expert

Someone who is qualified to comment on technical issues. Everyone thinks they're one of these, but it's important to listen to a real expert.

Target

The group of people who HAVE TO change. The difference between them and stakeholders is that stakeholders have a greater degree of choice.

Stakeholders

Beneficiaries of the change or people who may affect or be affected by it.

Change agent

Someone charged by the sponsor to bring the change about, but who has no power on his or her own.

Overview

Project management

- ◆ It should be collaborative.
- ◆ The methodology should be capable of being applied to any project.
- ◆ It should be results-oriented.
- ◆ It should be easy to use.

Stages of a project

In recent years, project teams and a project management approach have become common in many organizations.

The Initiation

The limits, constraints and priorities need to be defined.

Planning

- ◆ Team members need to be selected
- ◆ Scope of the project should be defined
- ◆ Potential 'risks' identified and planned for
- ◆ Resources required determined.

Execution

- ◆ Deliverables created
- ◆ Progress monitored and communicated
- ◆ Issues resolved and changes managed.

Closeout

- ◆ Customer satisfaction measured
- ◆ Lessons learned, analysed.

Criteria for success

- ◆ Customer satisfaction – expectations need to be managed
- ◆ Organization satisfaction – for example profit, development of capability
- ◆ Team learning – lessons can be learned and taken forward to other projects.

Reasons for failure

- ◆ Lack of appropriate expertise and approach from the project leader
- ◆ Lack of support from project sponsor
- ◆ Failure to communicate resources needed and reasons
- ◆ Lack of ability/necessary expertise of team members – need to select carefully
- ◆ Lack of 'buy-in' from end-users – need to involve them in the project.

Scope, definition and goals

- ◆ Project name
- ◆ Business case

- Objectives
- Deliverables
- Identify customers' requirements and needs
- Resources needed
- Planning, scheduling and resourcing.

Project plan

- Who – recruit the right skill base
- How – identify the interim deliverables
- When – schedule of delivery
- How much – the costs.

Budgets

- Staff costs
- Overheads
- Equipment needed
- Outside services
- Supplies
- Travel.

Controls

- Project team meetings
- Regular reviews
- Team member accountability
- Milestones
- Stakeholder meetings.

Post-project evaluation

- Customer and stakeholder evaluation
- Reviewing final status report with project team
- Recording lessons learned
- Reviewing final report with sponsor
- Celebrating success.

Seven steps to success

1   Use an effective method
2   Invest in planning
3   Involve the customer
4   Make it manageable
5   Involve the team
6   Communicate effectively
7   Learn from mistakes.

Project management may not always come easy to marketers, who may want to focus more on the 'creative' side of the work. Without a project management method, those who commission a project, those who manage it and those who work on it will have different ideas about how things should be organized and when the different aspects of the project will be completed. Those involved will not be clear about how much responsibility, authority and accountability they have and, as a result, there will often be confusion surrounding the project.

A project should possess identifiable goals, and a definite starting and finishing point. Project goals should be defined clearly. The major constraints on the completion of projects are time, resource availability and the need to achieve the required standard of performance for the project.

While marketing projects are getting more complex, marketing managers need to demonstrate a clear and strong return on marketing investment (ROI). One response to these pressures is the establishment of a 'project management office' – a team of people who use management methodologies and tools. Although such a structured approach might not be necessary or appropriate for every organization, many marketing professionals need to understand project planning and implementation.

Feasibility studies

Before a project is given the go-ahead, a feasibility study might be conducted. Support for a project could be important, so the aim of a feasibility study is to carry out a preliminary investigation to help determine whether a project should proceed further and how it should proceed.

The questions asked and the focus of a study will depend upon, for example, such things as the nature of the project that is being contemplated, the risk factors involved and its cost. The cost of carrying out a feasibility study needs to be weighed against the cost of a project not delivering what is expected of it. There is no point in carrying out an actual feasibility study if the cost of it would exceed the actual cost of the project. In this situation, the feasibility of a project would need to be determined in other ways on the basis of information that is already available.

However, a feasibility study will need to consider the following:

◆ **Cost** – Is it within the budget set by the organization or within the capabilities of the organization to finance it?

◆ **Timing** – Are there any time constraints and will it be possible to complete the project within these constraints?

◆ **Performance** – Will the project deliver the benefits that are claimed for it?

◆ **Effect on the organization** – Is it feasible in the context of the organization and the effect which it will have upon it? Does it fit the culture of the organization? Will it draw resources away from other important activities?

◆ **Resourcing** – Are the necessary skills, technology and physical infrastructure available? Or, if not, can they be easily recruited?

Aspects of a project

Project definition

Once the project has received formal approval to proceed, the objectives of the project and how the work will be undertaken can be determined. The project manager will carry out this work, in consultation with the client, and any sub-project manager if there are sub-projects. Large projects may be divided into sub-projects, with each sub-project requiring its own sub-project definition. The aim is to identify all prerequisites are in place. Before a definition can begin, there should be a project brief or terms of reference signed off by all parties involved in the project, giving the authority to proceed.

This is the stage where objectives, assumptions and constraints need to be identified so that everyone can be clear about the basis on which the project will proceed. As the project gets underway, there are likely to be changes to it because it is very difficult to know everything at the outset. Some of the assumptions made may need to change in the light of experience or, for example, the availability of resources or key personnel, and the original scheduling may need to be revised. All this is easier if the objectives, assumptions and constraints have been identified in the first place.

A project covers interrelated activities or tasks with definite start and finish times, identifiable objectives and an integrated system of complex but interdependent relationships. An activity or task is a unit of work whose scheduling is overseen by a project manager.

Projects have three elements:

1   Budget
2   Schedule
3   Deliverables.

The aim of project management is to ensure the effective scheduling of tasks and use of resources to deliver the objectives of a project on time, within cost constraints and with outcomes that meet the needs of the end-users.

Determine project scope

Determining the scope of the project helps to clarify objectives and set the boundaries of the project. It is often useful to state limitations, that is, what the project will not cover.

Project brief

A project brief should take the objectives and translate them into targets and goals. Any key constraints should also be identified and stated at this stage. This brief should be agreed by the client and communicated to the project manager. Success criteria should be established for the project, preferably criteria that are tangible and measurable. The success criteria should be provided in response to the conditions adhering to the project.

Contents of a project brief

A project brief will identify the following:

◆   **Objectives** – Why you are doing it, as listed in the client requirements definition, the business benefits that the project will provide when it is completed – often broken down to three basic project objectives: Time, Cost and Quality.

- **Scope** – Project boundaries.
- **Deliverables** – What it will provide.
- **Accountability** – Success criteria.
- **How you will be performing it** – Major milestones, change control procedures.
- **Constraints** – How would you know if your project had been successful?
- **Assumptions** – Listed unknowns about the project.
- **Resources**.
- **Key personnel** – Who is responsible for what? Who are the stakeholders?

The objectives form the basis of the project's strategic information. They also relate to one another; for example, a reduction in time may incur additional cost or may reduce overall quality. Project objectives are often a contractual agreement between the project manager, the project's client and the project's stakeholders.

The client is one of the stakeholders who will receive the benefits that the project will provide. He or she usually provides or authorizes the terms of reference and communicates strategic information to and from the project manager. Stakeholders are individuals or organizations with a vested interest in a project. The most obvious stakeholder is the sponsor.

Assumptions

Project assumptions can be checked with stakeholders who can critique them and, if necessary, a revised set of assumptions agreed when there are changes. A schedule can be revised when new information becomes available.

Areas where assumptions may need to be made include the following:

- The materials, resources, people and equipment that will be available.
- How long particular tasks will take to complete – Are the assumptions based on realistic information or are they the result of inspired guesses?
- How important is cost to the project – What are the arrangements if a budget needs to be increased?
- Will all the project tasks be completed in the timescale available and to an acceptable quality level?
- Are the project aims deliverable in line with the key stakeholders' expectations?
- What are the management arrangements for overseeing the project? Will there be a steering group to whom the project director or manager will report?
- What kinds of reports will be needed, by when?

Constraints

There can be constraints on the completion of projects, arising from the different objectives of: timescale; resource availability; quality factors and human factors.

- **Performance specifications** – These may be set out in terms of the ability to deal with certain demands. For example, this could be number of patients or transactions processed, or the number of enquiries dealt with.

- ◆ **Specific quality standards** – This could relate to technical standards and tolerance, or the achievement of a favourable report from an outside inspection agency.

- ◆ **Meeting deadlines** – For example, a new system may need to be implemented, ready for the start of the financial year, or a new development may have to meet time requirements as laid down in contract specifications.

Calculate resource requirements

Calculate requirements for each time period. Identify needs for each resource type (e.g. systems analyst, user staff) and identify needs for special skills or scarce resources.

Calculate costs

Calculate costs for the sub-project. This should include 'hardening up' items such as cabling, training, and so on for which an order of costs had been produced previously.

Determine overall costs of the project

The cost/benefit justification should have already been stated in the feasibility study. This stage provides the opportunity to review the case in the light of more detailed information. An important criterion may be to complete the project within a cost limit or budget which has been determined. Additionally, there may be requirements in terms of the ongoing cost of the completed project. For example, a new system may be required to make savings for the organization on a continuing basis.

Deliverables

A deliverable is a tangible verifiable outcome of work done to produce a product or service. To be verifiable, it must meet predetermined standards for its completion, such as design specifications for a product or a checklist of steps to be completed as part of a service. Deliverables have external stakeholders, such as customers, who receive the finished product or service and internal stakeholders, like a project manager and team members who work directly on the deliverable. A project may have one or many deliverables.

Define key project tasks

To help in breaking a project down into smaller and more manageable pieces of work, its objectives and scope are broken down into more detail in terms of duration, work and links. The most common approach is to plan from the overall objective, then to break this down into sub-objectives (or phases). These may relate to products, functions, disciplines and cost areas. The sub-objectives need to be broken down further into lower levels of detail until quantifiable tasks are at the bottom of the structure. The smaller the task, the more accurately it can be estimated. Tasks should be allocated to a named person, group or organization for implementation.

Once a project's tasks have been defined, the next stage is to determine how they relate to one another. This creates sequences of tasks within the project and identifies when each of the tasks can occur. In determining the sequence of tasks – those that must be accomplished before a particular task can take place – its predecessor(s) needs to be identified. This technique is known as precedence analysis and is the common way of determining how tasks relate.

These relationships are referred to as dependencies or precedences, and when planning a project it is important to establish the order of precedence of dependent activities, and to establish those activities which can be performed in parallel with other activities.

Not all tasks within a project start at the same time. There will always be some form of sequence. The simplest relationship is where the commencement of one task depends upon the completion of just one task that precedes it. This is a dependent relationship.

Building a project plan

The complexity of the project plan will depend on the size of the project, as larger projects demand greater planning and structure than smaller ones. Software such as Microsoft Project can be used to build project plans and will help with listing the project tasks, organizing them into phases, scheduling tasks, setting dependencies, deadlines and constraints, and specifying and assigning the resources to tasks.

If the timeline indicates that the project will run over its deadline, a check should be made to ensure that resources are not under- or overallocated. Resolving this is called 'resource levelling' and it may assist in sorting out the timeline. If it does not work, more resources may be needed. However, adding another person to a task does not necessarily mean that the task will be completed more quickly if the person needs to be trained and familiarized with the specific project. It may also slow down an existing member of the team if they need to brief and coach the newcomer. The timeline might be shortened through working overtime, though excessive overtime reduces productivity. If this does not work and the deadline is really unmovable, the project requirements may need to be reviewed so as to meet the deadline. When the project plan is agreed, it becomes a baseline that can be used to compare with the progress of the project.

RACI chart

RACI stands for:

R = Responsible (the role responsible for performing the task)

A = Accountable (the role with overall responsibility for the task)

C = Consulted (the roles that provide input to help perform the task)

I = Informed (the roles with vested interest who should be kept informed).

Responsibility charting is a technique for identifying functional areas where there are ambiguities, It enables managers from the same or different organizational levels or programmes to participate in a discussion a bout actions that must be accomplished in order to deliver a successful end product or service.

A RACI chart can help to ensure that the right people are involved in the right activities.

Action Items	R	A	C	I
1. _____	(Name)	(Other name)	May be	May be
2. _____			more than	next in
3. _____			one person	line
4. _____				
5. _____				
Etc.				

Determine work structure

Large projects are more likely to be successful if they can be divided into smaller units of work (sub-projects). Identify tasks which can be arranged into logical groups to form sub-projects. Grouping could be on the basis of, for example:

◆ Tasks relating to one functional area

◆ Tasks to be performed by staff in one geographic location

◆ Tasks relating to a particular deliverable

◆ Tasks to be performed by team members belonging to the same division or department.

◆ Ensure project structure and responsibilities are established.

Determine management systems

These will vary according to the size and nature of the project but should always include the following:

◆ A progress control system for recording planned and actual times. This could be an automated system or a manual one.

◆ Agreed procedures for formal review and agreement of each project deliverable.

◆ Scheduled management checkpoints.

If the project is divided into sub-projects, it is important that consistent management systems are used across them all.

Assign sub-project managers where appropriate. Clarify composition and responsibilities of the project steering group, and responsibilities of the project sponsor and the project manager.

Produce a project organization structure to show reporting lines.

Using IT

Computer software for project management

A wide variety of software packages is available to help with the scheduling and controlling of projects. Examples of the kind of software which an organization uses are as follows:

◆ ABC Flowchart
◆ Harvard Project Manager III
◆ On-Target
◆ Microsoft Project
◆ Suretrak
◆ Project Scheduler V5
◆ Super Project V2
◆ Time Line
◆ InstaPlan.

Assemble and organize the project team

Projects are sometimes carried out by a team of people assembled for that specific purpose. The activities of this team may be co-ordinated by a project manager. Project teams may consist of people from different parts of the organization, and in some cases, people from different organizations. The selection of the team will be dependent upon the skill requirements of the project, and upon the matching of those to individual members of the team. Within a project, roles and responsibilities define the relationships between the project team and the work that has to be done. Project work is often multifaceted, requiring a combination of skills and activities for planning, execution and completion. Every key project activity should be clearly defined in terms of roles and responsibilities. Some team members will have dual responsibilities of involvement in the project, in addition to a commitment to other projects or management of a functional area on a day-to-day basis. It is at this stage that a project manager should be appointed and responsibilities made explicit for all members of the team.

Project scheduling

The aim is to ensure that resources are available when they are needed. This needs to be checked before building a project plan.

Creating a cost schedule

This phase is primarily concerned with attaching a timescale and sequence to the activities to be conducted within the project. Materials and people needed at each stage of the project are determined, and the time each is to take will be set. When resources are assigned to tasks, they create measurable work. This work in turn can incur cost. One common occurrence when working with resource assignments is that demand will invariably exceed supply. Some key people will be overworked and others will have time to spare. This inefficiency can be overcome by first looking at how people are utilized, and then by looking at the tasks within the project and determining how much free time (slack) they possess. Once these factors are understood, actions can be taken and decisions can be reached regarding who does what (most efficiently), when.

Resource conflicts

If resource demand exceeds supply, this is known as a resource conflict and needs to be resolved. An assignment is the relationship between a task and a resource. This relationship creates work – somebody doing something to achieve the objective of the task. Work, time and cost are resources of the project that are consumed in its execution. Doing some work will take some time and incur some cost.

Milestones

Milestones are measurable objectives that signal the completion of a major deliverable and indicate that you have reached a significant point in the project. They can be established quickly if the project is on schedule, and can be useful when reporting on progress to management and clients.

Milestones are used to signify that something significant has been completed or something significant is ready to occur; for example, the start or beginning of a phase or the achievement of a key deliverable. The milestones and the information that need to be received and provided for different parts of the project need to be agreed with the project stakeholders. The information can be strategic and tactical.

Strategic

Strategic information would normally be provided for and by key stakeholders and include:

◆   Timing reports for the start and finish of major project phases

◆   Start and finish dates for discrete tasks within a project phase

◆   Cost schedules summarized by phase

◆   Start and finish dates for tasks assigned to a particular skill or resource

◆   Milestone date schedules for a task's sub-deliverables, or a to-do list.

Tactical

Tactical information would normally be shared between the project manager and members of their workgroup. This should include the following:

◆   Start and finish dates for discrete tasks within a project phase

◆   Cost schedules summarized by phase

◆   Start and finish dates for tasks assigned to a particular skill or resource.

Gantt charts

Gantt charts are particularly helpful when scheduling and controlling a project which has a number of repetitive activities within it. The graphic display afforded by the Gantt chart not only helps the operations management of the project but also helps to co-ordinate the various activities in an efficient way.

The Gantt chart takes its name from Henry Gantt, the American engineer who created it. It is a technique that can be used for sequencing project activities. The chart is the most common report in all project management systems. It is a form of bar chart with horizontal bars drawn against a timescale for each project activity. The length of each bar represents the time taken to complete an activity.

To construct a Gantt chart, the various activities are listed on a vertical axis, and the horizontal axis is used to represent time. Activity precedences are taken into account by starting a horizontal bar to represent the next activity at an appropriate point after its preceding activities, that is those activities which must take place before the next activity can start, have taken place. Normally, this would be at the earliest time that it could start after its preceding activities had finished.

The timescale should cover the duration of the project – from the start to the project finish date. In between these dates, it should be divided into equal increments. Gantt charts are sometimes known as milestone plans and they provide a useful way of monitoring the progress of a project (Figure 5.1). The advantages of using them are:

◆ All activities are planned for

◆ The sequence of activities is accounted for

◆ The activity time estimates are recorded

◆ The overall project time is recorded.

Task name	1 2 3 4 5 6 7 8 9 10 11 12 13 14 15 16 17 18 19 20 21 22 23 24 25 26 27 28 29 30

Figure 5.1: A Gantt timescale of 30 days

Once the chart's timescale has been created, tasks can be added. These tasks should be the complete list of sub-tasks as described within the network diagram, or from the lowest level of the outline (work breakdown structure). The chart's timescale can be in days, weeks, months and so on. It must be linear and in equal increments, for example one increment per day or one increment per week (Figure 5.2).

Task name	1 2 3 4 5 6 7 8 9 10 11 12 13 14 15 16 17 18 19 20 21 22 23 24 25 26 27 28 29 30
Design structure	
Write body text	
Set page layouts	
Create exercises	
Test exercises	
Create contents and index	

Figure 5.2: Example of a schedule for developing an online course

Displaying link lines between tasks

When a Gantt chart has a lot of links between tasks (especially cross-project links), the chart can become very busy with detail. When producing a Gantt chart for a client or a sponsor, decide if it is appropriate to tell them how tasks relate. They probably only need to know when tasks are scheduled to occur.

Once the project's schedule has been calculated (with critical path analysis) and a Gantt chart created, the next step in the planning process is to create some resource assignments. These assignments add the people dimension – someone doing something. What is important is a general understanding of the relationship between the task (something that needs to be achieved) and the resource (the individual that performs the work to achieve the task's objective). Gantt charts also provide a summary of the project as a whole, and can be used as a rough and ready means of assessing progress at the project control phase. At any date, the project manager can draw a dateline through the Gantt chart and see which activities are on time, which are behind schedule and generally record project status against plans.

	Apr	May	June	July	Aug	Sept
Marketing						
Broadsheet advertisement			░			
Face-to-face meetings with clients			░			
Direct mailing inserts into *Marketing Success*			░			
Arrange corporate ID		░				
Arrange printing of business cards		░				
Recruitment						
Recruitment period				░		░
London Recruitment Fair			░			
Programme starts						
Administration						
Administration support recruited			░			
Partnership agreement signed		░				
Arrange professional indemnity insurance		░				
Purchase domain name	░					
Register with Data Protection Act	░					
Finance						
Arrange online credit card payment system	░					
Arrange bank loan	░					
Website						
Design website	░	░				
Design activities for website		░	░			
Write web guide			░			

Figure 5.3: Six-month activity schedule

Activity 5.1

Choose a project that you will be involved with at work and, construct a Gantt chart which will provide an overview of the planned project.

When do you anticipate that you will start?

How soon could the project be completed?

Which activities need to be completed on time in order to ensure that the project is completed as soon as possible?

Show the shortest time it will take to complete the project.

Network analysis

The first step in network analysis is to divide the project into discrete 'activities' and 'events'. An event marks a point in time equating to the start or finish of an activity. An activity is a task or combination of small tasks that occurs between two events. Any activity that can be disaggregated and described by activities and events may be analysed within a network. The two most common and widely used project management techniques that can be classified under the title of network analysis are Programme Evaluation and Review Technique (PERT) and Critical Path Method (CPM).

PERT/CPM

There are six stages common to both PERT and CPM:

1   Define the project and specify all activities or tasks.

2   Develop the relationships amongst activities. Decide upon precedences.

3   Draw a network diagram to connect all activities.

4   Assign time and/or costs to each activity.

5   Calculate the longest time path through the network: this is the 'critical path'.

6   Use the network to plan, monitor and control the project. A network diagram is used to express how all the tasks in a project relate to each other. It helps to show how all the project tasks interrelate. A network diagram is also good for showing cross-project links.

Both models can help to answer the following questions for projects with thousands of activities and events, both at the beginning of the project and once it is under way:

◆   When will the project be completed?

◆   What are the critical activities (i.e. the tasks which, if delayed, will affect time for overall completion)?

◆   Which activities are non-critical and can run late without delaying project completion time?

◆   What is the probability of the project being completed by a specific date?

◆   At any particular time, is the project on schedule?

◆   At any particular time, is the money spent equal to, less than or more than the budgeted amount?

◆   Are there enough resources left to complete the project on time?

Probability analysis

Once the expected completion time and variance have been determined, the probability that a project will be completed by a specific date can be assessed. The assumption is usually made that the distribution of completion dates follows that of a normal distribution curve. If the project is to be completed in a shorter time, what is the least cost means to accomplish this and what are the cost consequences?

Critical path analysis

This is a method for scheduling when tasks will happen. A critical task is one that must be completed on schedule for the project to finish on time. If a critical task is delayed, the project finish date might also be delayed. A series of critical tasks make up a project's critical path.

As the tasks within a project have links between them, they cannot all happen at the same time. Critical path analysis (CPA) can be used to determine what can happen when. It calculates how quickly and how slowly the tasks can be performed, taking into account the sequence of tasks and their interrelationships. Gantt charts are created as a result of CPA.

Critical path analysis is a procedure that calculates a project's schedule. Taking each task in turn, it first calculates how quickly the task can be accomplished – its early start and early finish dates. Once all these dates have been calculated, the project finish date can also be determined. With this finish date known, CPA can then calculate how slowly each task can be accomplished (late start and late finish dates). Once all this information is known for each task, CPA will also calculate the slack that the task possesses.

The objective of CPA is to determine times for:

ES   Earliest Start Time. This is the earliest time an activity can be started, allowing for the fact that all preceding activities have been completed.

LS   Latest Start Time. This is the latest time an activity can be started without delaying the start of following activities which would put the entire project behind schedule.

EF   Earliest Finish Time. The earliest time an activity can be finished.

LF   Latest Finish Time. The latest time that an activity can finish for the project to remain on schedule.

ZS   Activity Slack Time. The amount of slippage in activity start or duration time which can be tolerated without delaying the project as a whole.

Once these values are known, the overall project can be analysed. The critical path is the group of activities in the project that have a slack time of zero. This path of activities is critical because a delay in any activity along it would delay the project as a whole. Finding the critical path is a major activity in controlling a project. Managers can derive flexibility by identifying the non-critical activities and replanning, rescheduling and reallocating resources such as manpower and finances within identified boundaries.

PERT

The major difference between CPM and PERT is that the latter employs three time estimates for each activity. Probabilities are attached to each of these times which, in turn, is used for computing expected values and potential variations for activity times. CPM assumes that activity times are known and fixed, so only one time estimate is given and used for each activity. The three time estimates specified for each activity in PERT are:

◆   The optimistic time

◆   The most probable time

◆   The pessimistic time.

These three time estimates are used to calculate an expected activity completion time which, because of the skewed nature of the beta distribution, is marginally greater than the most probable time estimate. In addition, the three time estimates can be used to calculate the variance for each activity. These values are then used exactly as in CPM. The variance values are calculated for the various activity times, and the variance of the total project completion time is the sum of the variances of the activities on that critical path.

Reviewing progress

It is the job of the project manager to make sure that the project stays on track and the deliverables meet the specifications detailed in the project definition document, as well as managing client expectations by keeping all relevant parties informed about the project's status. The project has a greater chance of success if the client is actively involved. The broad aims of reviewing are to:

Compare – Find variances between the baseline schedule and actual progress – cost variances and work variances.

Evaluate – Is it still possible for the project's objectives to be met? Do the variances indicate the development of a trend?

Decide – Perform a 'what-if' analysis to overcome the variances and get the project back on track. This is a method of experimentation to determine the optimum schedule of tasks or utilization of resources. A 'what-if' analysis may need to be carried out more than once.

Inform – Inform all project team members of revisions to the project's schedule, individual schedules and deliverables met. If certain tasks or resources are constantly going over budget or always taking longer than planned, could a trend be developing?

Managing communication

Effective communication with the relevant parties is the key to a successful project. The project manager should develop a communications plan in order to gather progress information from the team, supply timely reports and gather feedback from the management and the client.

Communication is Rational, Emotional and Political

	Speaking	**Listening**
Rational	The ability to convey knowledge and ideas	The ability to critically understand without making value judgements
Emotional	The ability to empathize with and stir an audience	The ability to recognize the emotional effect the speaker intends
Political	The ability to cause an effect	The ability to read between the lines

Note:
* Most listening happens outside the meeting
* Listening also means making an appropriate response

Collecting information from team members

Regular contact is needed with individual team members to evaluate the status of their work and to deal with any questions they have or issues that need to be resolved. There is no need to waste time by insisting on written reports when information can be gathered easily in other ways from face-to-face meetings, e-mail or telephone calls. Information should be gathered at regular intervals and any issues that are raised by the project team should be dealt with promptly.

Project meetings

Project meetings give the team, including management and the client representative, an opportunity to evaluate the project's status as a whole and to highlight issues that the team as a whole need to deal with. These meetings provide an opportunity to raise issues that concern the big picture even if they are only noted to be dealt with at a later time.

Reports to management and the client

Depending on the size of the project, status reports should be submitted to the management and the client to keep those who do not attend the project status meetings up to date. These may not be necessary for small projects, but for medium and large projects bi-monthly or monthly reports would be appropriate.

Managing client expectations

Managing client expectations is one of the tasks of the project manager and the project definition document is a tool that is useful in this process. By identifying clear project deliverables and constraints, the client should know what to expect from the outset of the project.

Once the project is under way, you then need to carefully manage scope change. Any changes to scope, whether suggested by the client or a member of the team, should be carefully discussed with the client. Pros and cons of the change should be weighed up, and if it is decided to go ahead, a formal scope change document should be presented to and signed by the client.

Managing the project plan

The progress of the project can be tracked by noting the status of each task at regular intervals. Software such as Microsoft Project offers three methods for tracking progress:

1   **Percentage of work complete** – This is the least accurate but fastest way to track. Asking team members to report their progress according to this method can result in misleading reports due to the human tendency to at times be 'almost done' for prolonged periods.

2   **Actual work completed** – This is more accurate, but also more time consuming.

3   **Hours of work completed per time period** – This is the most accurate but most time consuming, as people need to specify the exact hours they have worked in particular time periods.

Adding tasks

Sometimes the project will demand the addition of tasks that had not been previously identified, or the scope of the project may have changed. The project plan will need to be adjusted to create a new baseline.

Take note of when milestones are met and review the plan to ensure that it will meet the delivery date. If not, remedial action will be needed. Problems with the budget need to be resolved quickly, so it needs to be reviewed on a regular basis and reports submitted to the relevant parties.

Managing the scope of the project

The project manager is in charge of managing the scope of the project, so that only what was agreed is delivered unless changes have been formally agreed. The project manager needs to ensure that everybody involved remembers the project objective.

Mission creep occurs when the client or team members lose sight of the agreed project objectives. This can be avoided by creating a clear and unambiguous project and scope definition at the outset, and by constantly referring to this definition during the course of the project. The project's scope may also change upon request. Changing the scope of a project often means that a client has asked for extra work.

Budgeting

A budget is an expression of an organization's planned activities and serves a number of purposes. It is a forecast of the resources likely to be available to the organization and a plan for utilizing these resources to achieve the organization's objectives. It is also a framework for authorizing the expenditure of resources and for maintaining control over that expenditure.

Budgeting is the most common control mechanism of any planning process. Control is based on comparing actual against planned expenditure and investigating any variances calculated. It is important that sales and production targets are met and budgeting provides a standard against which the performance of the organization as a whole and the performance of individuals may be judged.

Budgeting systems also need to be flexible in enabling resources to be deployed quickly in response to changing demands from the environment and also motivate staff to use resources effectively and efficiently.

The control process

You want the *minimum* amount of information to meet your *needs*.

Rational

◆   Information is costly and burdensome to produce and maintain.

Emotional

◆   People resent giving information: they feel they are being checked on.

◆   People fear that information will be misused.

◆   People fear that it will allow others to interfere with their plans.

Political

◆   Collecting detailed information can put you in a position where you become accountable for the detailed performance.

◆   Having detailed information may tempt you to interfere.

◆   People adjust their behaviour to be able to report what they think powerful people want to hear.

Monitoring and control effectively contains four key activities:

1   Development or adjustment of objectives
2   Setting of performance standards
3   Evaluation of performance
4   Corrective action.

The first stage in the process after setting the objectives, by which performance will be measured, is setting performance standards. Performance standards are principally the level of performance against which actual performance can be compared. In the main, performance standards are presented in the form of budgets. The sole purpose of this will be to ensure that the amount of money given over to expenditure is not exceeded and that the proposed targets for income and profit are actually achieved. There are a number of methods of measuring performance overall, such as performance management. This consists of reviewing performance, giving feedback and, if necessary, re-examining and re-setting objectives and targets. To make monitoring easier, budgets are often broken down into a number of smaller manageable areas, often termed cost centres. For each of these, planned income and expenditure are monitored and compared with the actual results. In some organizations, each function may be a cost centre. For example, headings on a monthly or annual budget report could be as shown in the following table:

INCOME BUDGET – Marketing and sales division

	Actual year	Month	Budgeted amount	Variance under	Variance over
Sales					
Interest earned					
Sales commission					
Licence fees					
Royalty payments					
Property rentals					
Total income					

EXPENDITURE BUDGET – Marketing and sales division

	Actual year	Month	Budgeted amount	Variance under	Variance over
Sales					
Rent					
Advertising					
PR					
Sales promotions					
Travel					
Sales commission					
Total expenditure					

Evaluation

Variance analysis

One of the main things that control is likely to expose is constant variances from the planned budget. Variance analysis is used along with budgetary control. It compares a planned budget with an actual budget and seeks to explain any variations from what has been planned. A variance in itself is not good or bad, it is the interpretation and explanation of why there is a variance that will determine whether it is good or bad. As mentioned previously, figures do not speak for themselves, they need to be interpreted. The key to using variance analysis as a control tool is to be aware that variance in budgets is inevitable.

Benchmarking

In the words of Drummond, Ensor and Ashford (2008), benchmarkings is defined as:

> A systematic and ongoing process of measuring and comparing an organization's business processes and achievements against acknowledged process leaders and/ or key competitors, to facilitate improved performance.

It is concerned with demonstrating a commitment to continuous improvement and shows that the organization is a learning one, willing to learn from past mistakes and past successes, and to develop an approach to best business practice. It falls into three categories:

1 **Competitive analysis** – reviewing competitor activities, on an ongoing basis, to learn from their success.

2 **Best practice** – reviewing the best way of undertaking activities across the whole of the organization.

3 **Performance standards** – ensuring that targets are either met or surpassed.

Managing quality

The project manager should ensure that the project's quality standard is understood by everyone concerned and that deliverables meet that standard. Checklists and regular reviews focusing on the subject can assist in this process.

Post-project reviews

Some issues to consider:

◆ Were the main objectives met?

◆ Was enough time allocated to each task?

◆ Were there any warning signs that were ignored?

◆ Did everyone understand the project definition and their roles?

◆ Was the project on time and to budget and why?

◆ Was the relationship with the client satisfactory, or did unforeseen problems arise?

◆ Was the quality control process sufficient?

Successful project management

The effectiveness of project management is critical in assuring the success of any substantial undertaking. Areas of responsibility for the project manager include planning, control and implementation.

Knowledge, skills, goals and personalities are all factors that need to be considered within project management. The project manager and his/her team should possess the necessary interpersonal and technical skills to control the project activities.

The stages of implementation must be identified at the project-planning phase. In addition to planning, the control of the project is also a necessary condition of success. This means adequate monitoring and feedback mechanisms to facilitate comparisons of progress against projections. Monitoring and feedback also enables minor problems to be anticipated and addressed before they become major ones. Consulting with end-users is important for ensuring the success of a project.

Activity 5.2

Can you think of any examples where your organization needs to respond to change and a project management approach may be valid?

The reasons for project failure

Common reasons are as follows:

◆ Project goals are not clearly defined.

◆ The assumptions that are made at the outset of the project are incorrect but remain unchallenged.

◆ The project team is not sure of the project objectives or the deliverables.

◆ The planned schedule overruns.

◆ The budget is exceeded.

◆ Lack of co-ordination of resources and activities.

◆ Lack of communication with interested parties, leading to products being delivered that are not what the customer wanted.

◆ Poor estimation of duration and costs, leading to projects taking more time and costing more money than expected.

◆ Inadequate planning of resources, activities and scheduling.

◆ Lack of control over progress, so that projects do not reveal their exact status until too late.

◆ Lack of quality control, resulting in the delivery of products that are unacceptable or unusable.

Problems with project goals

◆ The project sponsor or client has an inadequate idea of what the project is about at the start.

◆ Failure of communication between the client and the project manager. This may be due to a lack of technical knowledge on the part of the client or an overuse of jargon by the project manager.

◆ Specifications may be subject to constant change. This may be due to problems with individual clients, decision-making processes at the client's end, or environmental changes. For example, the government may change the basic 'rules of the game' before the completion of the project.

◆ The project goals may be unrealistic and unachievable, and it may be that this is only realized once the project is under way.

◆ Projects may be complex and objectives may contradict each other.

There are perhaps two stages which can help the project succeed:

◆ Ensuring that goals are properly defined and achievable.

◆ Ensuring that the client specification is clear and understandable.

To do this the following objectives of the project must be established:

◆ What is it that the organization is setting out to achieve or is being asked to achieve?

◆ Will the suggested project fulfil these objectives?

◆ Have all the alternatives been considered, and is the chosen option the best one available?

◆ Have the full effects of the project, both inside and outside the organization, been considered?

Insight: : The value of soft and hard skills

Before I taught a nine-week course on project management for healthcare IT, I contacted CIOs of major hospitals and asked them what project management skills I should teach that most recruits are missing.

My students are mid-career clinicians that seek a role in IT project management. They want to manage healthcare IT projects to improve patient care and increase patient safety. For example, the Director of a Bone Marrow Transplant Unit and the Director of Clinical Operations each want to manage end-users through all phases of an EMR project in their respective hospitals. After 10 to 15 years as clinicians, they are back in school in the Master of Science programme on Clinical Informatics and Patient-Centered Technology at the University of Washington.

The CIOs responded to my question with the following list of skills:
◆ Leadership
◆ Listening
◆ Oral and written communications
◆ Team building
◆ Conflict resolution and management
◆ Critical thinking and problem solving
◆ Understanding and balancing priorities
◆ Balancing the big picture with attention to detail
◆ Understanding stakeholders' needs
◆ Change-readiness.

Responses emphasized the importance of 'soft' skills, which tend to influence how people interact with each other. In contrast, there was significantly less emphasis on 'hard' skills, i.e., more concrete technical capabilities, such as effective use of Microsoft Project software.

Everyone singled out the principle that the focus of projects is on how a business changes, not on the technology used as a tool to support that change.

The most important tools and techniques identified included:

◆ Scheduling
◆ Requirements definition
◆ Issue tracking
◆ Status reporting
◆ Project costing and control
◆ Risk analysis and control.

Almost all of the CIOs identified the need for a project management methodology flexible enough to meet the needs of their culture, no-one cited strict adherence to a single methodology as a workable approach.

The majority considered the best project management background to include versatile individuals who have deep clinical/business knowledge that understand IT. One cited that an excellent source for a project manager is administrative operations where you have a detailed understanding of business processes required 'to get the job done', e.g. managing central supply, purchasing or facilities management.

The response from the CIOs did not surprise me. Most project management methodologies focus on the tangible because it is easy to convey. The intangible, while less easy to express and learn, is just as important and requires equal time in the methodologies and while managing projects.

Source: The value of soft skills, *Project Management Matters*.
http://www.projectmanagementmatters.com/2007/11/the_value_of_soft_skills.html

Constraints on the completion of projects

Time

The definition of a project stated that it was an activity which had a defined beginning and ending point. Most projects will be close-ended in terms of there being a requirement for completion by a certain point of time. This point may be the result of an external factor such as new legislation, or may be derived from organizational requirements. It may also be partly determined by other constraints. There is likely to be some relationship between the time taken for a project and its cost. A trade-off between the two constraining factors may then be necessary.

Resource availability

There is likely to be a budget for the project and this will clearly be a major constraint. Cost constraints may be set in a number of ways, for example, as an overall cash limit or as a detailed budget broken down over a number of expenditure headings. Labour resources in particula,r may be a limiting factor. Whilst the overall resource available may be, in theory, sufficient to complete the project, there may be difficulties arising out of the way in which it has been scheduled. That is, there may be a number of activities scheduled to take place at the same time and this may not be possible, given the amount of resources available.

Quality factors

Whether the project delivers the goods to the right quality.

There are techniques which can be used to overcome the problems referred to above. These include:

◆ Budgeting and budgetary control

◆ Procedures

◆ Project planning and control techniques such as Gantt charts and network analysis.

The various constraints on project completion are likely to be interlinked with each other. For example, problems with time constraints or resource constraints may be overcome by spending more through working overtime, employing more people or purchasing better machines. Budget problems may have a knock-on effect on the achievement of deadlines.

Provided the project is not too complex in its activity relationships or simply too big to be mapped on reasonable size graph paper, Gantt charts can be very useful tools for the project manager and are graphically superior to the network analysis methods of CPM and PERT. They allow the critical activities to be found, that is those activities which must be performed on time if the project duration is not to increase, and any 'slack' or 'float' in the sequence of activities can easily be shown.

By timetabling the activities by horizontal bars whose lengths represent the activity times, the earliest completion date for the entire project can be mapped out on the Gantt chart, and then used as indicated above by the operations manager to check on progress as the project proceeds.

Management of projects

Gantt charts, PERT, CPM and other scheduling techniques have proven to be valuable tools in the management of large and complex projects. A wide variety of software packages are available for project managers, to assist in the handling of complex network problems. PERT and CPM, however, cannot ever purport to be able to solve all project scheduling and management problems in service or manufacturing industries. Good management practices, clear responsibilities for tasks, and accurate and timely reporting systems are the most essential qualities for successful project completion. As useful as these techniques are, they are only tools to assist the manager in making better, more calculated decisions in the process of conducting large-scale projects.

The role of the project manager falls into three areas:

1 Management of stakeholders

2 Management of the project life cycle

3 Management of performance.

Management of stakeholders

Stakeholders' interests must be monitored to ensure that their:

◆ Interest and support is maintained.

◆ Views and ideas are being adequately reflected in the project development.

◆ Personal success criteria are being pursued and achieved.

Management of the project life cycle

Feedback systems need to be set up to monitor key areas.

Management of performance

This is the least tangible but possibly the most important of the three categories. How it is tackled will depend upon what kind of project is being carried out. It is likely that the team will work apart most of the time, meeting up only occasionally and meeting only with the project manager from time to time. Issues that need to be considered are as follows:

◆ How to get the best out of the team when they are together?

◆ Ensuring people work when the team is apart.

◆ Disseminating information and keeping everyone informed is important.

◆ Ensuring continuing commitment by the team.

◆ Communicating change to team members quickly and effectively.

◆ Understanding the importance of looking at the team's performance, and also for the project leader to look at his or her own.

Project management and network techniques such as CPM and PERT are valuable tools for showing relationships between project activities, and identifying critical activities but the management of people is a major factor in whether a project will be a success or not. The ability to motivate staff, to create the structures and conditions in which they can be motivated and work effectively, and dealing with any people problems that arise are also essential features of project management. The human factors are as important as having the right tools and techniques. Working in teams and motivation have been looked at in other chapters so they would not be repeated here, but they are very important.

Five rules for delivering criticism

Project managers need to create and maintain good working relationships but they also need to monitor others' performance and act if there is a problem.

1 Think it through before you say something – A problem worth solving demands concentrated attention and focus to gain desired outcomes. This may mean not saying anything at all until you have mentally rehearsed your delivery and envisioned the receiver's response.

2 Criticize in private – Public criticism offends the receivers and observers. When a problem arises during a team meeting, acknowledge it and say that this is something that needs to be addressed 'later' 'without taking up everyone's time'.

3   Respond to problems in a timely fashion – Realize your own propensity to put off discussing problem behaviours. Remember the difficulty in reconstructing problems because everyone remembers them differently. Compare that to the benefits of a timely focus on correcting one problem at a time.

4   Criticize without comparison – Broad, unfavourable comparisons mean that individuals will end up finding fault with you rather than dealing with the ambiguous criticism levied at them.

5   Criticize with specificity, not labels – Examples of specific behaviours are inaccuracy, lateness, absenteeism, interrupting, missed timelines, incompleteness, incorrectness, assumptions, data, and so on. Criticism or feedback that cites specific examples such as these requires no interpretation of meaning. A missed commitment is a missed commitment. These concrete descriptions focus on quantifiable problems and achievable improvements.

Source: Paris (2000).

Activity 5.3

For a project that is under way in your organization, identify the key areas requiring monitoring, and suggest the kind of information and procedures that would be involved.

The project manager

Differences between a functional manager and a project manager

A functional manager is likely to be a specialist in the area being managed, such that when technical knowledge is required or a difficult issue arises, he should be able to make some realistic recommendations about how to tackle it (Meredith and Mantel, 1995).

Responsibilities of a project manager

1   To plan the project, soliciting the active involvement of all functional areas involved, in order to obtain and maintain a realistic plan that satisfies their commitment for performance.

2   To control the organization of human resources needed by the project.

3   To control the basic technical definition of the project, ensuring that 'technical' versus 'cost' trade-offs determine the specific areas where optimization is necessary.

4   To lead the people and organizations assigned to the project at any given point of time. Strong positive leadership must be exercised in order to keep the many disparate elements moving in the same direction in a co-operative manner.

5   To monitor performance, costs and efficiency of all elements of the project and the project as a whole, exercising judgement and leadership in determining the causes of problems and facilitating solutions.

6   To complete the project on schedule and within costs, these being the overall standard by which performance of the project manager is evaluated.

The skills of a project manager

The project manager is expected to integrate all aspects of the project, to ensure that the proper knowledge and resources are available when and where needed, and above all to ensure that the expected results are produced in a timely, cost-effective manner.

A project manager is more likely to be a generalist who is required to bring together a number of functional areas, each comprising specialists in their own fields. The project manager's task is to bring them together to form a coherent whole. He or she needs to be able to synthesize a wide range of information, whereas a functional manager must be more skilled in analysing a narrower area. The functional manager needs a depth of experience whilst the project manager needs breadth. Meredith and Mantel argue that an analytical approach breaks a system down into smaller and smaller parts, but a systems approach tries to understand the links between different elements. However, there is no doubt that an effective project manager needs the skills of analysis and synthesis.

Skill dimensions that a project manager needs to use at different points in the project management cycle are (Elbeik and Thomas, 1998):

Administrator

♦ Accomplishment of project tasks and goals
♦ Strong management of repetitive tasks and procedures
♦ Adhering to routines and systematic controls
♦ Focus on stability and consistency
♦ Able to meet deadlines and cope with workloads
♦ Organizing skills
♦ A concern for detail and accuracy.

Analyst

♦ Strong problem-solving orientation
♦ High level of critical thinking ability
♦ Ability to synthesize other people's thought and actions
♦ A strategic outlook – able to see the 'bigger picture'
♦ Able to balance short-, medium- and long-term requirements.

Negotiator

♦ Influencing and persuasion skills
♦ Diplomatic
♦ Willingness to challenge and tackle others
♦ Able to 'read' situations and identify motives and needs
♦ Determination to achieve objectives.

Verbal communicator

♦ Able to present arguments persuasively
♦ Able to communicate effectively with people from different backgrounds and levels of seniority
♦ Effective range of responses to most situations and able to think on his or her feet

- Able to secure people's attention
- Political sensitivity.

Written communicator

- Able to keep written communications brief and to the point
- Able to express complexity in a form that makes it accessible to the audience for whom it is intended
- Can write persuasively
- Can write with accuracy and precision
- Political sensitivity.

Listener

- Active listener – makes clear to the speaker that they are being listened to and understood
- Empathy and the ability to develop rapport.

Motivator

- Commands respect
- Persuasive and influential
- Able to enthuse people
- Highly developed interpersonal skills
- Able to achieve results through others
- Different people may respond to various techniques of persuasion in different ways, and it is important to know how to approach people so that they will be motivated to take appropriate action.

Decision-maker

- Capable of making decisions in the face of incomplete information
- Able to absorb a lot of information and identify what is significant about it
- Able to keep project aims and objectives in mind and not get bogged down in detail.
- Three questions face the project manager at the outset of a project:
- What needs to be done?
- When must it be done?
- How are the resources needed by the project to be obtained?

Managing large team projects

When managing a project it may be necessary to bring together partner firms, suppliers, subcontractors and team members who do not sit in the same building, or even in the same state or country. This presents challenges of monitoring, managing and integrating:

- Information flow (up, down and across the team)
- Scheduling, change control and logistics
- Work planning and staffing requirements.

All project team members need to be able to contribute their part of the project at the right time and place. This synergy of time, information and action depends on communication, collaboration and reporting. All of this is influenced by software capabilities.

Using a workgroup messaging system

The success of a project often depends on quick and effective communication between team members. Members can be linked through a workgroup messaging system; for example, Microsoft Project allows for almost instant exchange of project information. A workgroup messaging system is a network that is used to send and receive information about task status and assignments. Each team member should have access to this network, and be able to receive and send workgroup messages.

PRINCE

PRINCE (Projects in Controlled Environments) is a project management method covering the organization, management and control of projects. Since its introduction, PRINCE has become widely used in both the public and private sectors. Although PRINCE was originally developed for the needs of IT projects, the method has also been used on many non-IT projects. PRINCE2 is designed as a generic approach for the management of all types of projects. Each process is defined with its key inputs and outputs together with the specific objectives to be achieved.

Project evaluation

The main reasons for project evaluation and feedback are as follows:

◆ To ensure that the project remains on track

◆ To confirm whether the project meets user needs

◆ To determine whether the project delivers value for money

◆ To transfer the knowledge and any lessons from one project to other projects.

One reason for carrying out evaluation as an ongoing process during the project, rather than as a single post-project evaluation at the end of the project, is to ensure that important information and lessons are not forgotten.

Post-project review

A post-project review is performed by a project team at the end of the project's life cycle to gather information on what worked well and what did not, so that future projects can benefit from that learning. Participants in the post-project review process are members of the project team, key stakeholders and users of the project deliverables or results. Lessons learned from the review should be archived so that it is easy for project team members, process improvement teams and managers to find useful information. This is a formal review of a programme or project. It helps to answer the question of whether what was planned for has been achieved and if not, what should be done. It is undertaken when there has been time to demonstrate the business benefits.

Outputs and outcomes

There is a difference between outputs and outcomes. It is often possible to identify outputs during and not long after a project has been completed. With outcomes it takes longer to assess the impact of a project because objectives are often long term as well as short term. Implementation of outcomes-based monitoring can be difficult because while an organization may be able to control inputs (which resources are allocated in what amounts at what times to what activities) and to some degree outputs (in terms of products that are controlled by the organization), it cannot control the outcomes (impact) of a project.

Traditionally, success is measured by input–output analyses. Thus, for example, an anti-smoking campaign may be measured to see how many column inches of press coverage and other media coverage is generated (an output) but does it stop people smoking and lead to healthier people (an outcome)?

Post-implementation review (PIR)

The scope of the PIR will be dictated largely by the business case that will have identified the areas of business change and where benefits were to have been realized. A PIR will usually include an assessment of:

◆ The achievement (to date) of objectives

◆ Costs and benefits to date against forecast, and other benefits realized and expected

◆ Alignment with the overall business strategy

◆ Ways of maximizing benefits and minimizing cost and risk

◆ Business and user satisfaction.

Common problems

There are a number of common problems that may be encountered in carrying out PIRs. These include the following:

◆ When more than one organization is involved there may not be a common standard for measuring and recording the benefits and costs.

◆ A lack of documentation about aims and objectives.

◆ A lack of baseline measures. Measures of success can only be made accurately by comparing the level of performance before the project implementation against that at the time of the PIR.

◆ Management of expectations. The review process may lead to raised expectations of changes that may cost more to implement than the value of the benefits they would deliver.

◆ An organization may be too busy to undertake a systematic PIR and lessons may not be learnt or passed on when another project is implemented.

Some key success factors

◆ Focus on achieving continuous improvement through direction setting, evaluating achievements and identifying improvement actions.

◆ Performance management and measurement is an integral part of the business life cycle, helping the organization to evolve and change.

◆ Openness to constructive criticism and advice.

◆ Management commitment and readiness to learn lessons by adopting recommendations.

Post-implementation/post-project review checklists

The purpose of the review is to find out whether the expected benefits of the project have been realized and if lessons learned from the project will lead to recommendations for improvements.

Fitness for purpose checklist:

◆ Are all benefits mentioned in the project brief and is the business case covered?

◆ Does it describe each achievement in a tangible, measurable form?

◆ Are there recommendations in any case where a benefit is not being fully met, a problem has been identified, or a potential extra benefit could be obtained?

◆ Has this been conducted as soon as the benefits and problems can be measured?

◆ Was this scheduled in the project/programme plan?

Project review checklist:

◆ When the project was complete, did the outcomes meet user requirements without additional work?

◆ How close to scheduled completion was the project actually completed?

◆ What factors enabled the team to stay on schedule?

◆ What factors caused delays?

◆ What did you learn about scheduling on this project that will help you on the next?

Budget:

◆ How close to the budget was the final project cost?

◆ What did you learn about budgeting that will help you on the next project?

Team issues:

◆ What did you learn about staffing that will help you on the next project?

◆ What worked or didn't work about team communications?

◆ What was effective or ineffective about how information was distributed? Did you have the right skill mix?

Managing relationships:

◆ What lessons did you learn about managing the working relationship with clients?

◆ What lessons did you learn about managing working relationships with other departments or divisions?

◆ What techniques or systems did you develop for this project that could be used on other projects?

◆ List any recommendations you have for future development.

◆ If you could do the project again, what would you do differently?

Managing risks

'If anything can go wrong, it will.' Captain E. Murphy, US Army, 1978

'...and at the worst possible moment'

Types of risk:

◆ Risks to the success of the project

◆ Risks of the project on the wider organization

Dealing with risks:

◆ Remember Murphy's Law: make sure it can't happen

◆ Risks are associated with anxieties:

   ◆ a problem identified is a problem halved

   ◆ a problem shared is a problem halved again

Summary

In recent years, project teams and a project management approach have become common in many organizations. The basic approach to project management should be the same regardless of the type of project or sector in which the project is carried out. Project management is associated with a precise set of techniques, definitions and practices that can be used. These are all useful and demonstrate how a systematic approach can be used. However, skills in managing people are equally important. Many people are involved in managing projects as only part of their job and have to carry it out alongside other activities. A project should possess identifiable goals, and a definite starting and finishing point. Project goals should be defined clearly. Managing stakeholders' expectations is a major part of a project manager's role. The major constraints on the completion of projects are time, resource availability and the need to achieve the required standard of performance for the project.

Hints and tips

◆ It is useful to have an overview of the principles and techniques of project management. There are no surprises in the techniques that are used and they can be applied to a wide variety of situations where a systematic approach is needed.

◆ Good answers integrate project management theory and context specific development.

◆ There is not the time for very detailed development of Gantt charts or budgets in the examination. An appreciation of their role is necessary.

◆ Too much detailed development eats into time that could be spent better on other issues of project management.

Further study

Elbeik, S. and Thomas, M. (1998) *Project Skills*, Chapters 2–4. Oxford: Butterworth-Heinemann

Sample questions

June 2006, Question 5

a. What are the project management issues that need to be considered in the management of an international event?

(15 marks)

b. Make recommendations on how the issues may be managed.

(10 marks)

(Total 25 Marks)

December 2005, Question 4

The present website is only basic. A decision has been taken to completely re-launch it, to link in with the opening of the new facility. You have been assigned this project.

a. What information is needed before making a decision to launch the website?

(10 marks)

b. Outline project management theory that is relevant to this situation.

(15 marks)

(Total 25 marks)

Bibliography

Drummond, G., Ensor, J. and Ashfrod, R. (2008) *Strategic Marketing Planning and Control*, Oxford: Elsevier Butterworth-Heinemann

Elbeik, S. and Thomas, M. (1998) *Project Skills*, Oxford: Butterworth-Heinemann

Meredith, J. and Mantel, S. (1995) *Project Management – A Managerial Approach*, New York: Wiley

Paris, Claudine, E. (2000) Five guidelines for delivering constructive criticism, PM Talk Newsletter, available at: http//:www.4pm.com/articles/critic.pdf

Unit 6 Knowledge management and market research

Learning objectives

3.1 Explain the concept of information and knowledge management highlighting the role of marketing and employees within the organization.

3.2 Design a research project aimed at providing information as part of a marketing audit or for marketing and business decisions.

3.3 Manage a marketing research project by gathering relevant information on time and within the agreed budget.

3.4 Make arrangements to record, store and, if appropriate, update information in the market information system (MkIS) – a database created for a purpose or another system.

3.5 Analyse and interpret information and present, as a written report or oral presentation, appropriate conclusions or recommendations that inform the marketing and business decisions for which the research was undertaken.

3.6 Give examples of the application of information and knowledge management. Design a research project aimed at providing information as part of a marketing audit or for marketing and business decisions. Review and evaluate the effectiveness of the activities and the role of the individual and the team in this process.

Key skills

- ◆ Communication
- ◆ Develop a research brief
- ◆ Develop a research proposal or plan
- ◆ Present research results to decision-makers
- ◆ Present and justify a marketing or communications plan
- ◆ Produce effective marketing communications
- ◆ Assess the impact of a campaign.

Study guide

The *Marketing Research and Information* coursebook looks at marketing research issues in depth. For organizations to make informed decisions about the future, information is needed about a wide range of issues. This unit looks at information and knowledge management, and market research. Wilson (2003) defines marketing research as 'The collection, analysis and communication of information undertaken to assist decision-making in marketing'. One of the essential characteristics of marketing research is the gathering and analysis of information to inform decision-makers. This decision-making aspect is important. Marketing research provides a useful link between the supplier and the customer by keeping up to date with customer needs and wants.

Traditionally, marketers have used the marketing information system (MkIS) and its components to inform the decision-making process. Central to the process was the use of marketing research. Today with the development of customer databases, the marketer has a significant additional weapon in his or her armoury. There is more information than ever before but some companies still make poor decisions and still fail to meet their customers' needs effectively and efficiently.

This element of the syllabus explores the background to and the development of information management and the growth of the 'information-based' economy. It links this to the way in which organizations should determine their marketing information requirements and how information users should specify their needs within the organization in order to drive profitable lasting relationships with customers. It also explores formats and components of the technical systems that are available to marketers to manage information and support decision-making.

Key definitions

Data mining – The practice of automatically searching large stores of data for patterns, using computational techniques from statistics and pattern recognition.

Distribution – One of the four aspects of marketing. A distribution business is the middle-man between the manufacturer and retailer. After a product is manufactured by a supplier/factory, it is typically stored in a distribution company's warehouse. The product is then sold to retailers or customers.

Knowledge management – Refers to the technology, techniques or social practices for organizing and collecting 'knowledge' so that it is applied at an appropriate time or place. It includes the technology of databases and software applications collecting information.

Marketing research – A form of applied sociology which concentrates on understanding the behaviours and preferences of consumers in a market-based economy.

Market research – This is broader in scope and examines all aspects of a business environment. It asks questions about competitors, market structure, government regulations, economic trends, technological advances, and numerous other factors that make up the business environment.

Sample – A part or subset of a population taken to be representative of the population as a whole.

Sampling frame – A list of the population of interest that is used to draw the sample in a survey.

Probability sampling – A sampling method that uses objective sample selection so that every member of a population has a known probability of being selected.

Non-probability sampling – This involves a subjective selection of respondents. Therefore, the probability of selecting respondents is unknown. This means that, because the sample is not chosen objectively, it is not possible to state results with any degree of statistical certainty.

Quota sampling – A sampling method that selects a sub-sample based on known proportions in the population.

Convenience sampling – A sampling based on the convenience of the researcher. It may be that the selection is made in the street, in the office or from a database. As long as the sample fits with the population as a whole, it is legitimate.

Stratified random sampling – A probability sampling method in which the sample is forced to contain respondents from each of the key segments of a population.

Knowledge management

In recent years, the concept of knowledge management has become widespread in the business and management literature. Given marketing's focus on the effective gathering, analysis and use of information to yield insights into the behaviour of consumers in different markets, it is an important area. As with many business concepts, it is more common to read about it than to find concrete examples in the workplace. Thus, although there is agreement that it is a 'good thing', implementing a system for managing knowledge is by no means a straightforward proposition.

Knowledge management is concerned principally with how people are managed to collaborate and share their knowledge. Managing knowledge is concerned with developing a culture where people within the organization are willing to share knowledge so that the organization can be successful. This may involve changing the culture of the organization and putting processes in place to enable knowledge creation and transfer.

Knowledge management is the process through which organizations generate value from their intellectual and knowledge-based assets. This involves sharing them among employees, departments and sometimes with other companies. Knowledge-based assets can be explicit or tacit. Explicit assets usually refer to items that can be documented and archived such as patents, trademarks, business plans, marketing research and customer lists. Tacit knowledge refers to the know-how contained in people's heads. The challenge consists of being able to recognize, generate, share and manage it. ICT tools such as databases, access tools, e-learning applications, e-mail, groupware, instant messaging and related technologies, synchronous interaction tools, and search and data mining tools can all help to facilitate the dissemination of tacit knowledge but identifying it in the first place is a major challenge for most organizations.

Differences between data, information and knowledge

Data is unorganized words, numbers and images. It has no meaning and context. Information is data that has been organized or categorized and has meaning or value added to data. Knowledge refers to the use of information. Therefore, organizations can gather/capture information about their customers and competitors but they can become knowledge-driven only if they have the systems in place to use the information. Whether the organization becomes a knowledge-driven organization depends on leadership, culture and trust. Organizations such as management consultancies and R&D centres rely almost completely on their employees' skills and know-how for their success. Knowledge-intensive firms need employees who are able to spread knowledge across organizational boundaries.

Insight: Why ideas don't travel well

There are a number of reasons why good ideas that emerge in one part of an organization don't get picked up elsewhere. These include the following:

'What's in it for me?' – To get people to take on a good idea there must be something in it for them, which could be recognition, thanks, career progression or learning.

The 'not invented here' syndrome – Why should I learn from people I don't know much about? How do I know that what worked there will work here?

Lack of leadership – Many leaders do not spend any time promoting idea-sharing or rewarding those who contribute to it.

Lack of time – This is often a way of saying 'not enough of a priority'.

Failure to apply learning design expertise – Good ideas or business practices are turned into long documents that capture facts but are not designed to help people learn.

Lack of context sensitivity – Many organizations believe that what works well in one part of the organization (often the biggest part, such as the home country) can be applied without any modification in very different business environments.

Underinvestment in facilitating knowledge transfer – Leaders may say that 'sharing best practice' is a business priority but fail to give anyone the accountability or resources to make it happen.

All companies contain knowledge that they need to exploit and new technology makes it easier to share it. For example, conference calls mean that several people in different places can talk together and videoconferencing means they can see each other while they talk. Electronic databases make it possible to store vast amounts of knowledge, to which others can be given access. E-mail means people can communicate quickly, cheaply and over long distances. Company intranets mean staff can be given access to more information more quickly, and extranets enable organizations in the marketing channels to communicate more effectively.

Data mining can help businesses to handle and interpret large volumes of data so as to develop marketing, customer relationship and communication strategies. Advanced software can be used to analyse a terabyte of data – the equivalent of a million floppy discs – in a fraction of the time needed for human analysis. One of the challenges for companies that are serious about knowledge management is how to address the people and cultural issues. In an environment where an individual's knowledge is valued and rewarded, establishing a culture that promotes sharing can be difficult. It can seem as if people are being asked to give up something that enhances their value as individuals. Companies that manage knowledge most effectively tend to have three main characteristics:

1   Knowledge management programmes are intrinsic to their overall business strategy.

2   Human resources and IT policies that support the sharing of information.

3   A corporate culture that encourages staff to share what they know.

Case study: Nokia

Nokia dominates the world mobile phone industry with a market share of around 35 per cent. One of the keys to its success is its focus on knowledge management, on making sure that all parts of the organization communicate continuously with each other and with their suppliers. A large part of Nokia's success is ensuring that different groups constantly share their knowledge. A user-interface team is an eclectic group, made up of engineers, graphic designers, psychologists, sociologists and even a theatre director, who look at how people use mobile phones. While the design team thinks about what the phone should look like and the manufacturing group considers how it could be made, the user-interface team worries about how the customer will interact with it. While technology, such as e-mail, is important, it is not the foundation of the company's knowledge management. What is crucial is the constant attempt to break down barriers – between designers and engineers, or between factories and suppliers – and this is a task that never ends. What is important is seeking out the knowledge contained within the company and making it available to others in the organization so that they could use it. Many companies run up against a problem: their staff do not want to share what they know. They want to keep it for themselves. This is the most substantial obstacle to knowledge management.

Source: The change agenda, at www.cipd.co.uk/NR/rdonlyres/3E18B89D-4CE6-40DA-BDFA-2108DAA305CB/0/knowl_manage.pdf

'Do's' and 'don'ts' for effective knowledge management

The idea is to improve something or create new value so start with the business, the role of knowledge in it. Focus knowledge building on tools that justify the investment:

◆   **In-house Yellow Pages** – This system connects enquirers to experts and experience you can use, reduces errors and guesswork, and prevents the reinvention of countless wheels.

◆   **Lessons learned** – Insist that no project is complete until time has been spent providing insights into what went right and wrong and guidelines for others undertaking similar projects. Allow access via the company intranet.

◆   **Competitor intelligence** – Organize a database of customers, competitors and suppliers so that they are searchable, widely accessible and in a consistent format.

◆   **Use technology** to its fullest, but don't use it in place of human contact. In particular, don't rely on databases, encyclopedias, and libraries if there aren't 'librarians' who can help with navigation through the sea of information.

◆ **Share with people** how the company makes money. Many people are not aware of how this is achieved.

◆ **Deal fully with the obstacles** to sharing knowledge inside the organization.

◆ **Get learning** out of the classroom and into the marketplace. Action learning with project teams is a very powerful way to learn.

◆ **Speed up knowledge flows.** Encourage interactions via e-mail, in-house training programmes, cross-functional projects, and sharing best practices across departments and business units.

◆ **Don't manage knowledge for the sake of managing knowledge.**

◆ **Leverage the knowledge you have.** The most important function of knowledge management systems is connecting people to people, questions to answers.

◆ **Technology is an enabler** but don't think about knowledge management or knowledge management technology until it is clear what needs to be enabled.

Information

In his book *Marketing Research*, Alan Wilson (2003) identifies three main areas where information is needed by marketers if decisions are to be effective – information about customers, other organizations and the marketing environment.

Customers

Who are customers? – what are their characteristics? – what are the main influences on what, where, when and how they buy or use a product or service.

Other organizations

Comparison of performance relative to other organizations is used in the private and the public sector to improve competitiveness or, generally, to improve the quality of services. Benchmarking is an example of this. It involves learning, sharing information and adopting best practices to bring about step changes in performance.

Information and the marketing environment

The environment consists of many influences that are beyond the power of organizations to shape and control but have an impact on the organization. This includes factors such as social changes in the size and composition of households, age structure, legal framework, government policies and guidelines, economy and technology. The power of alliances such as the European Union, NAFTA, and ASEAN means that individual countries are less able to influence the trading environment in any significant way.

Marketing Information System (MkIS)

Information underpins successful marketing and can be of strategic importance as well as contributing to tactical and operational decision-making. Kotler defines an MkIS as:

consisting of people, equipment and procedures to gather, sort, analyse, evaluate and distribute needed, timely and accurate information to marketing decision makers.

A typical MkIS comprises the following:

◆ **The Marketing Research System** – gathers information about specific issues , such as testing products and evaluating the success of communications strategies.

◆ **Marketing Intelligence System** – gathers and processes critical business data from published sources, including government statistics, research reports, the national and trade press, transforming it into intelligence to support marketing decisions.

◆ **Decision support system** – The tools needed to make sense of data, statistical packages, the intranet and other tools that help marketers make decisions.

◆ **Internal records** – Sales records, account records, and other information that is available in the company.

Source: Housden, 2003

An MkIS can contain many different sources and types of information and, has a role in support of information gathering, evaluation, processing, dissemination, analysis and control. A good MkIS should encourage people throughout the organization to focus externally and provide quick, efficient and cost-effective information that is easily accessible. It can serve a number of purposes – it can help sales and service personnel in the field who want pricing information; marketers and planners who want to know about market and product trends so as to be able to develop marketing plans and adjust the marketing mix; and directors and senior managers who are interested in market developments that affect investment and other strategic decisions. Knowing what kind of information to obtain and how to make effective use of it are the key skills of strategic marketing.

Marketing research is an important element of the MkIS and is concerned with the provision of information about markets and customers and how they may or do react to different strategies. Marketing intelligence is concerned with information available from the marketing environment and may be less focused on immediate decision-making. Marketing productivity analysis uses internal information to quantify marketing inputs and outputs, for example measuring the response to a promotional campaign. Marketing modelling may involve, for example, the synthesis of profile and transaction information to develop profiles of individual customers. The MkIS is concerned with many areas of data collection.

Activity 6.1

How would you respond to these questions for establishing the scope of an MkIS if they were asked about your organization?

◆ What types of decisions need to be made regularly?

◆ What types of information are needed to make these decisions?

◆ Is this information available in a timely fashion?

◆ What types of information are needed but aren't available at the moment?

◆ What information is needed on a daily basis? weekly? monthly? yearly?

◆ What reports are needed on a regular basis?

◆ What types of data analysis programs need to be made available?

◆ What are the four most helpful improvements that could be made in the present marketing information system?

The critical function is how the organization uses information not the information system used to develop the information or the technology supporting it. Short-term advantage can accrue from IT but the results are not sustainable. Since the early 1980s, competitive advantage's focus has moved towards systems and away from technology. Systems that enable a business to create value for its customers include customer relationship management, supply chain management and knowledge management.

MkIS and customer relationship management trends

The development of technology is bringing closer the time when a company's information systems will lead to the generation of integrated profiles of individual customers. However, there are considerable difficulties in realizing the potential of technology. Whilst it is an important tool for marketers, human factors will always have a big influence on how effectively technology is utilized. The following trends are mostly enabled by increased technological capacity but still need an appropriate organizational structure and culture in order for any benefits to be realized.

1 **Highly successful companies will invest more in customers, not less** – Successful companies will focus on using customer information and applying technology and strategies to keep high-value customers, convert moderate-to-low-value customers to higher value, and minimize investments in customers that detract value.

2 **Companies will compete for customer share, not market share** – Companies will need to focus on how they are going to increase or maximize their share of each customer's spending by managing and increasing the value delivered to each.

3 **Customer relationship management (CRM) will evolve to CVM** – Customer value management (CVM) will become the standard approach to maximizing the return on customer investments. The measurement of customer value will evolve from revenue-based metrics to individual customer profitability.

4 **Companies will heighten their focus on data analysis and organization to avoid information roadblocks** – Companies will place a much greater emphasis on the analysis and organization of data so they can better differentiate their customers, establish clear customer value (profitability based) segments, and create richer and more measurable marketing campaigns.

5 **Companies will realize customer satisfaction doesn't translate to loyalty** – Companies will no longer be able to assume that a satisfied customer will remain a loyal customer. That's because people often make purchasing decisions based on shifting and migratory preferences with satisfaction being just one factor among many.

6 **Companies will focus on thoughtware, not software** – There's a reason why 55–75 per cent of current CRM projects don't meet their objectives. It's because companies often confuse CRM strategy with technology implementation, when in fact, CRM is a broader business strategy that technologies can enable.

7 **Companies will stitch their customer channels together** – The trend will be to create seamless interplay among all customer channels (customer service, field service, Web, marketing, sales, etc.) to create a consistent experience for customers, regardless of how they choose to interact with an organization. As these channels are integrated, the marketer will have one comprehensive view of the customer.

8   **Companies will embrace PRM as a means to maximize value to end-customers** – Organizations finally integrate their customer channels and focus on partner relationship management (PRM), a strategy to better serve end-customers by leveraging a company's business partner network.

9   **Companies will create CRM platforms** – We will start to see the integration and convergence of the Internet platforms with CRM platforms.

10   **Companies will shift to a long-term focus** – Organizations will think about long-term application viability, and focus on IT strategy to enable integrated CRM solutions.

Adapted from Braun Consulting (www.braunconsult.com).

Relationship marketing (RM) and (CRM)

This is an area of marketing that has been influenced considerably by the availability of IT solutions, particularly large interactive databases to enable companies to gather and maintain large amounts of data about individual customers and enable more individualized marketing. Customer databases and database marketing are the key to effective CRM. As Housden (2007) points out, the database does not have to be computer-based. It can be kept on hard copy. Simple software is capable of storing a significant number of records. Microsoft Access is perfectly serviceable for many businesses.

A marketing database as a comprehensive collection of interrelated customer and/or prospect data that allows the timely accurate retrieval, use or manipulation of that data to support the marketing objectives of the enterprise.

Wilson points out that the database differs from an accounting system in that the data must be relevant to marketing decision-making now and in the future. Wilson (2003) suggests that marketers develop customer databases for four reasons:

1   To personalize marketing communications

2   To improve customer service

3   To understand customer behaviour

4   To assess the effectiveness of the organization's marketing and service activities.

Database uses include:

◆   Identifying the best prospects

◆   Matching offers to customers

◆   Strengthening customer loyalty

◆   Re-activating customer purchasing.

Relationship marketing sees the concept of ongoing customer loyalty at the core of its customer relationship marketing strategy. The key aims are to ensure existing customers continue to purchase from them on a lifelong basis, that is achieving lifetime value to both the customer and the organization, rather than just one-off transactions. Sometimes, organizations concentrate solely on their customers, but there are other important relationships that should be considered. Typically, these groups are known as the stakeholder audience and include the following:

- ◆ **Internal markets** – If employees are treated as customers it should be possible to improve levels of customer service and quality throughout the organization.

- ◆ **Influence markets** – These are any bodies or groups that influence or have the potential to influence the organization's operations. They include government and regulatory bodies.

- ◆ **Employee markets** – The recruitment, retention and succession of skilled staff are important to the continuing success of the organization and companies need HR strategies to address this aspect.

- ◆ **Supplier markets** – In recent years, there has been a lot more emphasis on partnerships and alliances, and the synergy that is created from different forms of co-operative relationship.

- ◆ **Referral markets** – This is where organizations refer potential customers to third parties; for example, banks may refer mortgage customers to insurance companies and vice versa.

In order to successfully implement the ethos and culture of relationship marketing, the organization needs to look at internal markets – that is its employees and management. This aspect is considered in more detail in Unit 3 'Developing the Team'.

Knowledge management – At the heart of a CRM implementation is the acquisition of information about a customer, its analysis, sharing and tracking. Employees need to know what actions they need to take as a result of this knowledge.

Database consolidation – The consolidation of customer information in a single database and the re-engineering of business processes around the customer. All interactions with a customer need to be recorded in one place to drive production, marketing, sales and customer support activities.

Integration of channels and systems – Customers should be able to interact with a company through the former's channel of choice. The aim is to integrate all communication channels with the customer database. It also means the integration of CRM with other parts of a company's business systems and applications.

Technology and infrastructure – Tools exist to automate and streamline online customer service but there is a need to ensure that the technology infrastructure is able to cope with increased volumes.

Change management – CRM involves a change in philosophy and attitudes. A process for managing this change is needed to help a company move from a product-centric focus to a more customer-centric one.

Customer relationship management is a subset of RM and focused on the management of customer relations only. Relationship marketing is a broader type of marketing, encompassing relationships with customers, suppliers and intermediaries as well as strategies for the overall picture. Internal marketing can also be regarded as a sub-type of RM, focusing on the relationships within the company. A database is a tool in RM and might be able to provide information about trends that will help an organization to individualize its offer. Customization involves creating products and service offers specific for a particular individual or target group rather than analysing buying patterns to produce a 'best-fit' option. Thus, a prerequisite of customization is a detailed understanding of clients' needs and wants and this poses a considerable challenge for a marketing information system.

Benchmarking

Another complementary approach to an audit would be to use a benchmarking approach that compares one organization with another that is regarded as being very successful. Obviously, in some organizations, this can be difficult because of commercial sensitivities and the need to retain competitive advantage. However, a table could be constructed that could compare the organization along the dimensions that are felt to be important for marketing. The precise details will vary for each organization but, for example, it might look something like Table 6.1.

Table 6.1: Comparing the organization with high and low performing organizations		
Poor	**Good**	**Excellent**
Product driven	Market driven	Market driving
Mass-market oriented	Segment-oriented	Niche-oriented and customer-oriented
Product offer	Augmented product offer	Legendary offer

The EFQM Excellence Model

Another way of contributing to an audit is to use a recognized quality model. Usually, these kinds of models are very comprehensive and too detailed for a marketing audit because they cover the whole of an organization's activities. One of the most widely used models in the private and public sectors is the EFQM Excellence Model. It was introduced at the beginning of 1992 as the framework for assessing applications for the European Quality Award. It is a non-prescriptive framework that recognizes many approaches to achieving sustainable excellence. Increasingly, organizations use the outputs from self-assessment as part of their business planning process and as a basis for reviewing the organization.

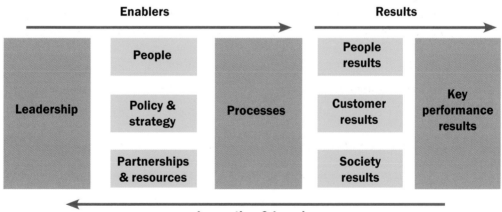

Figure 6.1 EFQM: Comparing the organization with high and low performing organizations. Source: www.efqm.org.

Within this non-prescriptive approach, there are some fundamental concepts which underpin the model. The framework is based on nine criteria. Five of these are 'Enablers' and four are 'Results'. The 'Enabler' criteria cover what an organization does. The 'Results' criteria cover what an organization achieves. 'Results' are caused by 'Enablers', and feedback from 'Results' helps to improve 'Enablers'. The model is based on the premise that:

'Excellent results with respect to Performance, Customers, People and Society are achieved through the enablers of Leadership driving Policy and Strategy, which is delivered through People Partnerships, Resources, and Processes'.

An Overview of the EFQM Excellence Model, http://www.efqm.org/Default.aspx?tabid=35

Results orientation – Achieving results that delight all the organization's stakeholders

Customer focus – Creating sustainable customer value

Leadership and constancy of purpose – Visionary and inspirational leadership, coupled with constancy of purpose

Management by processes and facts – Managing the organization through a set of inter-dependent and interrelated systems, processes and facts

People development and involvement – Maximizing the contribution of employees through their development and involvement

Continuous learning, innovation and improvement – Challenging the status quo and effecting change by using learning to create innovation and improvement opportunities

Partnership development – Developing and maintaining value-adding partnerships

Corporate social responsibility – Exceeding the minimum regulatory framework in which the organization operates and strives to understand and respond to the expectations of their stakeholders in society.

An example – Partnerships and resources element of the EFQM model

How is information and knowledge managed in the organization? The areas to address could include the following:

◆ How information and knowledge is collected, structured and managed in support of policy and strategy.

◆ How unique intellectual property is cultivated, developed and protected in order to maximize value.

◆ How appropriate access to relevant information and knowledge for both internal and external users is provided.

◆ How the organization seeks to acquire and use information and knowledge effectively.

◆ How the organization assures and improves the validity, integrity and security of its information.

◆ How the organization generates innovative and creative thinking within itself through the use of relevant information and knowledge resources.

RADAR

The method of assessment is based on the RADAR model, which looks at the evidence of what the organization achieves. This is based on documenting what it sets out to do, what evidence there is that its aims and objectives are actually translated into practice; whether it assesses the appropriateness of its approach and how successful its reviews have been. In this way, the self-assessment goes beyond what an organization claims it is doing to look for evidence that it is actually being implemented in practice.

◆ Results – What an organization achieves.

◆ Approach – What is it we are trying to do in order to address the issue?

◆ Deployment – How widely is the approach used across the organization?

◆ Assessment – Do we ever think about how appropriate the approach is?

◆ Review – Can we/do we measure success of the approach?

An example of the kind of format in which information could be collected is as follows:

Review your descriptions of the approaches as a whole, then record your views on where things have been successful, where improvements could be made and what actions are to be taken based on this analysis.

Market research is a cost-effective way of finding out what people believe, want, need or do. It is information that cannot usually be obtained from any other source. Until recently, limited budgets kept most types of market research out of reach of small organizations, but through the Internet there are more research options. The most important role of market research is to minimize risk by researching a product or service before it reaches the market. Thus, market research is a fundamental part of the marketing planning process.

This is dealt with in more detail in the CIM Professional Diploma coursebook, *Marketing Research and Information*. A market research project should include some form of a marketing audit, that is, an appraisal of an organization's marketing activities. This involves a systematic assessment of marketing plans, objectives, strategies, programmes, activities, organizational structure and personnel. There are a number of models that can be used for a marketing audit, for example a SWOT or a PESTLE analysis can each yield useful data that can inform an audit. The marketing audit and the models that contribute to it are discussed in Unit 7.

These are examples of the kinds of questions that could be asked in conducting an audit:

Objectives

◆ Are the marketing objectives of your department consistent with the overall company objectives? Should these be altered to fit changing environmental variables?

◆ Are objectives consistent with one another?

◆ How do objectives relate to marketing strengths and market opportunities?

Strategy

◆ What is the relationship between objectives and strategies?

◆ Are resources sufficient to implement the strategies?

◆ What are the company's weaknesses?

◆ How do you compare your strategies with those of competitors?

Product decisions

◆ How are new products developed within your business unit?

◆ How are existing products evaluated?

◆ How are products phased out of the line?

Pricing decisions

◆ How are pricing decisions made?

◆ How do pricing decisions reflect the influences of competitors and the concerns of channel members?

Distribution decisions

◆ How are channel members selected, evaluated and dropped, if necessary?

◆ How are channel members motivated?

◆ How are decisions to modify channel structures reached?

Promotion decisions

◆ How are promotion mix decisions made?

◆ How are sales people selected, monitored and evaluated?

◆ How are pay-offs associated with promotional efforts estimated?

Market information

◆ How is marketing research information transmitted to, and used within, the business unit?

◆ Is a global information system in place?

Activities and tasks

◆ How are tasks scheduled, described and planned? How are the responsibilities of individuals determined?

◆ What spans of supervision, reporting relationships and communication patterns exist? How are they evaluated?

Personnel

◆ What level of competence has been attained by personnel in each position?

◆ Are remedies to problems, if necessary, being planned? What are they?

◆ What is the state of morale? motivation? What are the present plans in these areas?

◆ Describe career development paths. Have potential replacements for personnel in key positions been identified?

The term 'marketing research' covers market research, marketing research, product research and research to support pricing, distribution and promotional activity. Market research is used to supply information about the market for particular products and services. Therefore, market research has a narrower focus compared to marketing research.

Market research

Characteristics of good market research

◆ **Scientific method** – The principles are careful observation, formulation of hypotheses, prediction and testing.

◆ **Research creativity** – Research should develop innovative ways to solve a problem.

◆ **Multiple methods** – The research should use more than one method to increase confidence in the results.

◆ **Interdependence of models and data** – A recognition that data is interpreted from underlying models that guide the type of information sought.

◆ **Value and cost of information** – A concern for estimating the value of the research against its cost. Costs are easy to determine but the value of the research is harder to ascertain.

◆ **Ethical marketing** – Market research should be conducted according to a recognized code of practice that respects informants.

The most important distinguishing characteristics of market research are that:

◆ Its primary objective is to apply research methods to the collection of information that will help in describing and understanding markets, planning strategies and monitoring outcomes.

◆ In most cases, it achieves this by studying relatively small, and usually representative, samples of the relevant populations.

◆ It is primarily, but not exclusively, concerned with analysing and reporting on aggregated groupings of those interviewed; it does not report information which can be linked to identifiable individuals.

◆ It guarantees the confidentiality of the information provided by respondents. Such information can be disclosed only with the respondent's consent, and then only for research purposes and to research organizations involved in the project.

Market research is concerned with a one-way channel of communication, from respondents to the client via the confidential filter of the researcher. It does not provide a facility for any form of commercial or similar communication in the opposite direction, from client to individual respondent, nor does it seek to influence the respondent's views or behaviour as a result of the research.

The characteristics of direct marketing are different from those of market research

◆ The primary objective of direct marketing is to conduct promotional and selling activities directed at specific individuals and organizations. Marketing analysis provides aggregated and cross-analysed information of various kinds – but this is normally a secondary rather than the primary objective of collecting the data, and does not affect the other characteristics of direct marketing referred to here.

◆ It normally involves the collection and use of personal data from very large numbers of the general population or from as many as possible of a specific group (e.g. customers). The emphasis is on maximizing the total number of the target audiences covered rather than on the representativeness of the final data.

◆ The data collected is purposely stored and made use of on an individually identified, disaggregated basis since it would not otherwise be fully exploitable in direct marketing.

◆ Since the personal data collected is permanently linked to the individuals who have supplied the data, there can normally be no guarantee of anonymity. In many cases, the personal data will be made available to a variety of users, most often for non-research purposes such as promotion and direct selling.

◆ Unlike marketing research, direct marketing is usually a two-way process whereby the individual who provides the data receives promotional and/or sales approaches based on the use of that data. Direct marketing is a form of 'commercial communication'.

The market research process: Stage 1

Defining the marketing problem and research objectives

This includes specifying the objectives of the specific research project or projects, to formulate the problem precisely. The art is to strike a balance between too broad and too narrow a definition of a problem. Too broad a definition can lead to a lot of information that is superfluous, whilst too narrow a definition means that some necessary information about issues that impact on the subject is not collected. It depends on how much is known about the problem. If relatively little is known, exploratory research may be used, for example qualitative research as well as secondary research. Some research is causal – its purpose is to test a cause and effect relationship. A marketing problem needs to be formulated as a marketing research problem. So, for example a marketing problem might be that sales are too low but the marketing research problem could be to assess customer perception of the price of the product in terms of its perceived value relative to the competition.

Sometimes, a researcher will be designing a research programme according to a research brief. However, the brief may not exist in a definitive form, and the researcher may need to work with the client to refine it and make sure that it can be operationalized.

Research briefs

When drafting a research brief for an agency to respond, as much detail as possible should be given. This helps to refine and clarify thinking about the project, including the target audience, the kinds of questions and issues that ought to be addressed, and why. Specify the deliverables expected. Below is a checklist of questions which could be used by the researcher to draw out the background to design a research programme.

Checklist to guide a researcher when taking a brief:

History

◆ How long has the company been established?

◆ How long has it concentrated on its present product/service range?

◆ Has the company always been sited in its present location?

◆ What factors have influenced its location?

Company background

◆ What is the principal business of the company? What are its subsidiary activities?

◆ What is its total turnover?

◆ Describe any holding companies/subsidiary companies.

◆ How many employees are there at the establishment?

Product details

- What are the important products (or services) in the range (by size, capacity, shape, material, etc.)?
- What proportion of the total turnover does each of the above groups account for?
- To what extent are the products standard/custom built?
- What proportion of an assembled product is made in-house or bought out?
- How important are spares in terms of revenue versus profit?
- Are any of the products built under licence?

Pricing

- What are the prices for each of the important products or services?
- How do prices compare with those of the competition?
- Is there a published price list?
- What is the discount policy?
- What power does the sales representative have to alter prices?
- How price-sensitive is the product?

Sales force

- Number of representatives.
- Are they a general or a specialized sales force – in what way are they specialized?
- How many calls a day do they make?
- Does the salesforce bring back orders or are they sent in independently?

Markets

- What are the major user markets for the products?
- What proportions of total sales are to each of these markets?
- Are any markets known for the product, where the company currently does not/cannot sell?
- Which markets are believed to offer the greatest scope for expansion of sales?

Decision-makers

- Who are the key decision-makers who specify and buy this type of product? What roles do they play?
- What do decision-makers look for from suppliers? Probe price, quality, delivery, sales service?

Competition

- Who are the most important competitors? Where are they based?
- What is their rank order/market share?
- What is each company's (including the client's) perceived strengths and weaknesses?
- To what extent do competitors rely upon this market for their turnover and profit?

Quality

- Where does the product fit against the competition in its quality?
- What are the special features of its quality?

- Where is it weak on quality?
- How long will the product last?
- When it finally fails, why will it do so?

Deliveries

- What is the current delivery period?
- What is the competition's delivery?
- What is the ideal delivery?

Distribution

- How is the product distributed?
- What proportion goes direct/indirect? What is the policy which leads to this split (e.g. size of account – OEM versus replacement, etc.)?
- What are distributors' margins?
- What other products do distributors sell?
- Do distributors actively sell, or just take orders?
- Who are the major distributors:
  - used by the company?
  - not used by the company?
- What is the average size of a direct account and a distributor account?

Promotion

- How big is the promotional budget?
- How does this break down between: (a) media (b) exhibitions (c) PR (d) print (e) direct mail (f) websites?
- Which media are used? Which are most successful?
- What proportion of sales leads come from promotion? How many? What is their quality?
- Which exhibitions are attended? What is their perceived value?
- What opportunities exist for e-commerce?

Other data

Full details of names (initials as well) of persons present at briefing, date of briefing, address of company, address to which proposals should be sent and how many copies of the proposal are required to be sent.

Preparing a research proposal

Having received the brief, the researcher, whether in-house or from an agency, must submit a written proposal to the sponsor which states an appreciation of the problem, the objectives, the research method and the timing. If an agency is preparing the proposal, a statement of cost must be given. An in-house job may omit this but many managers still like to see an estimate as a benchmark to compare with other surveys and as a perspective that they can use to relate to the size of any decision which may be taken. If the proposal is accepted, it becomes the contract between the researcher and the sponsor.

Stage 2 – Develop the research plan and research design

This involves developing an efficient plan for gathering the necessary information. A marketing manager needs to know the cost of the research before agreeing it can go ahead. One of the issues to be considered is whether there is a need for primary and/or secondary research. If primary research is needed, then what type? Research design specifies the type of research required. Secondary research usually precedes primary research to see whether the problem that needs to be investigated can be addressed without having to spend resources on acquiring primary data.

Exploratory research

The goal of exploratory market research is discovery. The underlying questions are 'What is new?' and 'What are we missing?'. The goal of confirmatory techniques is resolution: 'Is this the right choice?' 'What results can we expect?'. Exploratory market research is used to broaden a vision, whilst confirmatory research is used to narrow options and concentrate efforts (McQuarrie, 1996).

Exploratory and confirmatory market research techniques are used at different stages in a research project's decision cycle (Table 6.2). The decision cycle calls for sequential market research activities and questions as the research design and strategy are developed and implemented. Each activity requires different market research techniques as the researcher's informational needs change from initial exploratory information to final confirmatory information.

The four decision cycle activities in Table 6.2 are further described in relation to each activity's objectives and suggested market research techniques.

Research design

Table 6.2: Four decision cycle activities

Activity/Questions	Objectives	Techniques
Scan the environment How are we doing? What is going on? Supporting: Focus groups, surveys	Identify, describe, monitor	Main: Secondary research, user visits
Generate options What are the possibilities? Supporting: Secondary research	Generate, define, explore	Main: User visits, focus groups
Select an option What is the explanation? Which option is best? Supporting: Secondary research	Evaluate, test, select, prioritize	Main: Experiments, surveys, choice models, usability tests

Evaluate success	Measure, track, assess	Main: Surveys, secondary research
What will we achieve? How are we doing? Supporting: User visits		

Adapted from: McQuarrie (1996, p. 24)

A survey of the literature will usually precede all research designs. This is to learn from previous research in the area. Prevent expensive primary research being undertaken when research results are available.

Surveys of people with particular experience, or knowledge of the subject under investigation should be undertaken. For example, interviews of commercial directors to find out about trends in football merchandising. Examine the best and the worst examples to see if any conclusions may be made. For instance, a detailed investigation of top and bottom sales people to try to understand the factors that contribute to success or failure.

◆ Repeated investigations over time, for example monthly opinion surveys of consumers.

◆ Single investigation, for example a single survey of 100 business leaders to find out their attitudes to the training of their employees. Field experiments are carried out in the normal context, such as in a store, while a laboratory experiment is undertaken in an artificial environment.

◆ A field experiment is where, for example, the store changes the price of products in store and assesses changes in the quantity and value purchased. In this context, the experiment is in a normal environment and the consumer is unaware that it is taking place.

Sampling

As Housden (2007) points out, it is very unusual for an entire population to be surveyed. A population refers to the total number of people in a group of interest. Key to the accuracy of this is the determination of the characteristics of the sample. Wilson (2003) highlights five key questions that inform the sampling process:

◆ We need to understand the nature of the people we wish to survey.

◆ We need to know where they are.

◆ We need to know how we select them.

◆ We need to know the number of people we wish to survey.

◆ We need to understand how representative this sample is of the population as a whole.

Organizations will target specified customer groups for their marketing activity. These customer groups, or segments, will be the basis on which any marketing research is undertaken. They will be the focus of any sampling activity. The potential population in this context could be any target group ranging from large populations, such as the potential purchasers of television sets, to relatively small markets, such as buyers of widescreen plasma TV sets. Sampling allows conclusions to be drawn about the wider market, without the need to talk to everyone in the marketplace. Sampling estimates the numbers, attributes and beliefs of a population. The key to a good sample is to define the population of customers that are of interest and to select enough random members of that population. If the attitudes of buyers to a new type of hand-held computer were needed before planning a marketing campaign, the target population will be those who are affluent. This target population could be found, for example, by buying a mailing list from a computer magazine and specifying postcodes in a 30-mile radius of the store with the highest incomes.

However, what you really need to know is who has the highest disposable income with an interest in electronic gadgets. This may not coincide with the most affluent. A young person in a well-paid job, living at home with his parents may have more disposable income than an older person with twice the annual income. Therefore, you might want to cross-refer salary data with other data relating to marital status and age. However, marital status is not much of a guide to anything because many people are unmarried but living with partners. These latter points serve to illustrate the complexity of some of the factors when drawing up a relevant valid and reliable sample. The main decisions to be made when selecting a sample are as follows:

1   The process by which the sample is to be selected is known as the sample design. The quality of all statistical analyses and procedures is governed by the quality of the sample data. If it is not representative of the population, analysing the data and drawing conclusions from it will be unproductive and invalid. A representative sample will require the introduction of randomness in the sampling procedure.

2   From which list to draw a sample? This involves selecting a sample frame (i.e. a list of all members of the population) – unless people are just being interviewed randomly in the street.

3   How large a sample to select?

Sample design

The main approaches to sample design:

◆   Non-probability sample design
◆   Probability sample design.

A key issue is the cost of sampling versus the benefits. The main difference between probability and non-probability sampling is that with the former the result of a sample can be projected to the whole population whereas this cannot be done with non-probability samples.

Probability samples

Probability sampling requires the researcher to know the size of the population, and for each individual in the population to have a known and equal chance of being selected (using a sampling frame). The most commonly used sampling frames are telephone numbers and postcodes. There are four major ways to contact those being surveyed:

◆   Telephone
◆   Personal (e.g. door to door)
◆   Mail
◆   Internet.

Telephone, mail and e-mail provide the most control over the characteristics of those who are surveyed. The Internet and e-mail are the cheapest, but the respondents may not be representative of your target population.

1   Random sample – Everyone has the same chance. The advantage of the random sample is that it is the best representation of the population that can be obtained. The disadvantage is the difficulty of obtaining an entire population list. It works better with a small population because it is easier to get hold of that list. What does it mean to be random?

2   Stratified random sample – The population is divided into groups/levels of interest, for example socio-economic status. This is a more representative type of sample.

3   Cluster sampling – This is based on sub-sets of the population, for example geographic regions.

Non-probability samples

These are samples in which you do not know the chance of being selected. The precise size of a population or even who is in the population is not known. Examples of non-probability samples include the following:

1   **Convenience sample** – Samples are selected for interviews based on the ease of finding a sample from the researchers' point of view, that is from their convenience. They are not random and they use readily available subjects, for example, students.

2   **Quota sample** – Respondents are recruited because they possess particular characteristics – perhaps they may be selected on the basis of age or gender if these are believed to be important influencing factors in purchase decisions. Different individuals with different characteristics are sampled to meet the quota – for example, gender: 50 male, 50 female. This type of sample design attempts to reflect key attributes of the general population in the selection of the sample to be researched. It is a common technique used by commercial marketing research companies.

3   **Judgement sampling** – In this approach, the researcher believes that the results of the research will be improved if some judgement is exercised in selecting a sample, maybe by asking 'experts'.

Stage 3 – Data collection methods

Market research works because, by talking to a relatively small number of people, it is possible to find out about a far larger number, but it only works if the people who are interviewed (the sample) are a representative subgroup of the total group of interest (the universe), and if the right questions are asked. The universe might be the population as a whole or, parents, car drivers, the elderly, shoppers, voters, IT managers and so on.

Qualitative market research

The various types of qualitative market research methodologies are summarized below:

Market research depth interviews – a single respondent is interviewed based on various themes and topics (can be conducted either face to face or via the phone).

Market research paired depths – the same as a depth interview but there are two respondents. Particularly useful when ideas need to be 'bounced off' one another.

Triads – conducted with three respondents.

Market research mini-groups – contain 4–5 respondents.

Focus groups or group discussions – normally contain eight respondents. With groups you benefit from the interaction between the different personalities.

Market research observation – observing a respondent in their 'natural' environment.

Workshops – to elicit new ideas and to evaluate ideas.

The various types of quantitative market research methodologies are summarized below:

Face-to-face interviewing – either in the street or, for more complex projects, in people's homes.

Telephone interviewing – a quick and cost-effective way of gathering data.

Postal and self-completion market research – cheap but takes a relatively long time to collect data.

Omnibus market research surveys – useful when only a few questions need to be asked. Questions are attached to other larger surveys. Data is obtained at a low cost.

There are four basic data collection methods employed for surveys:

1   Personal interviews
2   Telephone interviews
3   Mail surveys
4   Web-based surveys.

The choice of the data collection method will depend on the objectives of the survey, and the relative importance of factors such as level of accuracy required, the amount of data to be collected, the sample bias acceptable, the budget required, speed and any administrative issues.

Primary data is information collected for a specific purpose

An example of this is the research required to identify the market for an innovative new product. It is unlikely that such research has previously been undertaken. Therefore, it is specially commissioned and, generally, the results belong to the organization commissioning the work. However, some research firms will conduct limited and less expensive primary research with the requirement that they can make the results available to other companies. More affordable primary research methods – both qualitative and quantitative – are available online as well. Inexpensive ways to conduct qualitative research via the Internet are through do-it-yourself online focus groups.

Compared with primary research, secondary research is generally:

◆   Quicker
◆   Cheaper
◆   Less relevant to the topic under investigation
◆   Out of date if it refers to fast-changing contexts or issues.

As someone else has conducted the secondary research, users of this material must look carefully at how the data was derived and how valid and reliable are the conclusions.

The following is an example of primary research. Does this count as market research?

Competitive analysis of French children's clothing market

New products should be aggressively marketed to appeal to French children's tastes and to influence their fashion preferences. The media has a tremendous impact on them. Music and television are influential at an early age, and are thus excellent means for promoting products that are specifically directed towards children. According to analysts, children spend an average of 2 hours per day watching television. Additionally, 25 per cent of French children have their own sets. US imports are expected to grow, given the fact that French children are greatly influenced by American trends and television. The easy-to-wear clothing of American colleges and the street wear of large cities appear especially attractive to French children. As a result, US products such as T-shirts, polos and jackets with names of football teams or American colleges are in high demand. Proof of the success of American brands in France can be seen in the opening of a Gap store for children in Paris. There appears to be numerous opportunities for US companies to successfully penetrate the French children's wear market.

Activity 6.2

Identify secondary research sources for your organization's products, services and markets. List specific reports that would be useful for marketing.

Evaluating secondary information

What was the purpose of the study? – Was it undertaken by an impartial source or by a pressure group that is attempting to put across a particular point?

Who collected the information? – In the UK, it is possible to obtain statistics on the number of vegetarians from the Vegetarian Society or from the meat industry. These two sources of information do not provide the same estimate for the number of vegetarians!

What information was collected? – Figures from two sources may differ because of the use of different sources of information, or because different timescales are used. However, sometimes it can be because each wants to prove a point.

When was the information collected? – If there has been a recent food scare, for example mad cow disease, consumption levels of beef will be low and consumption of substitutes will be high.

Is the information consistent with other information? – Most secondary information tends to be quantitative rather than qualitative.

Primary research

There are four main types of primary research:

◆ Surveys

◆   Observation

◆   Experimentation

◆   Simulation.

Personal interviews

Benefits

◆   The interviewer can select a good quality sample.

◆   The interviewer can interpret strange answers and ask for clarification.

◆   The interviewer can classify interviewees to save time.

◆   Longer questionnaires can be asked with this method.

◆   Visual images can be used.

Problems

◆   Costly.

◆   Possible interviewer bias.

◆   Possibility of fake interviews.

Focus groups

This is one of the most frequently used techniques in marketing research. Successful re-search requires a skilled moderator (i.e. the person who directs the topics of discussion and creates a balanced environment to encourage the contribution of all members of the group). Members of the focus group should be selected from the target population for the firm's products and services.

Benefits

◆   A wide range of ideas can be obtained.

◆   An in-depth understanding of consumer attitudes and purchase motivations may be obtained.

◆   Ideal when managers are looking for ideas or need to clarify some details.

◆   A certain synergy can be obtained from a group discussion that allows a deeper probing of issues.

◆   Visual images can be used.

◆   It is relatively easy to record (video and audio tape) for future analysis.

Problems

◆   Costly.

◆   Success is highly dependent on the skill of the interviewer and on the selection of the sample to attend the focus group.

◆   Possible problem of domination of the group by a strong and forceful individual, which will result in group conflict or in only the views of the forceful individual being obtained.

Focus groups can be used to cover a variety of topics, but they are best used to understand 'why' a particular group feels or acts in a particular way. If an interviewee says something of particular interest during a focus group, the interviewer can probe deeper into the topic, uncovering more information. Topics often covered in focus groups include reactions to product ideas and product prototypes, messaging tests, ad testing and customer-needs identification. The groups are taped (video and audio) for later analysis and can be observed during the focus group – either at a specially designed facility, or via a videoconference or Web-based hook-up when the session proceedings can be viewed remotely. Sometimes hard-to-reach people will not come to a focus group but they may be reached by depth interviews which are one-on-one discussions with a researcher. While qualitative data is very accessible, it can fall short on reliability.

Telephone surveys

Benefits

- Quick and easy to do.
- Reach geographically dispersed samples.
- Ease of sampling, for example random digit dialling.
- Complex routing through questionnaire is automated.
- Low cost.
- Possibility of recording to confirm that interview took place.

Problems

- The method can only handle very short, simple questionnaires.
- The sample obtained can be biased, depending on the type of people who are willing to complete a telephone interview.
- Lack of access to households without telephones.

Postal surveys

Benefits

- Low cost.
- Ease of contacting geographically dispersed samples.
- More complex questions can be asked.

Problems

- Usually quite a low response rate.
- The interviewee can misinterpret the questions.
- It can take a long time to get back replies.
- Minimal chance of interpreting the extent to which the respondent is answering truthfully.

Internet surveys

Benefits

- Very fast: instant analysis may be undertaken.
- Very low cost.
- Highly targeted.
- Ease of contacting the sample.

Problems

◆ The method can only handle very short, simple questionnaires.

◆ Very limited potential for 'open' questions.

◆ People with access to the Internet are not representative of the total population for all markets. They tend to be higher income and higher socio-economic groups. This is less of a problem for business Internet surveys.

Quantitative data

◆ Tends to be on large numbers of people.

◆ Findings are expressed numerically.

◆ Concerned with 'how many', 'how often' and 'what' rather than 'why'.

◆ Quantitative research problem: How many consumers buy the company's shampoo?

Qualitative approaches

◆ Fewer people.

◆ Deals with data difficult to quantify – concerned with 'why' rather than 'how many', or 'how often'.

◆ Concerned with attitudes and motivations.

Criteria for selecting methods

Some of the more important criteria, when selecting research methods, include:

◆ Cost.

◆ Speed.

◆ Access to target population (including ability to sample the target population).

◆ Type of questions that can be asked.

◆ Quantity of data.

◆ Response rate.

Qualitative research tends to be exploratory and directional in nature. It is designed to bring out issues associated with the subject matter as well as the best general direction to proceed. Qualitative methods can be useful in all stages of development and are very tangible to marketers and developers.

Observation

This is literally where the individual's behaviour is monitored and recorded. One of the most popular applications of this technique recently is in researching in-store shopping. Consumer movement through the store is observed and recorded. Researchers have been able to classify individuals in supermarkets according to their speed of movement through the store, their willingness to scan the shelves for products and to divert from a pre-planned shopping list, where one exists.

In-depth interviews involve one-to-one contact with respondents and are usually conducted face to face, although telephone interviews are sometimes used. The in-depth interview is different from the tightly structured interview used in quantitative surveys or opinion polls – it is not only longer (45–60 minutes), but also more discursive and open-ended. The interviewer also has a greater level of flexibility since they are not constrained by the order or wording of questions; she or he is able to cover the issues specified in the topic guide in a more context-sensitive way, as they 'naturally' emerge, and to probe responses to gain a full understanding of their meaning and/or implications.

Experimentation

This is where the researcher attempts to establish causality between two factors by varying one factor and holding all other factors constant.

Laboratory experiments

Laboratory experiments take place in an artificial environment created by the researcher, which allows one factor to be varied. For example, an advert can be placed within a magazine that has been created specially for research purposes. Consumers can be given the magazine to look through, and are then asked to comment on the advertising. If unfavourable comments are made, then the advert is changed and consumers are asked to repeat the procedure. In this way, researchers are able to assess the effect of changes in advertising on consumer response.

Field experiments

Field experiments take place in a more natural environment. Researchers often change a factor in order to observe the influence on purchase quantity/sales revenue. Examples of experimentation in a retail environment include changing:

- Shelf location
- Price
- Pack design
- Sales promotion activity.

As each of these factors is varied, the researcher observes the effect on sales volume and on revenue.

Simulation

Simulation is where researchers build a model (usually a computer model) of an environment and use this as the basis for experimentation. Simulation is employed when a problem is judged to be too complex for ease of mathematical formulation. In building a simulation, the researcher sets the framework (parameters) of the model and, within that framework, the researcher or business manager may experiment.

Cross-section versus longitudinal research

Researchers need to be clear about the type of data they require. Cross-sectional data is where a 'snapshot' picture of the current situation is obtained. A survey undertaken this month reports on the situation as it is for this month. For various reasons, the results may not be relevant at any other time. Longitudinal data is obtained over a period of time, often over many years.

Tracking studies

A tracking study may involve conducting a survey every month, or even every week, to establish and track consumer reaction. In such studies, advertising managers want to assess the peak level of responses, such as awareness, and the rate at which this decays between advertising activities. As longitudinal research is very expensive for individual companies to buy, groups of companies join together to purchase the same data using 'syndicated research'.

Syndicated research

Only companies within the syndicate have access to the data. A relatively low-cost method of collecting 'cross-sectional data' is usually the omnibus survey. A company will run a regular survey (say, every month) with a specified target population. Often a theme is specified, such as financial services or children. Any company is then able to pay to add their own questions.

Insight: How to find out if customers are happy

Portakabin carries out market research because it wants to find out what inspires loyalty in its customers, so that it can take steps to encourage them to remain loyal. Portakabin surveys its customers to find out what factors distinguished the company. Customers are impressed by the level of personal interaction with staff and with the overall level of support they received. The company carries out a regular customer satisfaction interview with the vast majority of its clients. This asks questions on all aspects of customer service and records scores on a scale of 1–10 (where 1 is very poor and 10 is excellent). The scale of responses provides quantitative data, showing how well the company is doing in each area. Portakabin uses the responses to identify excellent service so staff can be appropriately praised. It also uses the results to quickly tackle problems should they arise. Portakabin understands that if customers receive good service they are more likely to return.

http://www.thetimes100.co.uk/studies/view-summary--how-market-research-helps-portakabin-to-remain-at-cutting-edge--35-259.php

Stage 4 – Data collection

The most common approach to collecting information is the questionnaire. There are two main types of questions used in questionnaires: open questions and closed questions.

There are many types of closed and open questions. Some closed questions are able to achieve more than simply a count of people or attributes. They may be used to investigate attitudes held by consumers, in particular the intensity of attitude.

Open questions invite facts and opinions, whereas closed questions seek a simple response, such as 'yes' or 'no'.

Closed questions

Closed questions are most frequently used to count the number of people who exhibit a particular trait.

Closed question, for example:

Do you buy products made by the firm:

    a)   Never?

    b)   Once per year?

    c)   Once per month?

    d)   More frequently than once per month?

Closed questions may include two (dichotomous) or more (multichotomous) options from which the respondent selects an answer.

Semantic differential scale respondents are presented with a set of bipolar adjectives and asked to indicate the point on the scale which best describes the intensity of their feelings.

The danger of using too many closed questions is that they:

◆   Prevent people from expressing views

◆   Restrict the flow of information.

Open questions

Open questions are used when the researcher wants to explore some ideas. They may be used when trying to design a new product or explore consumer opinion about the company brand, for example, 'What features would you like in a robot vacuum cleaner?'

Open questions gather ideas and attitudes but they are time-consuming to analyse and require knowledgeable analysts.

Simple open questions leave the respondent free to answer as they wish.

Leading questions

These are phrased in such a way that makes it clear that you only expect one answer: 'I'm sure we all agree that ...?' 'Isn't it true that ...?' 'Don't you think that ...?'. They are to be avoided because they can cause resentment at trying to put words into respondents' mouths or trying to persuade them, against their own judgement, to agree with you. Ultimately, the data gathered is flawed because it may not represent what the respondent really thinks or believes.

Multiple questions

People can only answer one question at a time, so do not fall into the trap of issuing a stream of questions, such as, 'What's the situation with ... and how will we ... and when by?'

Listening

Questioning skills will not bring results unless equally effective listening skills are being practised. There are three levels of listening:

1   **Hearing the words** – to hear and understand the words that are being spoken.

2   **Understanding the meaning** – to be able to understand the overall meaning.

3   **Perceiving the inference** – to be able to perceive the inferences that lie behind the words.

Influence of researcher

When listening, and when you are being listened to, you should be aware of the stream of signals which are given off by somebody who is speaking. These verbal and non-verbal signals can transmit a significantly different message to other members of the meeting than the literal meaning of the spoken words.

◆ **Facial expression** – If the speaker's expression does not match the words, it is the expression which carries more weight.

◆ **Body language** – Shrugged shoulders or dismissive hand gestures have the same impact as facial expression.

◆ **Tone of voice** – Listeners can perceive strong signals through tone of voice and emphasis on certain words. The tone of voice, consciously or subconsciously, can significantly influence the way in which the question is perceived. For example, the question: 'Do you think this is achievable?' is apparently a neutral, closed question which seeks without expectation the answer 'yes' or 'no'. However, in a different tone, it could also imply that there is not the slightest chance that the results can be achieved. Conversely, the same question spoken in an enthusiastic voice would convey the impression that you were looking for a 'yes!' If you want the honest opinion of other members, you should take care to keep any expectation – either positive or negative – out of your voice.

Stage 5 – Analysing the results and reporting

This is the processing of data collected (which can be qualitative or quantitative data) within a market research project, which allows conclusions to be drawn in relation to the project. .As discussed earlier, Market Research is either quantitative, qualitative, or a combination of both. Qualitative and quantitative market research methods each provide different insights into behaviour. Normally, research results are more useful when the two methods are combined. The type of results that are required is a key factor in determining the data collection techniques used. Each technique yields different types of data and presents different problems of analysis. Broadly speaking qualitative techniques yield a lot of data about a comparatively small sample whilst quantitative techniques usually yield much less detail about a comparatively larger sample. In both cases the analytical challenge is to draw accurate conclusions from the data and to be able to focus on what are the key issues, sometimes in the midst of a sea of data.

The market research report should present findings that are relevant to the major marketing decisions facing management.

Online research

Online research covers all digital interactive media, including digital TV, Wireless Application Protocol (WAP) and new entertainment technologies. Online research can be appropriate if the target market is visitors to a specific website or Internet-users in general – but it is still not a medium for general public surveys. This may change eventually as Internet penetration grows among women and older groups. Internet research has an advantage for surveys among staff, employees and customers or subscribers to online services in any situation where the universe is known, and the e-mail addresses are available and up-to-date. Business e-mail addresses tend to be less volatile compared to those of consumers. The barriers to conducting online research are very low. The most important issue for research is declining respondent co-operation rates. Approaches like showing interactive stimuli material such as clips from ads all work well on the Internet. But while it is feasible to show TV clips, they can slow download times. With interactive digital TV, there is a lot more potential.

Case study: Online research

It is part of the mission at the Future Foundation to continually seek to innovate new research techniques both at the analysis stage and at the point of data collection. Online research can be used very successfully in our opinion if linked directly to specific sites, for example for site U&As, or if respondents are recruited through other means and then directed to a site to answer a questionnaire. Moving on to qualitative research, we have conducted both online groups and moderated e-mail groups for clients for a range of different projects. For example, for BT we invited a group of people who make purchases on the Internet to a group discussion in a moderated chat room. These individuals had been recruited using traditional techniques from sampling points all around the country. They had undergone a two-stage one-to-one interviewing process both face to face and on the telephone. The third stage was conducted online because it represented the most logical way of getting this group together for a discussion. We have utilized the moderated e-mail groups where more detail is required. We ask respondents a question, which we send to them by e-mail. All the replies are summarized and sent back to every member of the group who then responds again the next day. These groups take place over the course of one or two weeks. This technique does result in less interaction between group members but on the plus side the level of detail supplied by respondents in their answers can be better than any other research technique – both online and offline.

Source: www.futurefoundation.net/

Computer-assisted interviewing (CAI)

Computer assisted interviewing involves the use of a computer to collect, store, manipulate and transmit data relating to interviews conducted between the interviewer and the respondent(s).

Computer-assisted personal interviewing (CAPI)

Computer assisted personal interviewing (personal interview by an interviewer using a portable computer at the home or business of the respondent) is one component of CAI. Other components include computer-assisted telephone interviewing (CATI) and computer-assisted self-interviewing (CASI). The three chief theoretical benefits of CAPI are: better quality, improved timeliness and lower cost after the initial investment. Computer-assisted personal interviewing has the potential to provide improvements in the areas of data quality, survey timeliness and cost effectiveness, but cost savings directly attributable to CAPI are less well documented than the other benefits. On large-scale continuous surveys and on other operations where the hardware can be efficiently utilized and the costs spread over time, net savings might be expected but otherwise the costs might well be greater for CAPI. Computer-assisted personal interviewing also provides the opportunity to apply experimental design principles to survey testing, and the flexibility to enable collection of important policy-related data for difficult topics.

Online focus groups

An online focus group is essentially a formal chat session. A trained moderator leads a group of participants through a predetermined discussion over the Internet. Participants are often recruited through a research firm's own panel and are paid a fee for participating. A focus group could be set up inexpensively by using a chat room and recruiting your own participants. If a panel is used, the following checklist is useful to note.

Insight: Online panel users

A good online panel can offer real advantages over other approaches. But how do you know it's a good panel?

Here's a checklist of questions to ask a panel supplier.

Recruitment sources – How are the panel members found? What biases does this recruitment approach build in?

Screening – Are prospective panel members screened (off-line) to confirm age, residence, and so on? Many panel members belong to several different panels, to the point where some have become almost professional respondents.

Representative membership – How well does the profile of panel members match an independently derived profile of net users as a whole? Is there a bias toward the heavier or more experienced users?

Maintenance of representativeness – What steps has the panel supplier taken to ensure that the membership profile remains up-to-date? Drop-out and the changing profile of net users can lead to biases in the membership, if it is not regularly monitored.

Sampling methods – How are samples drawn from the panel membership? Is it a random sample from the whole database? Are quotas or over-sampling used to allow for differential response rates?

Differential response rates – What monitoring has the agency done on differential response rates? Some people respond every time, some rarely, so that the achieved sample for any survey may be biased, even if the panel as a whole is representative.

Survey frequency – How often are panel members asked to complete surveys? Professional respondents are not representative.

Lifestyle profiling – Are panel members profiled according to lifestyle criteria? If not, the panel could be less cost-effective if you are only interested in, for example people who have booked travel online, or who regularly work from home.

Source: http://www.mori.com/pubinfo, Online Research: ESOMAR Research World Interview

Feedback forms

A simple way to conduct ongoing qualitative research is through a feedback form. You can gain valuable insight by asking website visitors for suggestions, and/or asking them their opinions. You can do this through a form directly on your site and/or via e-mail to those on your opt-in list.

Primary quantitative market research

Quantitative research is used when you are looking for hard numbers and precision. To produce a top-quality primary quantitative research study, you must generally work through a research agency. For a small-budget business, this type of research is expensive. The Internet has made more inexpensive means of data collection and analysis possible. With the help of software or web-based tools, you can perform research through customer surveys and collect visitor-use patterns through web logs.

Customer surveys

The Internet has made conducting surveys quicker and less expensive. Options range from do-it-yourself programmes to research services with screened panels. You can use surveys in a variety of ways – segmenting your customers, improving/developing your product or site and gauging brand awareness, for example.

Use patterns

Another approach to quantitative research on the Web is to look for visitor-use patterns such as routes taken through your site, pages viewed or ordering behaviour. By studying web logs, you can know which pages are most popular, how visitors navigate through your site, common entry pages and where visitors often leave the site. You can also determine the number of different visitors to your site as well as the percentage of visitors converted to customers. By using a traffic-analysis service or software (often available through your hosting service), you can streamline the process. An alternative to conducting primary research is to find secondary research, or research that originated elsewhere. You can obtain secondary research either by purchasing the information or finding it through free resources.

Quantitative research

Quantitative research produces results that are more statistically accurate than qualitative research results. Often, companies first conduct qualitative research when developing a concept or looking for ideas, and later complete quantitative research to fine-tune and optimize. It is usually conducted via surveys or behavioural tracking. It is based on the principle that the characteristics of a randomly selected group of people will closely reflect the characteristics of the entire group from which the sample was taken. So, when marketers and site developers need to know, with relative certainty, the answers to specific questions, quantitative methods are used.

Insight

Quantitative research focuses on the left brain – objective, comfortable with logic, numbers and detailed, convergent reasoning rather than divergent reasoning. Qualitative research deals with the right brain – the hemisphere accountable for processing data such as words, emotions, feelings, colour and music. Traditional survey questionnaires are weak at eliciting follow-up data from respondents, as they usually require responses pre-categorized by the researcher. Often managers greeted the receipt of such surveys with the response 'So what?'. They answer questions related to such issues as market share, predicted revenue, statistical trends and past behaviour of customers well, but statistics are not good for answering questions about human behaviour, perceptions, future behaviour and involvement with a product. As a result of the need for companies to obtain richer data about their customers, prospective customers and the market as a whole, qualitative research became more in demand. While data collection techniques are now better developed, data analysis methodologies have not kept up. The new 'So what?' reaction from management is in response to the often confused summaries of the pages upon pages of focus group or interview transcripts. Running quantitative research alongside qualitative research offers a synergy whereby objective data can provide a structure to the analysis of subjective qualitative data. Generally, quantitative and qualitative research are presented as two separate entities. Yet, the smart market researcher knows how to combine both kinds of data.

Adapted from: http://www.asiamarketresearch.com/columns/market5.htm.

Case study: Beiersdorf

Creating new products

Analysing and understanding the data gathered on consumers' behaviours, needs, attitudes and opinions minimises the risks involved in making marketing decisions.

New Product Development (NPD)

How the NPD process is supported by market research	
The NPD process	**The market research process**
Identify consumer views and product needs	Primary & secondary research into consumer views and product needs
Product concept and packaging development	Concept, volumetric and packaging testing
Testing the product	Consumer usage research
Brand positioning and advertising development	Pre-testing of image and advertising research
Product launch and post launch	In-marketing monitoring

Market research serves two purposes:

1   To inform companies about consumer needs and desires. What are the trends in the market? What do consumers want?

2   To give consumers the opportunity to talk to the providers of products and services so that their views are taken into account.

Secondary research

In the deodorant category, NIVEA used many secondary research sources to discover consumers' views and their need for deodorants. These included:

i.   A consumer usage and attitude study. This had been conducted a few years earlier across various markets (UK, France and USA).

ii. An external study by fragrance houses. This covered the importance of scent and fragrance to people's well-being and mood.

Primary research

The research team felt therefore there was not enough recent knowledge about the consumer in the secondary research. They commissioned some primary qualitative research in key markets (Germany, France, UK and USA). The aim was to understand the motivations for using deodorant amongst the female consumer. The research involved small discussion groups of females. This helped researchers understand the beliefs and motivations of this group. There were several main findings:

◆   There is steady growth in females shaving. They wanted to look after their underarms throughout all seasons (not just in summer).

◆   Women cared increasingly about the condition of their underarms.

◆   Women desired attractive, neat underarms. This symbolized sensuality and femininity.

◆   The deodorant segment remained focused on functional rather than beautifying products.

Results of the research

The market research revealed an unexplored market potential for Nivea Deodorant. The brand did not have a specific product that addressed 'underarm beauty' for the female consumer. Consumers showed a need for a 'beautifying, caring deodorant'. The team generated ideas on how to address the consumer need.

From these ideas the marketing team created 'product concepts' which describe the product benefits and how they will meet the consumer needs. Several concepts were written in different ways. These explained and expressed unique product attributes.

The company needed to know which concept was preferred by prospective consumers. It carried out market research amongst the desired target market. For Pearl and Beauty, the desired target market was 18–35 year-old women who were beauty-orientated, followed fashion and looked for products with extra benefits.

Quantitative research was carried out in two test markets (France and Germany). A number of criteria were used to test the concepts:

1)   Deodorant category performance measures. These included wetness, dryness, and fragrance. The new concept must deliver generic core benefits.

2)   Product attributes specific to the new product and Nivea core values. The new Pearl and Beauty product has additional benefits to a 'regular' deodorant. For example, it leaves your skin feeling silky and gives you beautiful underarms. Consumers needed to understand and see these benefits.

3)   The product needed to be relevant and motivate a consumer to purchase it.

The team chose the 'winning' concept. This best conveyed beauty while remaining relevant to the deodorant category and Nivea brand.

Next the research team tested various name ideas for the product and developed different designs for the packaging. Packaging plays a very important role in helping to communicate the image of the product. Pearl and Beauty needed to communicate femininity and sophistication. Pink was a natural colour choice for the packaging. They also used a soft pearlescent container to emphasisz the 'pearl extracts' in the product.

Testing the product, brand positioning and advertising

The market research team conducted a product usage test. A de-branded sample of the product was given to the target consumer of females in several countries. The consumers were asked to use the new deodorant for a week. They kept a diary of when they used it and scored the performance of the deodorant against a list of criteria. These included:

Did it keep you dry all day?

Did you have to reapply it?

Did you like the fragrance?

Did it last all day?

Was the deodorant reliable?

Consumers applied the 'de-branded' deodorant under their right armpit and continued to use their current deodorant under their left armpit. This helped the users gauge if it was as good as or better than the brand they normally used. This gave a measure of how likely the consumer would be to swap brands. The results of the test were very positive. Most consumers loved the fragrance and the feel of the product on their skin. They felt it performed as well as their current deodorant. Most said they would swap their brands after trying the product.

Brand positioning

Now the marketing team had a new product idea that consumers liked. It had a name and packaging design that were well received. They now needed to check how this fitted with the rest of the Nivea Deodorant brand positioning and range.

Using qualitative research to inform advertising

The next stage was to brief an advertising agency to develop communication to support the launch of the new product. The company conducted qualitative research and presented ideas in the form of 'storyboards' of what a TV advert could look like. The objective was to evaluate which were the best ideas in terms of:

◆ Did they stand out as exciting or different?

◆ Were they relevant to the consumer?

◆ Did they communicate the right things about the new product?

◆ Did they persuade the consumer to want to purchase the product?

Evaluating success

Continuous consumer tracking can be carried out to find out consumers' views of the new product. This involves interviewing people every day to find out whether they are using the product, what they think of it and why they would purchase it. Beiersdorf uses other, secondary data sources such as consumer panel data and EPOS (electronic point of sale) data. These monitor the sales effectiveness of the product throughout the launch phase and through the product life cycle.

*Source:*http://www.shl.com/SHL/en-int/Company/Clients/Case_Studies/Case_Study _ List /Beiersdorfcasestudy.aspx

The market research industry

The market research industry consists of hundreds of firms and consultancies. Each of these will have their own areas of specialization. The leading agencies, and many of the smaller ones, have directors and executives who are members of the Market Research Society. The Society has a Professional Code of Conduct which lays down rules and good practices with respect to their responsibilities to clients (confidentiality), respondents (anonymity), the public as a whole and to each other. The following case study demonstrates how market research is becoming more complex and needs to become more sophisticated to match the complexity of consumers' lives.

A case study in complexity

An overwhelming majority of marketers surveyed – 92 per cent – believe that marketing has become more complicated as a result of the complexity of consumers' lives. Media fragmentation is identified as the root of their frustration, with 67 per cent of marketers citing it as the driving force behind increased complexity. The modern marketer is faced with a dramatically increased number of channels and platforms to deal with. Two-fifths of marketers believe that the increase in the number of media outlets has made consumers' media consumption less predictable and fostered a decline in consumer loyalty. Marketers are increasingly concerned that targeted outlets, which aim to capture specific consumers, have increased confusion rather than offering clarity. Marketers have to balance the need to develop an overall communications strategy with the need to target niche groups. The relationship between marketers and consumers embodies the complexity problem. The fragmentation of consumers' lives has led marketers to develop more sophisticated methods of marketing to reach them. This in turn has increased choice, making consumers' lives even more complex. Marketers are realizing that standard market research is no longer sufficient for understanding consumer needs. More than two-thirds of those surveyed agreed that there is a need for more innovative research, although only 20 per cent felt that they were already carrying out such research. Respondents to the survey believe that some companies are already getting it right: Tesco received the most praise, followed by Orange, Virgin, First Direct and EasyJet. Another interesting example is Ronseal, which is seen by marketers as a brand that achieves clarity and precision through the simplicity of its marketing.

Adapted from: A case study in complexity, *Marketing Week*, 18 September 2003, Caroline Parry, Emma Doniger and the Future Foundation.

On the theme of increased choice making consumers' lives ever more complex, the book *Sophisticated Consumers, Intricate Lifestyles, Simple Solutions* (Willmott and Nelson, 2003) reports how 14 types of dental floss were found in one UK pharmacy, a similar range of brandies were found in a Spanish supermarket and that there were eight kinds of orange juice available under the Tropicana brand alone.

Agency selection

It is possible to buy research and a reputable agency should give advice on the most cost-effective way of researching a target audience. It will discuss the advantages and disadvantages of different research options, and help to design and write questions. It will endeavour to achieve a representative sample and report the main findings in whatever form is preferred. The agency should also be willing to discuss the implications of any findings for the business.

The British Market Research Association (BMRA) website lists its member agencies with their specialisms. Smaller agencies are good for niche areas but larger agencies will tend to have specialists who focus on particular sectors, such as the voluntary sector, financial services, telecommunications, education, and so on.

Assessing the impact of marketing activity

Advertising

Pre-testing is the showing of unfinished advertisements to representative groups of the target audience.

Post-testing is concerned with the evaluation of a campaign once it has been released. Examples include the return of coupons, response cards, requests for further literature or actual orders. Recall tests attempt to assess how memorable particular advertisements are whilst recognition tests are based on the ability of respondents to reprocess information about an advertisement.

Evaluation of sales promotions

Evaluation methods include the following:

◆   Consumer audits – This will indicate if there has been a change in consumer behaviour as a result of the sales promotion campaign.

◆   Sales information – Increase in sales is one performance indicator.

- **Retail audits** – Specialist organizations can track changes in stock levels, distribution, market share immediately after the promotional campaign. This will provide an insight into the basis of an increase or decrease in sales.

- **Sales force feedback** – This is based on the uptake of sales promotion opportunities in their area.

- **Voucher/coupon redemption** – Usually based on coding to relate response rate to sales promotion activities. This can be used to endorse the right selection of media, the right kind of sales promotion activity and potentially the most frequently used distribution outlet.

Evaluation of public relations

Haywood (1991) suggested that there are seven commonly used measures of results:

- **Budget** – An assessment of whether the planned PR activity has been achieved within the budget defined and also within the timescales set.

- **Awareness** – The measure of awareness can be quite complex and is most likely to be established through a range of marketing research activities.

- **Attitude** – Combined with research on brand awareness can be research on brand attitudes, whether they are positive or negative, and whether they have resulted in any change in consumer behaviour.

- **Media coverage and tone** – First, it will be essential to establish the level of media coverage achieved as a result of planned-PR activities. Typical measures might include the number of different media which covered the case, the number of columns taken, key headings and perceived importance of the PR information. Second, the nature and tone in which the PR activities have been covered.

- **Positioning** – Measuring the perception of the position of the organization versus that of the competition.

- **Response generation** – Many of the enquiries or leads generated may be subject to some degree of code referencing, or sources of the enquiry will be recorded.

- **Share price** – For large public companies, this is an indicator of public confidence in the organization.

Evaluation of direct and interactive marketing communications

Evaluation is related to the pre-determined objectives of a campaign.

Typical measures for successful implementation of the direct marketing campaign will include the following:

- Response rate
- Conversion rate
- Order value
- Repeat orders.

This information will be gathered through a range of voucher and campaign response codes that will be able to distinguish the source of the direct mail or promotion. This may establish the most popular direct marketing technique.

Technology is developing quickly and click-through rates are a common measure for online activity. However, this evaluates only behaviour not attitudes.

Evaluation of personal sales

Sales performance needs to be measured against objectives on a regular basis. Other factors relating to sales performance that can be measured include the following:

◆ **Productivity** – calls per day, calls per account, total number of orders versus calls.

◆ **Account development** – total of new accounts, total of existing accounts, growth of sales from existing accounts.

◆ **Expenses** – expenses versus number of calls made, cost per call.

Sales measurement techniques are becoming more sophisticated and more effective and the speed at which information becomes available is of the essence.

Impact assessment

When assessing the impact of the marketing activity it is likely that a combination of measures will need to be used to support future expenditure. These could include:

◆ Sales growth

◆ Relationship measurement mechanism within centres (e.g. questionnaires)

◆ Qualitive and quantitive research

◆ Customer feedback mechanisms

◆ Footfall conversion measurement

◆ Indexed trading data (sales trends)

◆ Service charge savings

◆ Press cuttings with impact scoring mechanism (e.g. size of article)

◆ Car counting

◆ Dwell time measurement

◆ Frequency of customer visits

◆ Retailer demand for units

◆ Community relationships

◆ Retailer feedback mechanisms including surveys and retailer consultations

◆ Use of website, where appropriate.

Source: http://www.rics.org.uk

Summary

There are many different approaches to market research but the most important aspect is to choose an approach that is fit for the purpose and will deliver the kind of data that will be useful. Sophisticated market research is costly so it is important to conduct a cost/benefit analysis of any proposal. No approach is perfect and the main choice is between knowing a lot about a little, or a little about a lot.

Further study

Boddy, D. (2002) *Management: An Introduction*, Harlow: Pearson Education, Chapter 7 'Managing marketing'.

Hints and tips

◆ You need to be able to show that you know the issue that needs to be decided when designing a research project aimed at providing information as part of a marketing audit or for marketing and business decisions.

◆ On a practical level, you will need to be able to analyse and interpret information and present, as a written report or oral presentation, appropriate conclusions or recommendations that inform the marketing and business decisions for which the research was undertaken.

Sample questions

June 2005, Question 2

'@ Medi Wrap' is a new venture for '@ Wrap'

a. What information will the company require for the development of the market for '@ Medi Wrap'?

(15 Marks)

b. How might this information be obtained?

(10 Marks)
(Total 25 marks)

December 2004, Question 2

The online digital business will be a radical departure for Pinnacle Pictures from its traditional overnight developing and printing business via high street agents.

a. What information will the company require for the development of the online digital business?

(15 Marks)

b. How might it be obtained?

(10 Marks)
(Total 25 Marks)

Bibliography

Haywood, R. (1991), *All About Public Relations*, London: McGraw-Hill

Housden, M. (2007) *Marketing Research and Information*, Oxford: Butterworth-Heinemann

McQuarrie, Edward F. (1996): *The Market Research Toolbox: A Concise Guide for Beginners*, Thousand Oaks ,California, Sage Publications

Public Sector Benchmarking Service (2004) http://www.benchmarking.gov.uk

Willmott, M. and Nelson, W. (2003) *Complicated Lives: Sophisticated Consumers, Intricate Lifestyles, Simple Solutions*, Chichester: Wiley

Wilson, A. (2003) *Marketing Research*, Harlow: FT Prentice Hall

Unit 7
Developing and implementing marketing plans

4.1 Develop an operational marketing plan, selecting an appropriate marketing mix for an organization operating in any context such as FMCG, business-to-business (supply chain), large or capital project-based, services, voluntary and not-for-profit, or sales support (e.g. SMEs).

4.2 Use the main techniques available for planning, scheduling and resourcing activities within the plan.

4.3 Identify appropriate measures for evaluating and controlling the marketing plan.

4.4 Review and evaluate the effectiveness of planning activities.

Related statements of marketing practice

Jc2 Manage and report on delivery against plan and objectives.

Kc.1 Define measurements appropriate to the plan or business case and ensure they are undertaken.

Kc.2 Evaluate activities and identify improvements using measurement data.

Malcolm McDonald, Cranfield University School of Management, defines the overall purpose of planning at this stage as: 'the identification and creation of sustainable competitive advantage' (Quoted in Dibb et al, 2001, p. 689) The purpose of your studies is to prepare you to add value to your organization, with a combination of knowledge, understanding and application abilities and skills that could really enable your organization to achieve 'sustainable competitive advantage'. An ability to apply marketing in different contexts is important. You will be in a stronger position to add value to your own position within the organization as well as to the organization as a whole. Dibb et al.'s (2005) five-stage planning cycle is useful. The planning cycle involves:

◆ The development or revision of marketing objectives relative to the organization's previous year's performance.

Key definitions

Corporate planning – Continuous process of making present risk-taking decisions systematically and with the greatest knowledge of their futurity; systematically organizing the efforts needed to carry out these decisions, and measuring the results of these decisions against the expectations through organized, systematic feedback.

Environmental scanning – This is fundamental to the planning process and should form an integral part of all localized planning and strategic decision-making. The process involves the research and assessment of known or proposed changes in the areas of politics, the environment, social and demographic change, technology, economic issues or legal issues, in the short, medium and long term. A PEST analysis is part of this process.

Marketing audit – The systematic collection, analysis and evaluation of information relating to the internal and external environments that answers the question 'Where are we now?' for the organization.

PEST – A framework for analysing the political, economic, social and technological trends, issues and so on in the external environment that are likely to have an impact on the business. Sometimes this is written as 'PESTLE' where Legal and Environmental categories are added.

Strategic planning – Long-term plans based on the organizations overall business objectives. Strategic plans are typically multiple years and reach out 5 or 10 years (or more) using scenarios or other planning methods that identifies assumptions, risks, and environmental factors.

SWOT – A matrix that categorizes information about internal strengths and weaknesses and external opportunities and threats. The aim is to minimize the threats and address the weaknesses whilst capitalizing on strengths and aligning them with the opportunities that exist.

Introduction

The Marketing Management in Practice module is intended to give participants guidance in developing and implementing marketing plans at an operational level in organizations. A key part of this is working within a team to develop the plan and managing teams implementing the plan by undertaking marketing activities and projects. Its aim is to encourage you to integrate and apply knowledge from all the modules, particularly as part of a team. The focus should be on implementing a marketing plan as a team activity and careful attention needs to be given to the issues surrounding the actual implementation of a plan. The *Marketing Planning* Coursebook, (Beamish and Ashford 2008) covers all these areas in detail. That book focuses on the process of effectively 'doing' marketing. It looks at the concepts and applications of 'the marketing planning process', from the marketing audit through to developing objectives and marketing strategies. It covers:

◆ Explaining the role of the marketing plan within the context of the organization's strategy and culture and broader marketing environment (ethics, social responsibility, legal frameworks and sustainability).

♦ Conducting a marketing audit considering appropriate internal and external factors.

♦ Developing marketing objectives and plans at an operational level.

♦ Developing the role of branding and positioning within the marketing plan.

♦ Integrating marketing mix tools to achieve effective implementation of plans.

♦ Selecting an appropriate co-ordinated marketing mix incorporating appropriate stakeholder relationships for a particular marketing context.

♦ Setting and justifying budgets for marketing plans and mix decisions.

♦ Defining and using appropriate measurements to evaluate the effectiveness of marketing plans and activities.

♦ Making recommendations for changes and innovations to marketing processes based on an understanding of the organizational context and evaluation of past.

Implementing the marketing plan is one of the most challenging areas of business strategy. Ultimately this can often result in one of the most dramatic changes of all, that is change in the organizational structure. It is necessary to consider carefully the nature, structure and culture of any organization, in order that it can clearly meet the challenges to achieve a sustainable competitive advantage and remain at the heart of the marketplace. Culture and structure were discussed in Unit 1 of this book.

Planning

Marketing planning and corporate planning

Corporate or strategic company planning comprises the following sequential steps:

1 **Mission statement** – is a statement of the company's overall business philosophy or purpose. It is normally a set of guidelines, rather than something that is stated in hard and fast quantitative terms.

2 **Situational analysis** – means evaluating external and internal factors that will affect the planning process and asks the question 'Where are we now?'.

3 **Organizational objectives** – describes where an organization wants to be and how it wants to fulfil its mission. They are often expressed in achievable quantitative terms.

4 **Strategies to achieve these objectives** – which are the concrete ideas that set about achieving company objectives and they relate to how the mission will be accomplished.

In large organizations, corporate planning is often a separate function reporting directly to top management. How corporate planning is organized in different organizations and sectors is influenced by factors such as the size and structure of the organization. Corporate planning provides an overview and brings planning functions together from across the organization. A key aspect of corporate planning is to ensure that there is consistency and coherence across the organization and all plans will contribute to achieving overall organizational objectives. Corporate objectives are derived from the corporate plan, and inform the direction and focus of the marketing plan. Marketing objectives cover issues such as increasing the awareness of a product or service among a target audience in a particular time frame. Marketing objectives are likely to be linked to market share or sales targets.

Strategic planning

In his book *The Rise of Fall of Strategic Planning*, Henry Mintzberg describes how strategic planners make the mistake of thinking that the future will resemble the past and tend to gather 'hard' data on their industry, markets and competitors, whilst ignoring 'soft' data such as talking with customers, suppliers and employees. Many organizations now make use of the term 'strategic intent' defined by Gary Hamel and C.K. Prahalad in their book *Competing for the Future* as 'an ambitious and compelling dream that provides the emotional and intellectual energy for the journey to the future, conveying a sense of direction and destiny'. Strategic intent is more flexible than a strategic plan and recognizes that the best laid plans may need to change in response to market conditions. The pace of change means that it is not always possible to anticipate change and, for example, cataclysmic events such as September 11 and its aftermath, which was not and could not have been anticipated, can completely transform the business context. The upshot of this is that planning is important but it needs to incorporate flexibility. The days when vast resources were put into creating gigantic strategic plans that were out of date by the time they had been produced are probably over for the present.

Marketing planning

Strategic marketing planning is the application of a number of logical steps in the planning process. There are different ways in which this can be done. One specific model would not suit every marketing planning situation. The planning process:

The market planning process

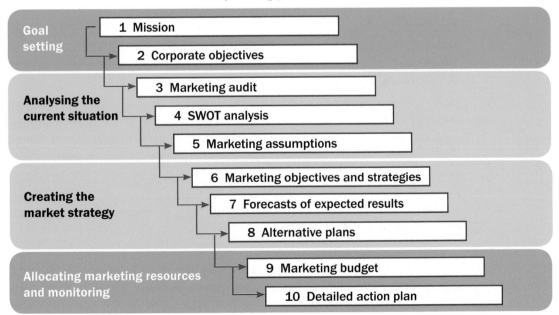

Example of a structure for a marketing plan linked to corporate planning

Mission Statement

Macro-Environment Situational Analysis

Political, economic, socio-cultural audits of all major company and technological (PEST) functions – marketing, finance, hrm, production, distribution

- Strengths, weaknesses, opportunities, threats, analysis (SWOT)
- Marketing objectives
- Forecast market potential
- Generate marketing strategies
- Assumptions and contingency plans
- Prepare detailed marketing mix programmes
- Budget Resources including staffing
- Agree timescales
- Implement the plan
- Measure and control

Other ways to develop a strategic approach

Value disciplines and market leadership

In *The Discipline of Market Leaders* (1995), Michael Treacy and Fred Wiersama argue that there are four new rules that competing companies must obey.

1   Provide the best offer in the marketplace, by excelling in one specific dimension of value. Market leaders first develop a value proposition, one that is compelling and unmatched.

2   Maintain threshold standards on other dimensions of value. You can't allow performance in other dimensions to slip so much that it impairs the attractiveness of your company's unmatched value.

3   Dominate your market by improving the value year after year. When a company focuses all its assets, energies and attention on delivering and improving one type of customer value, it can nearly always deliver better performance in that dimension than another company that divides its attention among more than one.

4   Build a well-tuned operating model dedicated to delivering unmatched value. In a competitive marketplace, the customer value must be improved. This is the imperative of the market leader. The operating model is the key to raising and resetting customer expectation.

Treacy and Wiersema describe three generic value disciplines in their book. Any company must choose one of these value disciplines and consistently and vigorously act upon it. An enterprise cannot be successful unless it actively pursues one of three value propositions: operational leadership, customer intimacy, or product leadership. This does not mean the other two dimensions should be completely neglected, but rather that the company should aim to be merely 'OK' in these other two disciplines.

◆ **Product leadership** – innovation and the best quality goods and services, e.g. Nike and Nokia; very strong in innovation and brand marketing; the focus is on development, innovation, design, time to market, high margins in a short time frame; flexible company cultures.

◆ **Operational excellence** – low cost and process efficiency, e.g. Dell and Southwest Airlines; focus is on efficiency, streamlined operations, supply chain management, no-frills, volume is important; most large international corporations are operating out of this discipline; measuring systems are very important; extremely limited variation in product assortment.

◆ **Customer intimacy** – Providing the best total solution (service/relationship building), e.g. Nordstrom; excels in customer attention and customer service; tailors its products and services to individual or almost individual customers; large variation in product assortment; focus is on: CRM, deliver products and services on time and above customer expectations, lifetime value concepts, reliability, being close to the customer.

The value disciplines model is similar to the three generic strategies from Porter (cost leadership, differentiation, focus). However there is at least one major difference: according to the value disciplines model no discipline may be neglected: threshold levels on the two disciplines that are not selected must be maintained. According to Porter, companies that act like this run a risk of getting "stuck in the middle".

Value disciplines	Value focus	Image driver	Image
Customer intimacy	Service	Create relationship	Best friend
Product leadership	Quality	Unique attribute(s)	Best product/ service
Operational excellence	Cost	Low cost	Best deal

Source: Treacy, M. and Wiersema, F. (1997) *The Discipline of Market Leaders*, Perseus Books Group

3Cs model

The model is another useful way of looking at the focus and direction of the company. Kenichi Ohmae (1991) believes that successful business strategies do not result from rigorous analysis but from a particular state of mind. In the construction of any business strategy, three main players must be taken into account: the corporation itself, the customer, and the competition.

Ohmae believes that founders of successful businesses follow a five-step process for successful, foresighted management decision-making:

1 Clear definition of the business domain.

2 Logical hypothesis based on an extrapolation of forces at work in the business environment.

3 Focus on a few strategic options, instead of the many open to the business.

4 The company must pace its strategy and not overreach itself.

5 Management must be prepared to change the basic direction of the business, if conditions demand it.

Each of these five steps are discussed in detail. In the final chapter of the book, the author discusses strategy formulation: 'to bring insight to fruition as a successful strategy takes method, mental discipline, and plain hard work.' He also discusses the creativity required for the development of business strategy.

The strategic triangle

Only by integrating the three Cs (customer, corporate, and competitor) in a strategic triangle, can a sustained competitive advantage exist.

1   **Corporate-based strategies**: These aim to maximize the corporation's strengths relative to the competition in the functional areas that are critical to achieve success in the industry.

The corporation does not have to lead in every function to win. If it can gain a decisive edge in one key function, it will eventually be able to improve its other functions.

2   **Customer-based strategies:** Clients are the basis of any strategy. In the long run, the corporation that is genuinely interested in its customers will be interesting for its investors.

3   **Competitor-based strategies:** These can be constructed by looking at possible sources of differentiation in functions such as: purchasing, design, engineering, sales and servicing.

Ohmae, K. (1991) *The Mind of the Strategist: The Art of Japanese Business*, McGraw-Hill

Marketing plan components

The following are examples of what can be included in a marketing plan but it does not necessarily follow that every plan will have all of these components. Marketing plans tend to vary by industry, size of company, stage of growth and organizational goals. The process of preparing it is as important as the particular form it takes. The process should make you think about goals and the marketing strategy that will be used to achieve them. A marketing plan may contain all or just some of the following components.

Executive summary

Introducing the organization:

◆   Explain the major points of your plan

◆   Describe briefly the nature of the business and the products or services offered

◆   Include a mission or values statement and objectives

◆   List the structure of your organization and the senior management team

◆   Summarize the marketing objectives and strategies that are in the plan.

Marketing audit

A good marketing audit is:

◆   Systematic – It follows a logical, predetermined framework, an orderly sequence of diagnostic steps.

- ◆ **Comprehensive** – It considers all factors affecting marketing performance, not just obvious trouble spots. Marketers can be fooled into addressing symptoms rather than underlying problems. A comprehensive audit can identify the real problems.

- ◆ **Independent** – To ensure objectivity, outside consultants are sometimes used to prepare the marketing audit. Using outsiders may not be necessary, but having an objective auditor is important.

- ◆ **Periodic** – Many organizations schedule regular marketing audits because the environment for marketing is dynamic.

A typical marketing audit consists of a number of sections, examples of which are given below.

Marketing environment audit

This is based on an analysis of the internal and external environment. It should include information about target markets, including information about other individuals or organizations that offer similar products and services. Identify key issues in the competitive environment, for example challenges, such as new legislation or the impact of technological changes.

The marketing audit is important to the planning process because it provides the analysis that supports the corporate and the marketing decision-making process. An audit should provide information on the external and internal environment. Understanding trends and trying to anticipate changes that will have an impact on markets, customers, suppliers and competitors are important aspects of strategic development. Decisions about product and service development and investment decisions should be informed by the outcome of the marketing audit. The challenge is to use data intelligently and be prepared to respond to changes that influence consumer preferences and behaviour as well as to be proactive and to try to influence that behaviour.

Internal marketing audit

The goal of the marketing audit is to assess the effectiveness of a company's marketing function and process, and provide recommendations for improvement. Philip Kotler introduced the concept of the marketing audit in *The Marketing Audit Comes Of Age*.

The issues that are addressed as part of the marketing audit include:

- ◆ How well is the present role of marketing defined?

- ◆ Is there adequate co-operation between marketing and other functional areas?

- ◆ Is the right information gathered? How good is it?

- ◆ How effectively is it used?

- ◆ Are the right processes in place (e.g. market planning and new product development)?

- ◆ How effective are they?

- ◆ How well are basic marketing concepts understood?

- ◆ How well is the understanding translated into practice?

There are several other models that can be deployed to assist the auditing process. The 7-S framework of McKinsey describes the key factors that shape the way that an organization operates. Changes in one area often have implications in others. This is why it is important to examine and anticipate the potential intended and unintended consequences of change. A SWOT analysis can be used for both the internal and external environments.

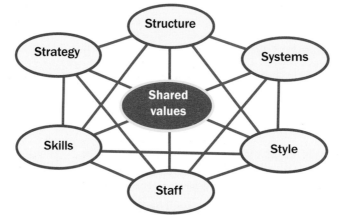

Shared values: What the organization stands for and its core beliefs and attitudes.

Strategy: Plans for the allocation of a firm's scarce resources, over time, to reach identified goals.

Structure: The way the organization's units relate to each other: centralized, functional divisions (top-down); decentralized (the trend in larger organizations); matrix, network, holding and so on.

System: The procedures, processes and routines that characterize how important work is to be done: financial systems; hiring, promotion and performance appraisal systems; information systems.

Staff: Numbers and types of personnel within the organization.

Style: Cultural style of the organization and how key managers behave in achieving the organization's goals.

Skills: Distinctive capabilities of personnel or of the organization as a whole.

The company's capabilities and competences

Distinctive capabilities

Organizations with distinctive capabilities have attributes which others cannot replicate. In 'Foundations of Corporate Success', John Kay argues that outstanding businesses derive their strength from a distinctive structure of relationships with employees, customers, and suppliers. He identifies three distinctive capabilities a company can have to create added value and achieve competitive advantage through relationships:

Architecture (a structure of relational contacts within or around the organization with employees and with customers and suppliers). A firm with a distinctive architecture gains strength from the ability to transfer information which is specific to the firm, product or market within the organization and to its customers and suppliers. It can also respond quickly and flexibly to changing circumstances. It has often been through their greater ability to develop such architecture that Japanese firms have established competitive advantage over their American rivals.

Reputation (built up through customer's own experience, quality signals, demonstrations and free trials, warranty, guarantee, word of mouth, association with other brands, staking the reputation once it is established). An important element of the strategy of many successful firms has been the transformation of an initial distinctive capability based on innovation or architecture to a more enduring one derived from reputation.

Innovation (provided it is translated to competitive advantage successfully). This is an obvious source of distinctive capability, but it is much less often a sustainable or appropriable source because successful innovation quickly attracts imitation.

Core competences

In their article 'The core competences of the corporation' (1990) Prahalad and Gary Hamel argue that a corporation should be build around a core of shared competences.

Three tests to identifying a core competence (CC) are as follows:

1   Should provide potential access to a wide variety of markets;

2   Should make a significant contribution to the perceived customer benefits of the end product(s); and

3   A CC should be difficult for competitors to imitate.

Core competencies are built through a process of continuous improvement and enhancement. They should constitute the focus for corporate strategy. Once top management (with the help of divisional and Strategic Business Unit managers) has identified an overarching CC, it must ask businesses to identify the projects and the people closely connected with them. Care must be taken not to let core competencies develop into core rigidities. Corporate competences are difficult to learn, but are difficult to unlearn as well.

Analysing the market

Environmental scanning

This is the systematic collection and evaluation of information from the wider marketing environment that might affect the organization and its strategic marketing activities. It is undertaken by marketing planners. Key issues are as follows:

◆   Making sure that data is up to date, particularly for markets that are volatile and where consumer behaviour can change quickly.

◆   The ability to identify what is significant amongst a myriad of detail. It is important not to drown in a sea of information.

◆   Collecting data on a regular basis may be too expensive for an organization to undertake itself but the data that is available for purchase from market research analysts may not be specific enough about particular markets and products.

◆   Marketing managers need to be able to understand the environment in which they are operating.

Marketing analysis tools

Analysis tools commonly used for this purpose are PEST, Porter's five-force analysis, gap analysis, BCG matrix and the GE matrix. The PEST model has several variations and is shown sometimes as STEP. PEST is also extended to seven or even more factors, by adding Ecological (or Environmental), Legislative (or Legal), and Industry Analysis, which produces the PESTELI model. Other variations on the theme include STEEP and PESTLE and SLEPT which allow for a dedicated Ethical section. STEEPLED refers to Political, Economic, Social and Technological – plus Ecological or Environmental, Ethical, Demographic and Legal.

You should use whatever version works best for you given your communication objectives.

A SWOT analysis usually measures a business unit whereas a PEST or SLEPT analysis measures market potential and situation, particularly indicating growth or decline, and thereby market attractiveness, business potential, suitability of access, market potential and 'fit'.

A market is defined by what is addressing it, be it a product, company, brand, business unit, proposition, idea and so on, so be clear about how you define the market being analysed. The PEST or SLEPT subject should be a clear definition of the market being addressed, which might be from any of the following standpoints:

- A company looking at its market
- A product looking at its market
- A brand in relation to its market
- A local business unit
- A strategic option, such as entering a new market or launching a new product
- A potential acquisition
- A potential partnership
- An investment opportunity.

A PEST(LE) analysis is a logical framework for identifying and assessing the various influences on the present and future development of the organization. It is usually a precursor to developing a SWOT analysis of the internal strengths and weaknesses of the organization compared with the opportunities and constraints in the external environment.

Political factors – such as changes in government and the ramifications of their strategies such as tax levels, education and training issues, employment legislation and so on. Any changes in policy – impact on strategic direction – timing? Change of legislative foreign exchange, taxation policy, interest rates, funding sources, exports.

Economic factors – such as the impact of the trade cycle, levels of disposable income and inflation.

Typical questions are as follows:

- What are the effects of competitors (their products, services, technologies) on your operation?
- What major developments in income, prices, savings, taxation and credit will affect the organization?

Social/cultural issues – such as the ageing consumer, increases in one-parent families, changing values, attitudes to smoking.

Informal networks, health – population under 14 years, Population over 65 years, education, professional development.

Typical questions to ask are as follows:

◆ What population trends are expected to affect existing and planned strategy?

◆ What social and psychological patterns (attitudes, lifestyle, etc.) are expected to affect buyer behaviour patterns? How are environmental trends monitored?

◆ How are present and pending legal developments affecting your operation?

Technological factors – such as the increased rate of computer capability, production methods, information management, privacy of data, reliability, updates on technology, protection of intellectual property, ease of transferring funds with technology.

Legal issues – such as changes in advertising legislation for tobacco, regulations and codes of practice for promotions, and so on.

Environmental issues – Kyoto protocol, biodiversity, climate change, desertification, nuclear test ban, ozone layer protection; safety and health, cultural heritage of the land, environmentally responsible corporate citizens, attitudes towards pollution, energy use, fair trade, slave labour and so on.

Case study: SLEPT analysis – McCain's

McCain is the world's largest producer of potato chips and also one of the world's largest frozen foods companies.

One of the biggest environmental factors affecting McCain in recent years is the growing concern about obesity.

SLEPT analysis

A SLEPT analysis helps to analyse the environment.

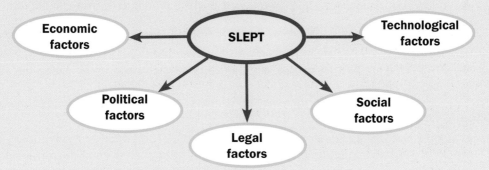

To create a SLEPT analysis the company needs to examine the key environmental factors that affect its business. These are broken down into:

Social factors

Social trends include consumer buying patterns. Just as the demand for clothes are determined by fashion, demand for food products is determined by eating patterns. Recently, food producers have seen a slowdown in sales as a result of campaigns to encourage healthier eating. McCain has responded to this challenge in two main ways:

◆ Reducing quantities of salt and oil throughout its product range.

◆ Communicating the message that all McCain potato products are made from simple ingredients such as whole potatoes and sunflower oil. It does this through public relations campaigns and advertising.

Legal factors

Food labelling

The UK government's Food Standards Agency has recommended that firms put 'traffic light' labels on food to help people understand what they are buying:

Red represents high levels of ingredients such as fats and salts.

Green represents low levels.

All of McCain's potato products are able to display the green label for saturated fat and none of its products show a red label.

Advertising

McCain makes sure that all its advertising sticks rigidly within the requirements of the Advertising Standards Authority (ASA) which stipulates that all adverts must be:

◆ legal
◆ decent
◆ honest and
◆ truthful.

Legislation

McCain's products comply with:

◆ The Food Safety Act, covering the way in which food is prepared and served.

◆ The Trades Descriptions Act, which states that goods and services must be exactly as described.

◆ The Weights and Measures Act – governing such aspects as giving the right weight on packs.

Economic factors

As people become cash-rich and time-poor they prefer to switch to ready meals and simple to prepare foodstuffs that they can quickly heat in an oven or microwave. With growing affluence people are prepared to buy oven chips rather than cook chips themselves or buy them at a fish and chip shop. The convenience of being able to heat them up on demand is a powerful driver.

Political factors

On political factors, the UK government has increased the pressure on food suppliers to come up with healthier foods. The government publicises and supports healthy eating by creating initiatives such as 'Healthy Schools'.

Technological changes

Food technology involves researching and developing techniques for resolving problems such as how to:

◆   freeze while retaining flavour

◆   maximize natural nutritional characteristics

◆   turn a frozen product into an oven heated product.

McCain needed a solution that reduced fat and salt but also retained flavour. Its solution was to use sunflower oil which reduced saturated fats by 70 per cent across its potato product range. Consumers are increasingly aware of food issues and they look at food labelling and information in the press about what is good for them. The challenge is to prepare potato products in the healthiest way possible. McCain's advertising supports the company's message that chips are nutritionally acceptable provided they are made in the right way.

Source: http://www.fleishmanhillard.co.uk/index.php?pid=89

SWOT analysis

This should be a summary of the marketing audit and indicate the key issues which need then to be considered further.

Strengths

Every organization has some strengths. In some cases this is obvious, for example dominant market shares. In others, it is a matter of perspective; for instance, a company is very small and hence has the ability to move fast. It is important to note that companies in a bad position also have strengths. Whether these are adequate is an issue for analysis.

Weaknesses

Every organization also has some weakness. In some cases, this is obvious: for example, a stricter regulatory environment. In others, it is a matter of perspective: for example a firm has 99 per cent market share and is open to attack from every new player. It is important to note that companies that are extremely competent in what they do, also have weaknesses. How badly these weaknesses will affect the company is a matter of analysis.

Opportunities

All organizations have some opportunities that they can gain from. These could range from diversification to sale of operations. Identifying hidden opportunities is the mark of an astute analyst.

Threats

No organization is immune to threats. These could be internal, such as falling productivity. Or they could be external, such as lower priced international competition.

A SWOT analysis is undertaken to help plan the marketing mix, which includes:

◆ Strengths of the product/service/organization

◆ Weaknesses of the organization

◆ Opportunities available to the organization (external factors)

◆ Threats which may come from the competition.

One way to improve upon the basic SWOT is to include more detailed competitor and business environment information in the analysis. SWOT analysis can also be augmented through surveys, for example customer awareness, interest, trial and usage levels.

Case study: SWOT analysis – Starbucks

Strengths

Starbucks Corporation is a very profitable organization, earning in excess of $600 million. The company generates revenue of more than $5000 million. It is a global coffee brand built with almost 9000 cafes in almost 40 countries.

The organization has a strong ethical ethical mission statement: 'Starbucks is committed to a role of environmental leadership in all facets of our business.'

Weaknesses

Starbucks has a strong presence in the United States with more than three quartersof its cafes located in the North American market. It needs to invest in other countries to spread the business risk. The company is dependent on one main competitive advantage, ie coffee retail and this makes it potentially vulnerable if it needed to diversify into other market sectors.

This could make them slow to diversify into other sectors should the need arise.

Opportunities

Starbucks are very good at taking advantage of opportunities.

◆ In 2004 the company forged a commercial relationship with Hewlett Packard to provide a CD-burning service in one of their cafes in California. Customers are able to create their own CDs.

◆ New products and services that can be retailed in their cafes, such as those sold under the Fair Trade label

◆ The company has the opportunity to expand its global operations. New markets for coffee such as India and the Pacific Rim nations are beginning to emerge.

◆ Co-branding with other manufacturers of food and drink, and brand franchising to manufacturers of other goods and services is a possibility.

Threats

No-one knows if coffee will remain a popular worldwide drink. Health scares could have an impact on sales. Will another beverage or leisure activity replace it in the future?

Starbucks are exposed to rises in the cost of coffee and dairy products.

Since its conception in Pine Place Park, Seattle in 1971, Starbucks' success has lead to the market entry of many competitors and copycat brands that pose potential threats.

Starbucks mission statement is: 'Establish Starbucks as the premier purveyor of the finest coffee in the world while maintaining our uncompromising principles while we grow.'

Source: www.mhhe.com/business/management/thompson/11e/case/starbucks.html

GAP analysis

A gap analysis is something which needs to be monitored and considered in terms of filling the gap, should one occur. A gap is where corporate sales and financial objectives are greater than the current long-range forecasts in marketing planning. A gap could be filled in various ways, for example by improving productivity, reducing costs, increasing prices, stimulating increased usage, increasing market share, finding new user groups, developing new market segments, product development.

The marketing audit should ensure that the method chosen to fill the gap is consistent with the company's capabilities and builds on its strengths. For example, it would normally prove far less profitable for a dry goods grocery manufacturer to introduce frozen foods than to add another dry foods product. Likewise, if a product could be sold to existing channels using the existing sales force, this is far less risky than introducing a new product that requires new channels and new selling skills.

Marketing objectives

Corporate objectives are derived from the corporate plan, and inform the direction and focus of the marketing plan. Marketing objectives cover issues such as increasing the awareness of your product or service among your target audience in a particular time frame. They are likely to be linked to market share or sales targets. Long-, medium- and short-term objectives should be identified, some of which should be SMART. Examples of objectives are as follows:

◆ **Profitability objectives** – To achieve a 25 per cent return on capital employed by August 2010

◆ **Market share objectives** – To gain 30 per cent of the market for umbrellas by September 2009

◆ **Promotional objectives** – To increase awareness of the dangers of hepatitis to travellers from 15 per cent to 30 per cent by April 2010

◆ **Objectives for survival** – To survive the current double-dip recession

◆ **Objectives for growth** – To increase the size of our operation from $200,000 in 2006 to $400,000 in 2009

◆ **Objectives for branding** – To make Y brand of bottled beer the preferred brand of 21–28-year-old females in North America by February 2009.

Goals and aims tend to be more vague and focus on the longer term compared with objectives. They will not be SMART.

Deciding on the market

Marketing mix decisions

The strategy will inform the decisions in relation to pricing, product, place, promotion and the extended Ps – people, process and physical evidence. Here, the marketing communications plan will be developed. This enables the organization to meet the needs of its target markets and achieve its marketing objectives. Consideration should be given to each of the areas of the 'four Ps' plus customer considerations in terms of segmentation, targeting and positioning.

Market segmentation

This involves aggregating prospective buyers into groups that have common needs and will respond similarly to the marketing action. The groups that result from the process are called market segments, a relatively homogeneous collection of prospective buyers.

Criteria for market segmentation are:

1   Potential for increased profit and return on investment (ROI)

2   Similarity of needs of potential buyers within a segment

3   Difference in needs of buyers among/across segments

4   Feasibility of marketing action to reach a segment

5   Simplicity and cost of assigning potential buyers to segments.

Positioning

It refers to the place an offering occupies in consumers' minds on important attributes relative to competitive offerings.

Approaches

Head-to-head positioning – involves competing directly with competitors on similar attributes in the same target market.

Differentiation positioning – involves seeking a less competitive, smaller market niche in which to locate a brand. Consumers generally use a small number (2~4) of product attributes when they think about a particular product or product class. In determining a brand's position and the preferences of consumers, companies obtain three types of data from consumers:

◆   Evaluations of the important attributes for a product class

◆   Judgments of the existing brands with the important attributes

◆   Ratings of an 'ideal' brand's attributes.

Criteria for target market

1   **Size:** The estimated size of the market to determine whether it is worth going after.

2   **Expected growth:** The size of the market may be small, but if it is growing significantly it may be worth going after.

3   **Competitive position:** The less competition the more attractive the market.

4   Cost of reaching the market: Is the market accessible to a firm's marketing actions? If not it should not be pursued.

5   Compatibility with the organization's objectives and resources.

All parts of the marketing mix should work together to achieve an organization's objectives. This part of the plan is concerned with who will do what and how it will be done. In this way responsibility, accountability and action over a specific time period can be planned, scheduled, implemented and reviewed. Budget decisions will need to be taken throughout the strategic and operational areas of the plan. Marketing mix decisions describe how you intend achieving your marketing objectives. It is, essentially, the heart of your marketing plan and covers the 4 Ps of marketing.

Product – Describe your product or service in detail. Include features and benefits.

Price – Describe your pricing strategy and payment policies. There are a range of approaches to pricing strategies considering cost, volume and profit.

There are four key factors that affect pricing decisions, also known as the 4 Cs:

1   Cost – Related to the actual costs involved

2   Consumer/customer – Related to the price the consumer will pay

3   Competition – Related to competitors' prices for substitute/complementary products

4   Company – Related to the company's financial objectives.

Promotion – Describe the promotional tools or tactics (a promotion plan) you will use to accomplish your marketing objectives.

To sell an offering it must be effectively promoted and advertised. There are two basic promotion strate gies, Push and Pull.

◆   The **Push** strategy maximizes the use of all available channels of distribution to 'push' the offering into the marketplace. This usually requires generous discounts to achieve the objective of giving the channels incentive to promote the offering, thus minimizing your need for advertising.

◆   The **Pull** strategy requires direct interface with the end user of the offering. Use of channels of distribution is minimized during the first stages of promotion and a major commitment to advertising is required. The objective is to 'pull' the prospects into the various channel outlets creating a demand the channels cannot ignore.

There are many strategies for advertising an offering. Some of these include:

◆   **Product comparison advertising:** In a market where your offering is one of several providing similar capabilities, if your offering stacks up well when comparing features then a product comparison ad can be beneficial.

◆   **Product benefits advertising:** When you want to promote your offering without comparison to competitors, the product benefits ad is the correct approach. This is especially beneficial when you have introduced a new approach to solving a user need and comparison to the old approaches is inappropriate.

◆   **Product family advertising:** If your offering is part of a group or family of offerings that can be of benefit to the customer as a set, then the product family ad can be of benefit.

◆ **Corporate advertising:** When you have a variety of offerings and your audience is fairly broad, it is often beneficial to promote your enterprise identity rather than a specific offering.

Of course, making a decision about pricing, promotion and distribution is heavily influenced by some key factors in the industry and marketplace. These factors should be analysed initially to create the strategy and then regularly monitored for changes. If any of them change substantially the strategy should be re-evaluated.

1   **Place** – Describe how and where you will place your product so that customers have access to it and how you will make the sale – your sales and distribution methods. These could include the following:

   a) **On-premise sales** involves the sale of your offering using a field sales organization that visits the prospect's facilities to make the sale.

   b) **Direct sales** involves the sale of your offering using a direct, in-house sales organization that does all selling through the Internet, telephone or mail order contact.

   c) **Wholesale sales** involves the sale of your offering using intermediaries or 'middlemen' to distribute your product or service to the retailers.

   d) **Self-service retail sales** involves the sale of your offering using self-service retail methods of distribution.

   e) **Full-service retail sales** involves the sale of your offering through a full-service retail distribution channel.

2   **Action plan** – Describe what will be done, when it will begin or be completed and who will accomplish the tasks.

3   **Budget** – List the cost of the activities you are describing in the marketing plan.

4   **Measurements** – Describe the specific numerical targets that will be used to measure the results of implementing your plan. Control involves setting standards and comparing progress against them. Corrective action needs to be taken if it looks like the standards would not be met. Include time limits for achieving goals.

5   **Monitoring and control** – The plan will need to identify the methods of monitoring and evaluating the plan. Decide which controls are important, how they should be implemented and who should be involved.

6   **Control factors** – There are four main areas where control mechanisms should be considered within the marketing plan, that is management control, financial control, efficiency control and strategic control.

   a) **Management control** – This includes areas such as performance appraisal for staff and the workforce, benchmarking procedures and so on against other organizations.

   b) **Financial control** – This includes financial controls which most companies are adept at calculating. It could include trend analysis, comparison, liquidity ratios, debt ratios, activity ratios and so on.

   c) **Efficiency control** – Here, this area considers the optimum value from marketing assets.

   d) **Strategic control** – The easiest method of control is to measure marketing activities against market performance or objectives set.

Case study: Experian

As a credit reference agency (CRA), Experian enables different lenders, such as banks, to share information about their customers' credit accounts. Lenders pay a fee to the CRA each time they search its records.

As organizations develop their businesses, they face a range of choices and opportunities. One way of representing these choices is through Ansoff's matrix:

Product Market	Present	New
Present	Market penetration	Product development
New	Market development	Diversification

Alternative marketing strategies

By relating product opportunities to markets, this mix identifies four broad alternative marketing strategies open to Experian:

a) Market penetration. This involves selling more of existing products to existing markets, increasing the market share. Experian's is the largest credit reference agency in the UK and in this field the company has two main competitors.

b) Product development. This means developing new products for existing markets. Experian is a customer-focused organization. Its customers are businesses. Knowledge of individuals and markets enables Experian to build and develop a wide range of products relevant to its customers.

c) Market development. This strategy takes existing products and finds new markets for them. Experian uses market research to target and develop its markets.

d) Diversification. This involves moving away from core activities and developing new products for new markets. It stands apart from the other strategies and carries the greatest risk. It requires new skills, new techniques and different ways of operating.

In a world where credit is part of modern living, Experian diversified with a new product CreditExpert. This decision recognized that many consumers wanted to be more in control of their credit status, to be able to monitor their credit report at any time and protect themselves against identity fraud.

The market

CreditExpert has enabled Experian to target a new market with a new product. It enables consumers to access their credit report online to check whether the information held about them is accurate and up-to-date and that they have not been targeted by an identity fraudster. CreditExpert sends its members a text or e-mail, or both, every time there is a significant change to the information on that individual's credit report. They can also check that any credit accounts opened belong to them and have not been opened by a fraudster using their name and address.

Market segmentation

The marketing team at Experian wanted to identify the nature, characteristics and type of consumer who would be interested in CreditExpert. Experian used its knowledge of consumers who had applied for their statutory credit reports in the past to help segmentation. It built up a profile of the consumer it wanted to target. This took into account people's ages, where they lived, their gender and socioeconomic grouping.

Experian wanted to attract people with certain characteristics, such as those who were:

◆ Internet users

◆ credit users

◆ keen to manage their financial affairs well.

This profiling helped marketers at Experian to identify which groups they would then target with information about the new CreditExpert service. Having a profile of the most likely customer also helped Experian to develop a promotional campaign that would position the product in the minds of its potential customers.

Marketing mix

Product

The CreditExpert service enables members to check online that their credit report is accurate and up to date. It enables them to see their credit history online as often as they want. The CreditExpert alert service helps them to identify whether somebody has been asking for credit using their name and address, which enables them to spot identity fraud. If there is a problem, consumers get free phone advice from credit reference specialists. Members can also order a credit score based on their Experian credit report, which gives them an idea of how a lender would view the information if they were to apply for credit.

Price

Before making a decision to use CreditExpert, consumers can take up a free 30-day trial. During this time, they have to pay to see a credit score. If they are happy with the service, they can use it to help manage their credit history for a monthly charge.

Place

CreditExpert developed because of the growth in e-commerce communications technology. Its 'place', or channel by which it reaches its users, is the Internet. Experian developed CreditExpert as an e-commerce product to be available online for consumers.

Promotion

Above-the-line promotion includes the traditional forms of advertising such as radio and television. Below-the-line promotion carries a one-off cost. Examples include special offers and exhibitions. Experian has developed a range of different promotional strategies. Until recently, Experian worked mainly in the business-to-business (B2B) market. Its expertise was in personal selling. To succeed in the business-to-consumer (B2C) market Experian had to use a different promotional mix.

CreditExpert used a public relations agency to help advertise the new online credit report with press releases and a television advertising campaign. Experian was the official sponsor, of Credit Awareness Week 2007, which aimed to help consumers understand those credit issues that might confuse them.

In order to help people understand the issues surrounding identity fraud, Experian sponsored a comedian whose identity was stolen and used by a fraudster. He uses a stand-up routine to tell people what being a victim of this fraud feels like and how a monitoring service like CreditExpert can help protect against such a crime.

Source:http://www.experian.co.uk/www/pages/why_experian/client_case_studies/understand_customer_behaviour.html

Other ways of analysing markets

Some organizations group their analysis into the following areas:

Financial analysis

This includes ratio analysis, variance analysis, cash flow monitoring, and capital expenditure monitoring. Financial analysis of competitors is relatively easy to perform because the financial accounts should be readily available. The main problems arise when the competitor is a division of a major corporation and is not a limited company in its own right, and so is not obliged to publish its accounts; or when the company is present in markets where accurate financial reporting is not in evidence.

Market analysis

This covers analysis of total market demand and market share. Market share information may not be as easily obtainable, although most organizations have access to some means of measuring this, such as through marketing database companies, market research periodicals, trade associations and journals.

Sales analysis

This involves analysis of sales targets and selling cost budgets. As with market share, this information may not be easily obtainable. Checking out the effectiveness of a marketing campaign from a product sales standpoint is critical. Begin the review process early, and repeat it often. The plan can be tweaked along the way to eliminate or shift schedules if some element of the mix is not working.

Physical resource analysis

This would involve analysis of plant and equipment utilization together with other measures of productivity and product quality. Operational effectiveness, for example, process technology, people, information systems and so on impact on operational efficiency. This affects costs and business performance, including the speed and efficiency of service, customer perception, quality and reliability of product or service and warranty claims.

Systems analysis

This deals with the effectiveness of strategic implementation and analysis of marketing resource applications.

Companies may benchmark best practice at different levels of the organization in a variety of ways:

◆ In an organization in another industry.

◆ Internally, for example comparing operations in business units in different locations.

◆ With competitors, though they may be unwilling to share the secrets of their success.

The way an organization prioritizes these factors has a bearing on its performance. This leads to the following questions:

◆ Which factors are absent from your organization? Do these need further investigation?

◆ Which factors do competitors pay more attention to, compared to you and why?

◆ Which factors are given low priority by your organization? Do these indicate areas for improvement?

Monitoring progress

Assumptions and contingency plans

Assumptions relate to external factors over which the company has little control and should be as few as possible. For each assumption, a contingency plan should be formulated. They should consist of a sentence or two that give a general indication of what would happen if assumptions prove to be incorrect.

Budget resources and staffing

Budgeting covers general marketing expenditure and salaries and expenses for staffing. If the plan is based on increasing sales and market share this will normally have resource implications for the marketing department, perhaps in terms of more representation or increased advertising costs. Financial considerations might well cause the organization to tone down its original marketing objectives.

Timescales

Most plans are for a period of one year but a plan must also contain timescales which detail marketing activities normally on a month by month, or a quarter by quarter, basis. However longer-term issues can also be addressed in the marketing plan. This will mean different things in different business sectors. In the case of technology long term may not be longer than three years, whereas in car production long term may mean ten years or more. When long-term planning is addressed as part of a marketing plan it is usually a directional marketing plan which does not contain a lot of detail. Some companies have rolling plans that are modified in the light of experience. As one planning period finishes (one month, one quarter, one year) the rolling plan will be modified in the light of what has happened and a further planning period will be added on to the end of the plan.

Implement the plan

The plan is now put into action. Those who are involved in implementation need to know what part they must play in its implementation to ensure its success.

Measure and control

The marketing information system provides information from market intelligence, marketing research and the organization's own internal accounting system. It can also be a control mechanism because customer reactions are also fed into this MkIS from market intelligence through the field sales force or from marketing research studies. Information on sales analyses is also fed into the system so assessments can be made as to whether forecasted sales are being achieved or not. The plan should be reviewed on a regular and controlled basis and then updated as circumstances change. Such controls can address the tactics in terms of sales analyses that will commence with a comparison of budgeted sales revenue against actual sales revenue. Variations might be due to volume or price variances.

Tools for monitoring and control

Control involves setting standards, measurement, evaluation, and monitoring. Resources are scarce and costly so it is important to control marketing plans. A marketing manager will compare actual progress against the standards. Corrective action (if any) is then taken and, an investigation undertaken to establish why the difference or variance occurred.

There are many tools to help with control and monitoring:

◆ Market share analysis

◆ Sales analysis

◆ Budgets

◆ Marketing information systems (MkIS) and customer relationship management (CRM) systems (see Unit 6).

◆ Feedback from customer satisfaction surveys

◆ Cash-flow statements

◆ Performance of any promotional activities.

Tracking procedures

This section of the plan should include plans and procedures for tracking each type of media you are using and which seems to be the most effective.

◆ **Display advertising** – With traditional consumer publications, tracking can be done through the use of different phone numbers, special offers (specific to an advertisement or publication), or reference to a specific department to call for information.

◆ **Reader service cards** – Many trade publications also include cards that allow the reader to circle a number that corresponds to your ad on a mail-in postcard in order to get more information about your product or service.

◆ **Direct marketing** – With postal mailings, tracking is relatively simple. Include on the mailing label a code (called a key code or a source code) that corresponds with the mailing list. For telemarketing campaigns, tracking is also relatively simple since someone is communicating with the customer throughout the entire process in most cases.

◆ **Internet marketing** – Usually this is easily tracked because it is based on click-throughs, or page impressions.

◆ **Promotions** – Most closed promotions are basically 'self-tracking' because they require the customer to do something such as fill out an entry form (trackable), turn in a coupon, return a rebate slip (trackable), or log on to a website to claim a prize (also trackable).

Supporting documentation

Include any supporting documents referenced in other plan sections here, such as CVs or key management resumés, spreadsheets, market research results and so on.

Summary

This unit has provided examples of marketing plans and demonstrated that there is no uniform pattern. However, it has also demonstrated that there are key issues that a marketing plan needs to address even if the formats are sometimes different.

Hints and tips

◆ In an exam context you may not have time to go into great detail, so an outline marketing plan with some elements described in detail might be the most appropriate strategy.

◆ Remember that any tools that are used need to be applied to the context. There are no marks just for knowing about different models. Application of knowledge is the key activity.

Sample questions

June 2005, Question 1

Part A – Compulsory

a. Outline a marketing plan to introduce the '@ Medi Wrap' product in 'New Territory'.

December 2004, Question 1

a. Outline a marketing plan to develop a profitable regional business for the art gallery opportunity (incorporated in your role). This should include partnership arrangements with local organizations such as art galleries, museums and theatres for the art images.

Bibliography

Beamish and Ashford (2008), *Marketing Planning*, Harlow: Elsevier Butterworth-Heinemann.

Birch, A., Gerbert, P. and Schneider, D. (2000) *The Age of E-tail*, Milford, CT: Capstone, 4th European edition)

Carlzon, J. (1987) *Moments of Truth*, New York: Harper and Row,

Christopher, M., Payne, A. and Ballantyne, D. (2002) *Relationship Marketing: Creating Stakeholder Value*, Oxford: Butterworth-Heinemann

Dibb,S., Simkin, L., Pride, W. M. and Ferrell, O. C. (2006) *Marketing: Concepts and Strategies*, Boston, Houghton Mifflin, (5th edition)

Hamel, G and Prahalad, C. K (1994) *Competing for the Future*, Boston, Harvard Business Press

Kotler, P. (2005) *Marketing Management*, New York: Prentice Hall, 12th edition

Ohmae, K. (1991) *The Mind of the Strategist: The Art of Japanese Business*, McGraw-Hill

Peck, H., Payne, A., Christopher, M. and Clark, M. (1999) *Relationship Marketing: Strategy and Implementation*, Oxford: Butterworth-Heinemann

Mintzberg, H. (2000) *The Rise and Fall of Strategic Planning*. London: FT Prentice Hall.

Porter, M E (1980) Competitive Strategy: Techniques for Analyzing Industries and Competitors, New York, The Free Press

Treacy, M. and Wiersema, F. (1997) *The Discipline of Market Leaders*, Perseus Books Group

Porter, M E (1980) *Competitive Strategy: Techniques for Analyzing Industries and Competitors*, New York, The Free Press

Prahalad C. K. and Hamel, G (1990) The core competence of the corporation, *Harvard Business Review*, May-June

Unit 8 Marketing communications and customer service

5.1 Plan the design, development, execution and evaluation of communications campaigns by a team of marketers, including external agencies and suppliers.

5.2 Use appropriate marketing communications to develop relationships or to communicate with a range of stakeholders.

5.3 Manage and monitor the provision of effective customer service.

5.4 Use marketing communications to provide support for members of a marketing channel.

5.5 Use marketing communications techniques for an internal marketing plan to support management of change within an organization.

5.6 Review and evaluate the effectiveness of communications activities and the role of the individual and the team in this process.

Key definitions

Communications mix – The way in which a company allocates its marketing budget between the various communications media. It would include deciding on how much of the budget to allocate to the print, radio, visual and other forms of communications media. Understanding the communication process, as described by Kotler (2005), helps with understanding what motivates an audience and in determining what is the most effective medium or media.

Customer service – The set of behaviours that a business undertakes during its interaction with its customers. It can also refer to a specific person or desk which is set up to provide general assistance to customers.

> **Direct marketing** – The sales technique in which the promotional materials are delivered individually to potential customers via direct mail, telemarketing, door-to-door selling or other direct means.
>
> **E-marketing** – Increasingly, organizations are adopting 'e' methods – electronic media – within their integrated marketing communications mix. Examples are websites, e-mail, intranets, extranets, mobiles, telephone and fax. Websites are a key form of corporate communication. They can be used to advertise the company, provide customer service and technical support, sales transactions and gathering customer data. E-mail is a major tool used to communicate with customers. An intranet is an electronic system of internal communication throughout an organization. An extranet is used to communicate with selected people outside the organization, e.g. distributors, suppliers and so on. They allow for fast, accurate, cost-effective exchange of information. Fax, telephones and mobile phones are also major forms of communication.

Introduction

Marketing communications strategy is concerned with how an organization can successfully communicate and deliver its marketing strategy. The Marketing Communications units of the CIM syllabus are intended to provide the skills and knowledge that enable marketers to manage marketing communications and brand support activities within organizations. The Marketing Management in Practice module builds on the underpinning knowledge developed in the Marketing Communications module. The *Market Planning* coursebook, Beamish and Ashford (2008), also considers the importance of managing marketing relationships effectively, to maximize customer retention opportunities. The book makes the point that the key to success within any marketing environment will be the realization that managing marketing relationships is crucial to long-term customer loyalty and customer retention, as is the necessity to manage each market differently in order to optimize customer relationships and the associated benefits. The coursebook focuses on the importance of customer relationships to the organization and how they can be developed and supported by the marketing mix. It examines the following themes:

◆ Relationship marketing

◆ From transactional to relationship marketing

◆ The scope of marketing relationships

◆ Planning for relationship management

◆ Customer retention management

◆ The marketing mix for customer retention management.

The communications mix

Sometimes referred to as the promotional mix, the communications mix lists all of the communications tools available to a marketer:

◆ Selling

◆ Advertising

◆ Sales promotion

- ◆ Direct marketing
- ◆ Publicity (and public relations)
- ◆ Sponsorship
- ◆ Exhibitions
- ◆ Packaging
- ◆ Point of sale and merchandising
- ◆ Word of mouth
- ◆ E-marketing
- ◆ Corporate identity.

Different types of enterprise put different emphases on certain communication tools. An FMCG manufacturer is likely to put greater emphasis on advertising, packaging, sales promotion and point of sale while an industrial machine manufacturer may consider selling, exhibitions and word of mouth to be the most important.

Formats for a marketing communications plan

There are a range of formats that can be used for developing a marketing communications plan. The following is an example from a university:

Insight

Deciding where, when and how to get the right message to the right audience at the right time is the essence of a marketing communications plan. The plan is a tool to promote an event, unit or activity and is based on the following fundamentals:

- ◆ Targeted audience
- ◆ Perceived university image
- ◆ Overall marketing strategy
- ◆ Results/expected outcome
- ◆ Resources available and capabilities
- ◆ Timing of these activities
- ◆ Measuring results.

Checklist to complete a marketing communications plan

1. Do your homework – Before you contact your account executive to begin planning, assemble the relevant background information for review. Think through your key messages and audiences, timeline, budget, challenges, resources, measurable goals, sources to contact and what you want accomplished.

2. Plan – Meet with your account executive and other appropriate personnel to think through communication strategies linked to the university's marketing goals, past efforts and external factors.

3. Assign responsibilities – Determine who will communicate all vital information, facilitate meetings among key staff, faculty and students and ensure timely approvals and reviews through plan completion.

4 Write – Determine who will gather information, read reports, interview key sources, review what has been done and how the project relates to the university marketing goals.

5 Approve plan – Identify who will edit, update and approve the plan at various administrative levels.

6 Assign responsibilities – Determine who will carry out the plan's tactics on time, on budget and within university identity and style compliance and ensure payment of services.

7 Distribute – Send plan to all appropriate personnel.

8 Evaluate – Track, monitor and evaluate plan's effectiveness and distribute evaluation. Ensure goals are successfully met.

Source: http://www.map.wayne.edu/checklists/marketing.pdf.

Designing a communications campaign

A communications campaign is the dissemination of messages using appropriate channels, to a well-defined audience in order to educate and create an informed public. Designing and implementing a communications campaign could be carried out entirely in-house, or it could be devolved to an agency, or the campaign could involve a combination of internal and external input. Obviously the size of the campaign and that of the budget, as well as its aims and objectives, will be important factors in determining which approach to use. The key barrier to integrating the communications mix is people, and the way they work. The best way to overcome this barrier is to motivate the key players to work as a team. An effective team is one that includes client and agency, across the entire communications mix.

Full-service agency

When using an external agency the most straightforward approach is to use the services of a full-service agency that is able to assemble a team including representatives from all the agency services that the client needs. Full-service agencies can provide a comprehensive range of services such as creative and strategic planning, production, media planning and buying and market research. The advantage of using a full-service agency is the range of skills that can be drawn upon when needed, and the fact that all the elements of the promotional mix and marketing communications operation can be brought together making the whole process easier to manage and control. However, this strength is also a potential weakness because if the relationship breaks down, it will be difficult to find another agency to take on the work at short notice and still keep to the envisaged timescale.

Limited service agency

An alternative to the full-service agency is a limited service agency that specializes in particular elements of the marketing communications process. The advantage in using a limited service agency is that a client can use different agencies for the different skills that best suit their needs. This gives choice and flexibility but it can take a lot of time to manage the different relationships involved. Selecting an agency should be based on explicit criteria based on the aims and objectives of the communications. Key issues are whether the agency fully understands the requirements of a brief, and whether it will be able to work with the client as a team. In some cases, companies are establishing online communication services which may make it more difficult to tell whether or not the chemistry is right between the client and the agency.

Developing an agency brief

Elements that could be contained in an agency brief are as follows:

◆   **Current situation** – This will cover the history of the brand, previous campaign successes (or failures) and the reasons for mounting the new campaign.

◆   **Promotional objectives** – Having set marketing objectives, the promotional objectives need to be identified. These will vary but could include, for example, encouraging product trial or direct sales or increasing distribution outlets.

◆   **Target markets** – This should include socioeconomic details (e.g. age, class, sex) and also psychographic information on users. This will have a bearing on the focus and content of the promotional activity.

◆   **Product/service** – In providing the agency with a detailed brief, this section should include any available research that has been used to establish the perceived benefits so that these can be promoted strongly.

◆   **Budget** – The budget should include funds for the cost of the media and the production of promotional material.

◆   **Competitors** – Find out about these and include the results of your findings in the brief.

◆   **Timescales** – Media scheduling will play an important role at this stage.

The creative team will be responsible for the artwork, ensuring that visualization and copywriting match the needs of the organization, and they will be directed by the accounts manager within the agency who will also brief the media and planning functions.

When agencies are used, the process of briefing will be followed by the 'agency pitch'. An agency will carry out research into the marketing and communications situation, and then present creative and media plans to the client.

What type of campaign is it?

There are different types of marketing communications campaign. An educational campaign targets a specific audience with information that benefits the consumer, for example health-related matters, or how to obtain benefits. A marketing campaign promotes, for example, a new service or product, or repositions an old service or product, and focuses on price, promotion and product. A public relations campaign would focus on image and name recognition. The following is an example of an integrated campaign that was the result of extensive research carried out over a year involving marketers and professionals working in the anti-drug field.

Insight: The US national youth anti-drug media campaign

The campaign's five-year initiative to reduce and deglamorize youth drug use targets middle-school-age adolescents (approximately 11–13 years old), parents and other influential adults. The integrated communications campaign delivers anti-drug messages to kids and parents where they live, work and play through advertising, the Internet, movies, music and television, public education efforts and community partnerships. The campaign will spend about $180 million per year in advertising – and receive a pro bono match of equal value from the entertainment industry, media, corporations and other advertisers – to expose young people to innovative anti-drug messages that reinforce the ads. For more than a year, TV ads have run nationwide during prime time. Nearly a year of research went into designing the campaign. Hundreds of specialists were consulted, including experts in behaviour change, drug prevention, teen marketing and advertising communications, as well as representatives from professional, civic and community organizations. The campaign will be constantly monitored, evaluated and updated to ensure that it effectively reaches teens and their parents.

http://www.mediacampaign.org/newsroom/factsheets/overview.html

Who is the target audience?

Communication should be tailored to meet the needs and interests of a given audience. Does the audience comprise potential buyers, current users, deciders or influencers, individuals, groups, or the general public? Are the members of the target audience consumers, businesses, non-profit organizations or government agencies? The target audience is a critical influence on decisions about what to say to whom, when and how.

What are the aims and objectives of the campaign?

Try to devise both quantitative (measurable) and qualitative objectives. A quantitative objective would be, for example, to increase the number of users by 20 per cent per year. A qualitative objective would be to improve public understanding of the benefits of recycling by the autumn, measured by pre- and post-survey responses. The campaign may be trying to elicit a cognitive (attention), affective (feeling) or behavioural (doing) response.

Designing the message

This is concerned with what to say, how to say it and who should say it. The aim is to find a theme, idea, appeal or unique selling proposition. The message can try to appeal on moral, rational or emotional grounds. Rational grounds emphasize the benefits of a product or service such as quality, value or performance. Emotional appeals try to stir up negative or positive emotions to motivate purchase. Moral messages appeal to the audience's sense of propriety and the right way to behave. The structure of a message is important, that is whether it is a one-sided or two-sided presentation mentioning benefits and shortcomings, and the order in which arguments are presented. The credibility of the message source depends on expertise, trustworthiness and likeability.

Select the channels

This involves choosing between a range of personal communication channels, for example face to face or through telephone or e-mail, and non-personal communication channels.

Activity 8.1

Think of a marketing campaign that you have been involved in or which is memorable to you.

◆ What type of campaign was it?

◆ Who do you perceive was the target audience?

◆ What was the key message?

◆ What channels were used?

◆ What made it stand out for you?

Internet marketing

Companies that have achieved the greatest success with Internet marketing have leveraged the strength of multiple marketing and sales channels. This includes the use of more traditional marketing and sales channels: brand advertising in broadcast media, demand generation and promotional communications in print media, direct mail and e-mail channels, and sales and service support from field sales, telesales and business partners.

Insight

What is the single biggest prerequisite for successful Internet marketing? – customer-centric thinking and delivery. Marketers still talk about 'campaigns' whereas customers want to take control of the relationship. And the second biggest lesson for successful online marketing? It's a multi-channel process, not just a collection of separate web pages. Customers experience you as a journey that is a sequence of interactions across any number of channels towards their end goal.

The really successful marketers really understand that journey and how the channels, including the Internet, best work together. The real challenge here is getting your organization galvanized and incentivized to work together, as opposed to by channel or departmental silo, to help the customer towards his or her end destination, wherever that may be within your company.

Companies that have achieved the greatest successes also have defined and deployed Internet marketing strategies from a cross-functional perspective and leveraged the strength of multiple marketing and sales channels. Customer-facing marketing, sales and service activities have not simply been automated or moved to the Internet. Instead, they first have been freshly redesigned to provide greater value, reliability, responsiveness and service quality to customers – and second to provide improved transaction economics to the company. Such a redesign, of course, suggests that the company has already gained a thorough understanding of customers' buying behaviours and their channel preferences.

The Internet has been an integrated element of the marketing mix, not an isolated or stand-alone marketing activity. Years of management research and practical experience have demonstrated that changing customers' buying behaviours and motivating them to accept and adopt innovations, like Internet marketing, can be difficult and costly. The most successful 'Internet marketing' companies have recognized that integrating new e-channel capabilities with traditional marketing and sales channels can accelerate the innovation process for customers and themselves.

Source: www.insightexec.com

Until recently, consumers often learned about a product and made their choice at the same time. People would often visit a department store or dealership to seek advice from a salesman, look at his recommendations and then buy. Now, for many, each of these steps is separate. Reaching these better-informed consumers with a marketing message is not easy. Some Internet search firms are offering more localized services on PCs and mobile phones. So local consumers will be able to find a local store and then check the offers from nearby outlets even as they browse the aisles, or listen to a salesman. Consumers are in a more powerful position to take control of the way they find out about products. There is more spending on 'below-the-line' advertising, or marketing services.

Case study: Procter and Gamble

For P&G, brands are the chief medium through which it communicates with customers. Traditionally, that communication has gone in a single direction, with P&G spending billions of dollars a year to tell consumers through bold, persistent advertising.

The PG.com team successfully pushed to include two features on the site that would have been almost unthinkable in the old world of P&G. In Try & Buy, which has become the site's most visited section, consumers can purchase new products before they show up in the supermarket or drugstore. In Help Us Create, P&G conducts virtual test markets where consumers can tell the company which kinds of new products it should make, or how it might improve existing products.

P&G has stepped up its experimentation because it has discovered an ideal laboratory for doing so: the Internet. Using test markets – auditioning a product in selected locations in order to find out what sells and what doesn't – is old-time religion at P&G. Before rolling out a new product nationally, the company typically spends several months and millions of dollars to conduct field tests in a handful of midsize, middle-American cities. But the Internet has fostered new, more efficient ways to sound out customer attitudes toward product innovation. By doing a test online P&G can do it for a tenth of the cost in a quarter of the time.

Source: http://www.icmrindia.org/casestudies/catalogue/Marketing/MKTG075.htm

Media planning

Media planning needs to be co-ordinated with marketing strategy and with other aspects of an advertising strategy. The strategic aspects of media planning involve four steps:

1   Selecting the target audience towards which all subsequent efforts will be directed.

2 Specifying media objectives, e.g. in terms of reach (What proportion of the target audience must see, read, or hear our advertising message during a specified period?); frequency (How often should they be exposed to it during this period?), gross rating points (GRPs) or effective rating points (ERPs) (How much total advertising is necessary during a particular period to accomplish the reach and frequency objectives?)

3 Selecting general media categories and specific vehicles within each medium.

4 Buying media.

The concept of media neutral planning has been developed to counteract the perceived power of creative teams that may be regarded as considering only themself and their peers when developing new ideas. This has led to media choice, being biased towards those options deemed to show off creative talent to best effect, rather than necessarily being the best at meeting the needs of the consumer.

Media neutral planning – buzz word or a new world order?

Looking back for a moment we can see that each decade through the second half of the twentieth century brought our predecessors face to face with their own key issues. Starting in the 1950s with the development of the creative team as we now know it, which then contributed in the 1960s to the move away from linear models of communication to a more humanistic approach, through the advent of account planning in the 1970s, to the break up of the full-service agency in the 1980s which, in turn, led directly to the issue of integration in the 1990s. So here we are in a new century facing our own particular issue – media neutral planning. But what is it? What, if anything does it owe to these preceding trends? And is it just a passing fad or is it here to stay? To set my stall out from the beginning, I should say that, in my view, media neutral planning is probably the biggest issue of all, being a culmination of all those issues that came before. To put it in its own context, I believe that media neutral planning is far greater than merely a creative or 'advertising' issue. It is fundamental to the way in which a brand does and should touch consumers' lives. It is the planning of those brand touchpoints without bias toward or against any particular mediums or channels, from conventional above the line media, through traditional below the line options to new media, ambient media, PR, sponsorship, events, design, point of sale, collateral material and so on. Currently, planning tends to be heavily media-centric dependent on where the planner sits, who pays his/her wages and what his/her particular prejudices are. Media-neutral planning, on the other hand, seeks to put the consumer firmly at the centre of the planning process, viewing media from his/her perspective as defined by the particular brand relationship in question.

Source: Tina Kaye, www.marketing-society.org.uk

Determining the marketing communications budget

A key task within the framework of marketing communications is the appropriate determination of the levels of expenditure required to fulfil the task established. The amount of money spent on marketing communications differs widely among companies, even within the same industry. There are various methods to choose from, each with a slightly different focus and with different advantages and disadvantages.

♦ **Percentage of sales** – A widely used method of budget determination is based on the calculation of a ratio between past expenditure and sales. The model creates a situation in which the budget only increases against an expectation of higher sales and fails to acknowledge that marketing can create sales for a brand.

♦ **Percentage of product gross margin** – A percentage of either the past or expected gross margin – net sales less the cost of goods – is used.

♦ **Percentage of anticipated turnover** – This approach is based on the allocation of a fixed percentage of future turnover to the marketing communications budget.

♦ **Unit or case/sales ratio method** – This method is based on estimating sales volumes, and a fixed sum per unit is allocated towards marketing communications expenditure. Multiplying the expected sales volume by the fixed allocation gives producers the size of the budget. The expenditure patterns reflect past achievement and tends to benefit growth brands and disadvantage those that are declining.

♦ **Competitive expenditure** – Another frequently used approach is to base a brand's expenditure levels on an assessment of competitors' expenditures. However, the difficulty is how to make an accurate assessment of the level of competitors' spend. While it is possible to obtain a reasonable fix on advertising spend from published information, the same is not true of sales promotional spend and other categories of marketing communications.

♦ **Share of voice** – This approach is based on the relationship between the volume share of the product category and the expenditure within the category as a whole. It is primarily related to advertising expenditure.

♦ **Media inflation** – This makes the assumption that the previous year's budget should be increased in line with the growth in media costs.

♦ **Objective and task method** – This method is based on the specific objectives that the marketing plan needs to achieve. The objective and task method requires that specific objectives for the campaign are defined, for example increasing brand awareness, encouraging sampling and trial, promoting repeat purchase and so on. A numerical target is given and the costs of achieving this target are calculated. The budget is based on present goals rather than past or future results.

♦ **What can be afforded** – This is based on a management assessment of, for example, the return on investment, and the marketing communications budget is the amount that remains after calculating that level and other claims on the budget.

Planning a social marketing campaign

When planning programmes or awareness campaigns, it is important to target programmes and messages to reach and meet the needs of the intended audience. In health communications, these concepts take on the following meanings:

♦ **Product** – is the knowledge, attitudes or behaviour you want the audience to adopt.

♦ **Price** – can be interpreted as what the target audience must give up in order to receive the programme's benefits.

◆ **Promotion** – is the means for persuading the target audience that the product is worth the price.

◆ **Place** – refers to how the message is disseminated, such as through electronic or print media, or community programmes.

Case study: Vodafone – cause marketing

To identify an appropriate cause Vodafone carried out research with a number of groups:

◆ Customers

◆ Employees

◆ Public

◆ Opinion formers (e.g. the press)

◆ Cause marketing experts.

A variety of research techniques were used, including:

◆ In-depth interviews with customers

◆ Discussions with 60 charities

◆ Identifying the best examples of cause marketing programmes

◆ Testing various propositions to gain feedback from stakeholders

The results of the research showed that partnering with an organisation dealing with communication disabilities was a clear favourite. Three charities were identified as having the closest fit. They were then assessed against 15 criteria, including:

◆ Impact on society

◆ Clear fit with the Vodafone brand

◆ Impact could be measured

◆ Employees and customers felt that it would be an appropriate partnership

◆ Fit with communication theme.

The National Autistic Society was eventually chosen because it provided the best fit. Communication is central to Vodafone's business and people with autism find communicating with others very difficult.

Source: www.indiainfoline.com/content/bschool/Site_Manager/2006/07/19072006 /cause_marketing.pdf

Stage 1 – Planning and selecting the strategy

This stage provides the foundation for the entire social marketing process. An assessment of the problem, the target audience and the available resources is conducted before moving ahead. During this planning process, the target audience should be increasingly segmented. This segmentation will aid in the development of appropriate messages. Goals and objectives for the programme will be developed at this time.

Stage 2 – Selecting channels and materials

Channels are how the message will be delivered, whether it is face to face, group, mass media, or a combination of channels. The more the channels selected, the more the target audience will be exposed to the message. Determining the channel prior to producing materials is important because different materials work better in different channels.

Material selection involves using what you have learned about your target audience to your advantage. Time and money can be saved by selecting materials that are specific to the audience you are trying to reach.

Stage 3 – Developing the materials and pre-testing

Draft the materials, pre-test them with the target audience and, if necessary, revise them. Determine if materials get the intended results, or revise them accordingly. Pre-testing adds time to the project but it can help to avoid producing materials that the target audience do not read.

Stage 4 – Implementing the programme

A method for tracking and evaluating the programme should be in place before it starts. The tracking method should help to identify those areas where changes may be needed.

Stage 5 – Assessing effectiveness

The type of evaluation conducted at this stage will depend upon several factors, including money, time, policies regarding the ability to gather information, the level of support for evaluation and the overall design of the programme.

Types of eval uation

- ♦ **Formative evaluation** – includes pre-testing of materials, and is designed to test the strengths and weaknesses of a programme before it is ready for implementation.
- ♦ **Process evaluation** – reviews the tasks of implementing the programme.
- ♦ **Outcome evaluation** – is used to gather descriptive information. It gathers information about knowledge and attitude changes, expressed intentions of the target audience and the initiation of policy changes.
- ♦ **Impact evaluation** – is the most comprehensive of the four types. It focuses on the long-term outcomes of the programme and long-term behaviour change.

Stage 6 – Refining through feedback

If the programme is to be continued, revisions of the programme should be undertaken. If this is the end of the programme, documentation of what was learned should be made so as to assist others who may undertake a similar project in the future. An evaluation report should be prepared that could be used to secure funding to continue the programme and assist others conducting similar activities.

Integrated marketing communications

Creating an integrated marketing communications (IMC) plan is important for achieving maximum effectiveness. The elements of the communications mix need to be used in a co-ordinated way so as to achieve the objectives of a promotion. Usually, a combination of marketing communications tools are used to meet specific campaign objectives. For example, advertising campaigns are often supported with sales promotions activities, or public relations or both. The role of marketing communications is to:

◆   Differentiate a product/brand (to make it different to a competitor's brand or seem different through effective positioning).

◆   Remind and reassure a target audience with regard to benefits (to encourage (re) purchase).

◆   Inform a target audience by providing new information (e.g. of a new brand or flavour).

◆   Persuade an audience to take a particular action (e.g. visit a theatre, stop smoking).

This example shows how companies see the advantages of an integrated approach.

Case study: Integrated marketing communications

Washington State University (WSU) uses integrated marketing as a disciplined approach to communicating about the university to both internal and external audiences for the purpose of advancing its goals and strategic vision. In sum, itsintegrated marketing programme is the communication process for achieving WSU's strategic plan.

The integrated marketing programme is focused on four goals:

◆   Increasing the enrolment of high-performing students

◆   Building awareness and support among influencers

◆   Increasing the enrolment of top graduate students

◆   Improving organizational communications.

Now in its fourth year, the programme began with an in-depth analysis of the university's programme strengths, target markets, and communication practices, together with the identification of marketing goals critical to its success. A focused campaign to increase the number of high-performing students choosing to enrol at Washington State University led the first two years of this effort. Now ongoing and well established, that campaign continues as the core focus of the programme. It has also laid the groundwork for the integrated marketing programme to shift to the second phase of work.

In the second phase of the programme, WSU has expanded its work toward building its reputation with leaders statewide and increasing the enrolment of top graduate students. Using the successful model of the student recruitment campaign, WSU's strategy for influencing leaders focuses on two issues simultaneously:

◆   Building WSU's reputation with identified, influential audiences

◆   Building relationships with those audiences to actively engage them with the university in advancing WSU's strategic priorities.

Major executions aimed at immersing these audiences in the progress of WSU include leadership tours, WSU Connections in Seattle, world-class face-to-face showcase, and work supporting the university's state and federal agenda. That work is supported by continued awareness-building through broad markets that influence these individuals, such as *Washington State Magazine*, major news media exposure, and leveraging the image advertising that supports the student recruitment campaign.

Source: http://marketing.wsu.edu/

Types of marketing communications

There are many different terms to describe the various methods used by organizations to communicate with customers and other stakeholder groups. They include personal selling and non-personal selling (advertising, sales promotion, public relations and direct marketing). Sales promotion is a short-term incentive to encourage the purchase or sale of a product. Public relations aims to build and sustain good relations with the organization's stakeholders and the public through favourable publicity, building up a good 'corporate image', and handling or heading off unfavourable rumours, stories and events. Direct marketing is direct communications with carefully targeted individual consumers to obtain an immediate response through the use of non-personal tools (mail, telephone, fax and e-mail).

With push strategies, marketers use personal selling to promote their product to retailers and wholesalers, not the end-user. They include special incentives such as discounts, promotional materials and cooperative advertising. Advertising and sales promotions are part of pull strategies, which build consumer awareness so that the consumer will ask retailers to carry the product. The strategies are not exclusive and, in fact, most companies use both to increase their promotional effectiveness. By selecting a combination of promotional mix elements, marketers attempt to achieve the organization's promotional objectives: to provide information, differentiate a product, increase demand and add to a product's value.

Personal selling

Personal selling is often the most expensive element of the marketing communications mix because it is resource-intensive, and involves high contact and customer maintenance costs. In some instances, personal sales have been replaced by direct mail, telemarketing and e-mail. Personal selling includes activities such as:

◆ **Prospecting** – Gathering information to gain sales leads and prospective clients.

◆ **Communicating** – Being the provider of information about the organization, its products, services and after-sales care.

◆ **Selling** – Persuading a potential customer to adopt the product.

◆ **Market research/information gathering** – Environmental scanning, competitor intelligence, customer intelligence.

◆ **Servicing of accounts** – Maintaining and providing ongoing customer service, including technical support, financial contractual arrangements and logistical arrangements.

◆ **Allocating** – Ensuring that the allocation of products to customers is undertaken at all times, in particular in times of production shortages.

◆ **Customer relationship building** – Building and sustaining long-term customer relationships.

Evaluation of personal sales

Evaluating and measuring sales performance is based upon the sales objectives set for the organization. But the objectives set will be SMART, and therefore clearly defined and clearly linked with marketing objectives and overall corporate performance goals.

It is likely that sales performance will be measured against objectives on a regular basis, anything from weekly to quarterly. However, in most organizations sales performance against actual planned achievement is measured on a monthly basis.

It is also likely that other factors relating to sales performance will be measured, such as:

◆ **Productivity** – calls per day, calls per account, total number of orders versus calls.

◆ **Account development** – total of new accounts, total of existing accounts, growth of sales from existing accounts.

◆ **Expenses** – expenses versus number of calls made, cost per call.

With the evolution of IT, sales measurement techniques are becoming more sophisticated and more effective, and the speed at which information becomes available is of the essence. A drastic reduction in sales performance can mean that other elements of the promotional mix might be subject to increased activity to compensate for the drop in sales. However, the drop in income often inhibits too much marketing expenditure of a contingency nature to be undertaken.

Insight: Britain provides a glimpse of the future of advertising

Why Britain? For a start, the British online-advertising market is 'exploding'. The Internet accounts for 14 per cent of companies' total spending on advertising in Britain, compared with about 5 per cent worldwide. Britain is now the leading market for online advertising. Eventually, says Sir Martin Sorrell, chief executive of WPP, the Internet will grow to account for 20 per cent of worldwide advertising spending, at the expense of traditional media (broadcast and cable TV, print, radio and outdoor advertising). A catalyst of the growth of online advertising is Britons' enthusiasm for online shopping. In Britain 47 per cent of households have broadband, compared with 44 per cent in America and 33 per cent in Germany. The attraction of online ads is obvious. Britons spend an average of 23 hours a week online, compared with 14 hours per week for Americans. Advertisers also like the efficiency of the medium: much of the advertising on the net is 'pay-per-click', which means that advertisers pay only when consumers click on an ad, so they can be relatively confident that their advertisements are reaching a receptive audience. In 2007, a new mobile-phone service for young people, called Blyk, was launched in Britain before being rolled out across Europe. Users can earn airtime in exchange for receiving advertisements on their handsets.

Adapted from: *The Economist*, 13 December 2006

Advertising

Advertising is one of the most influential forms of communication in the promotional mix and is particularly effective at reaching large audiences with specific messages. Depending on the media, costs of reaching individuals can be low compared to other forms of communications. It can be used at different stages of purchasing, or for awareness creation at the early stages of a product launch. Its main purpose is to inform, persuade and remind customers to purchase products and services. Advertising objectives are expressed in terms of promoting products, organizations and services, or stimulating demand, increasing sales, brand and product awareness, and reminding and reinforcing perceptions of a product or service.

Measuring advertising effectiveness is important for understanding how well ads are performing and what changes need to be made to improve performance. Promotion research consists of media and message research. Media research measures audience composition and size for media vehicles as a basis for determining ratings. Audience measurement services include magazine, local radio, national radio and television. Multiple measurement methods are usually preferable to single techniques to assess advertising effectiveness. There has been a trend towards greater use of sales promotion in comparison with advertising. This shift is part of the movement from pull- to push-oriented marketing, particularly in the case of consumer packaged goods. The factors that underpin this shift include increased brand parity, growing price sensitivity, reduced brand loyalty, the fragmentation of the mass market, reduced media effectiveness, growing short-term orientation, and favourable consumer responsiveness to sales promotions.

Sales promotions

Sales promotions often complement advertising, and may be planned and executed in parallel with associated advertising and possible public relations campaigns. They are used to encourage customers to trial products and services, and then to purchase them. The main aims and associated objectives of sales promotions are, for example, to increase brand and product awareness, attract new customers, increase trial and adoption of new and existing products, increase brand usage and to encourage trading up to the next size or the next range. Sales promotions can be a highly targeted and flexible form of communications and evaluation of their effectiveness is usually an integral part of the communication through, for instance, coupon redemption, money-off vouchers/coupons, buy one get one free, discounts, trial-sized products and so on.

Insight: Promotion

Promotion is divided into two areas: above-the-line and below-the-line. Above-the-line promotion is that which is paid for directly. It includes spending on TV, radio, poster and press advertising and on other paid-for media such as the Internet. Below-the-line promotion refers to those methods of promoting a product that do not use direct advertising. These include public relations, such as getting stars to endorse products, or news and magazine stories featuring the product. They also involve packaging and point-of-sale material. Companies may also separate below-the-line spending between consumers and the trade. For example, Kelloggs offered the trade, a 'buy three for the price of two' for a Star Wars™ event. For consumers, there was a free insert in the box and the chance to win some prizes.

Public relations

Some commonly used measures of results are as follows:

◆ **Budget** – Has the planned activity been achieved within budget and timescale?

◆ **Awareness** – Established through using market research activities.

◆ **Attitude** – Positivity or negativity; whether there is any change in consumer behaviour.

◆ **Media coverage and tone** – Coverage in a range of media – number of column inches, key headings and the tone.

◆ **Positioning** – Comparative information about the relative position of the organization and the competition.

◆ **Response generation** – Enquiries or leads linked to reference codes or enquiry sources, for example a particular newspaper.

◆ **Share price** – Highly publicized scandals such as WorldCom show that share prices can be manipulated, especially when exceeding a particular level is a management target, and achieving it earns large bonuses. During the so-called 'dotcom boom', some worthless stock was also heavily promoted by brokers. A share price can also be affected by a myriad of external factors outside a company's control so a healthy degree of scepticism is needed before relying on this as a guide to anything.

◆ **Sales** – When an organization suffers from negative perception, sales tend to drop. The challenge is to rehabilitate the image in order to increase sales.

Direct marketing activities

Direct marketing may take the form of direct mail, telemarketing, electronic and online marketing. It is immediate, customizable to individual consumers or groups of consumers, and interactive. E-mail marketing includes unsolicited bulk e-mail and opt-in direct e-mail. Generally, direct marketing allows for easy measurement of effectiveness. Data mining (the extraction of hidden predictive information from large databases) is used to 'drill down' into the data to any level of detail needed to identify common characteristics of high-volume users. Clusters of consumers who share specific characteristics, such as income, education and brand loyalty, can be identified as targets for marketing efforts. Direct mail is the most commonly used direct-marketing advertising medium and marketers are able to target messages to specific market segments and quickly evaluate the success of a mailshot. It also enables greater personalization compared to mass media advertising.

Evaluation of direct marketing activities is based upon the predetermined objectives of the campaign. Typical measures for successful implementation of the direct marketing campaign will include the following:

◆ Response rate
◆ Conversion rate
◆ Order value
◆ Repeat orders.

Often, this information will be gathered through a range of voucher and campaign response codes that will be able to distinguish the source of the direct mail or promotion. However, the cost per enquiry and per order needs to be identified. Click-through rates are a common online measurement.

Trade promotions

Good trade promotions, that is, a good 'push strategy', highly incentivized, backed up by appropriate merchandising and advertising, may be advantageous. Specific methods might include, allowances and discounts, free merchandise, selling and marketing assistance, co-operative advertising, merchandising allowances, market information and product training. This case study from Toshiba demonstrates its integrated approach to marketing.

Case study: The integrated marketing disciplines

Toshiba has a long history of developing marketing programmes that are the result of direct consumer research and input. With insight into its consumers' wants and behaviours, Toshiba can be more effective in its unified product sales, training, advertising, public relations, trade show and online teams with consistent, integrated messages and themes. Toshiba's advertising campaign promotes the brand as well as its full line of TVs and digital audio video products. The new advertisements focus on Toshiba's lifestyle appeal and on the overall breadth of their line of products and their ease-of-use features, modern space-saving designs and convenience.

Toshiba's public relations programme has focused on the impact of consumer electronics on lifestyles, particularly the benefits, features and overall experience. Using a combination of media relations, product reviews, creative mailers, product placement, media tours, trade events and more, the programme continues evolving to communicate, educate and increase consumer awareness of Toshiba products to a larger yet targeted audience.

Toshiba's website (www.tacp.toshiba.com) provides access to product information and registration, owner's manuals and service information as well as enabling consumers to purchase accessories including portable DVD batteries and TV stands. The look and feel of the site integrates a lifestyle theme that connects all of Toshiba's marketing disciplines. Online communications and the unveiling of www.gigabeat.com were also key for the launch of gigabeat™ as Toshiba re-entered the portable digital audio category.

As part of its integrated marketing strategy, Toshiba positions its Training and Dealer Support Team in metropolitan areas around the USA to provide support for key retail partners. This team is composed of dedicated and knowledgeable product trainers (field support representatives) who help the salesforce make it easier for consumers when they are looking to buy their next Television or digital audio video player. Toshiba understands the importance of building relationships at the store level and arming front-line sales people with the tools necessary to sell Toshiba products successfully.

Toshiba has also developed a full array of product materials including catalogues and product-specific brochures to meet customers' needs. Catering to different sets of needs, Toshiba offers catalogues devoted to its main TV and digital audio and video lines, its Cinema Series™ line, the new integrated HD television line, accessories and stands, and dimensional drawings which include measurements and weights and carry tell-tale lifestyle images to reinforce the Toshiba brand and products. The result is an integrated marketing campaign and strong partnerships that allow Toshiba to leverage its brand at retail in order to develop a solid presence in the crowded MP3 market.

Source: http://www.tacp.toshiba.com/news/

Marketing channels

Increasingly, organizations are examining the whole demand chain that links raw material, components and manufactured goods, and how they are moved to their customers. The starting point should be the customer needs for which the organization needs to mobilize its resources. However, the term 'supply chain' is challenged because it suggests too linear a view of purchase, production and consumption. A more contemporary term is 'value network'. Philip Kotler in his book *Marketing Management* (2005) expresses the wish that marketers will look more widely than the customer side of the value network and participate in upstream activities. This would mean that they became network managers, not only customer and product managers.

Marketing channels are an integral part of the marketing mix, and they provide the means by which products and services are made available to end-user customers. They link manufacturers with their target markets, and are the means by which customers can access the products and services that they want. They consist of a number of different organizations each of which fulfils a particular role. Typically, a conventional channel will consist of a producer, wholesaler, retailer and end-user customer who need to collaborate and co-operate with each other. Intermediaries assume particular roles in relation to the other members of the marketing channel according to their position.

Hybrid channels

There are also 'hybrid' channels with different strategies used to reach different types of customers. For example, IBM uses its salesforce for its largest accounts, telemarketing for medium-sized accounts, direct mail for small accounts, retailers to sell to even smaller accounts and the Internet for speciality items. The Internet has had a major impact on established marketing channel structures because it allows direct contact between, for example, a service provider and the customer. Low-cost airlines is an example of this. Overall, the effect of more direct selling has been to reduce the number of intermediaries.

Distribution channels

A distribution channel consists of individuals and organizations who ensure that a product or service is available to the customer at the right place and time. A channel comprises marketing intermediaries, for example transportation companies, merchants, agents, wholesalers, warehouses and retail outlets. The successful management of the supply chain depends on motivating and controlling distributors and distribution outlets. Investing in intermediaries and their activities motivates them to undertake marketing within their network, thus adding value to the customer–supplier relationship. Traditionally, manufacturers operated within the area of production and marketing of brands, and retailers focused on selling activities. Interaction between the two was often based on manufacturers acting as 'order takers' and retailers as 'sales outlets'.

The challenge of making products and services available to customers around the world when, where and how they want them is complex. Technology transfer has made product advantages difficult to maintain but distribution is seen as having the potential for achieving a competitive advantage if marketing channels can be designed to provide excellent customer service. This means that members of the channel need to work together to create added value. A competitive advantage gained through better distribution is not so easily copied and may offer more of a sustainable competitive advantage. The main objective of physical distribution is to decrease costs while increasing service to the customer. The manager will need to consider the order processing, materials handling, warehousing, inventory management and transportation issues. Managers strive for a good balance of service, costs and resources. Therefore, effective planning is paramount to ensure that this happens by determining what level of customer service is acceptable, yet realistic in terms of costs. As physical distribution affects every element of the marketing mix, it is important that the customers' needs are at the top of the list. An effective physical distribution programme should have a positive impact on customer satisfaction; for example, some companies offer guaranteed 'next day' delivery.

◆ **Track record** – The supplier partner should have a history of successfully driving the retailer's business.

◆ **Data management** – The supplier partner should have the skills and resources to deliver state-of-the-art, business-building information, insights and ideas. Does the candidate have access to data for use in better understanding category dynamics and benchmarking performance? Can the candidate interpret data and develop business-building recommendations?

◆ **Personnel** – Does the proposed team have high-quality members? Do you get along with the candidate's team members?

Wholesaler

Wholesalers buy products from the manufacturer, store them within their warehouses and sell them on to the trade. Producers try to increase demand, and support marketing activity through various push and pull strategies. Both wholesalers and retailers want their respective customers to perceive a high level of service and value in the goods and services they purchase.

Retailer

Nowadays, retailers often have a presence on the high street and the Internet. They provide the link between the customer and the producer, and may require a lot of technical support, customer services backup, stock ordering facilities, systems underpinning the sales process, information and merchandise. Retailers provide wholesalers with sales contacts and outlets and help them by purchasing small quantities of stock on a regular basis. Retailers focus on end-user consumers and consider their buying motivations.

Distributors and dealers

Distributors and dealers stock products for manufacturers and sell them on, including after-sales service, warranties and credit facilities. Dealers often specialize in a particular brand and sell them to the end-user, making the channel shorter.

Agents and brokers

Agents and brokers act on behalf of the manufacturer to bring buyers and sellers together.

Franchisee

A franchisee holds a contract to market and supply a product or service that has been very strictly designed and developed by the franchiser. There are often restrictions on store design and layout, and what is sold within the retail outlet.

Merchandiser

Merchandisers are responsible for promotional displays in stores for different products.

Channel management

Power is not distributed evenly in most distribution channels and conflict can occur which is either horizontal, involving disagreements between channel members at the same level in the distribution chain, or vertical, occurring between channel members at different levels. Conflict in marketing channels can occur for a variety of reasons over issues such as stock levels, pricing and sales order processing. Sometimes it is because channel members have different priorities, and are focused on different business elements. A manufacturer might be focused more on products and processes, and a retailer may be focused more on customers and the processes necessary to meet their needs. Poor communication between channel members can be a cause of conflict but communication is an important co-ordinating mechanism for all members of a marketing channel. The willingness of members to share information and associated resources is an important factor because it enables an openness between parties, through which full information can be exchanged. This means that the producer must be willing to share sensitive information, and the distributor must be willing to share information about themselves, their customers and markets.

Horizontal conflict occurs when, for example, dealers in an area can complain about other dealers who are too aggressive in their pricing and advertising or are selling outside their assigned territories.

To overcome this, sometimes companies implement a vertical marketing system (VMS), a planned network of distribution channels designed to reduce conflict among channel members and resolve other distribution problems. This is where producers, wholesalers and retailers act as a unified system. One channel member owns the others, has contacts with them, or has so much power that they all co-operate.

The promotional mix in the marketing channel

A marketing channel is an organized network of agencies and institutions which in combination perform all the functions required to link producers with end-customers to accomplish the marketing task. It enables goods and services to be moved from producers and providers to consumers. Within a channel, upstream trading partners for a retailer are, for example, wholesalers, manufacturers and producers. Downstream activity takes place along the distribution chain, for example, from manufacturer to retailer to customer.

Channel communications help to hold together a channel of distribution and they are important in the development of channel relationships. However, the nature of marketing communications in a marketing channel is different from communications aimed at consumers because different audiences have different information needs. For example in comparison with consumers, distributors tend to make a smaller number of high value orders less frequently. The promotional mix in a marketing channel is aimed mainly at conveying information relating to product features and benefits. For this purpose, advertising is expensive and relatively inefficient, whereas personal selling, combined with activities such as direct marketing, the Internet, exhibitions and sales literature, could provide an effective promotional mix.

Advances in marketing communications

Difference between consumer and business-to-business marketing communications

	Consumer-orientated markets	Business-to-business markets
Message reception	Informal	Formal
Number of decision-makers	Single or few	Many
Balance of the promotional mix	Advertising and sales promotions dominate	Personal selling dominates
Specificity and integration	Broad use of promotional mix with a move towards co-ordinated mixes	Specific use of below-the-tools but with a high level of co-ordination and integration
Message content	Greater use of emotions and imagery	Greater use of rational, logic and information-based messages although there is evidence of a move towards the use of imagery
Length of decision time	Normally short	Longer and more involved
Negative communications	Limited to people close to the purchaser/user	Potentially an array of people in the organization and beyond
Target marketing and research	Great use of sophisticated targeting and communication approaches	Limited but increasing use to targeting and segmentation approaches
Budget allocation	Majority of budget allocated to brand management	Majority of budget allocated to sales management
Evaluation and measurement	Great variety of techniques and approaches used	Limited number of techniques and approaches

Source: Fill (2002) cited in Beamish (2007). Used with kind permission.

Marketing communications in the B2B sector have been transformed by technological advances (Beamish, 2007). In the B2B sector, marketing communications can fulfil a variety of specific objectives which will vary according to the circumstances:

1 To create and maintain awareness

2 To generate sales leads

3 To pre-sell sales calls

4 To contact minor members of the decision-making unit

5 To build corporate and product images

6 To communicate technical information

7 To support the promotional effort.

The CIM 2008–2009 coursebook on Marketing Planning (Beamish and Ashford, 2008) uses the DRIP acronym to describe the use of marketing communications in a marketing channel.

Focus of the message	Potential needs
Differentiation	Downstream so that channel members understand how a particular manufacturer (or particular products) adds value and is different from its competitors and other products that they carry
	Upstream to flag attention and to secure stock, support and resources
Reinforcing	Reminding downstream members of any superior product features and support facilities that are available
	Reassuring them of the benefits of continuity and reliability
	Reminding upstream members of their needs, problems and the support that is available
	Reassuring them that the business is working hard on their behalf, that they have their interests in mind
Informing	Providing downstream members with suitable levels of customer support and upstream members with market and performance information
Persuading	Encouraging downstream members to carry extra stock, provide facilities and meet service levels
	Stimulating upstream members to allocate stock, promotional support and favourable financial arrangements

Personal selling is a major communications tool in the marketing channel because face-to-face meetings between buying and selling organizations help to develop and maintain inter-organizational relationships. The willingness of organizations to share information is important to the development of sustainable relationships.

Intranets

An intranet uses a company's internal network to publish, distribute and display information for anyone directly connected to the network. Intranets allow authorized staff to access the information they need and it can encourage the sharing of knowledge from the different parts of an organization. Different types of information, prepared by different people in different parts of the business can be integrated into a single document. Staff can have easy access to information at their computer, even photographic images and technical drawings. Information can be shared rapidly when transmitted through e-mail, either within a company or outside via the Internet.

Extranets

Extranets can be used to engage distributors and producers, and allows for fast, accurate, low cost exchange of information. It involves building bridges between the public Internet and private corporate intranets, and can be seen as part of a company's intranet that is made accessible to other companies, to the public, or comprises components that enable the collaboration with other companies. Maximizing accessibility will mean that many partners can be involved and the more the participants, the greater the rates of return from the system. Extranets can also help companies to finally realize the benefits of just-in-time (JIT) inventory systems.

Other uses of extranets include the following:

◆ Private newsgroups that co-operating companies use to share valuable experiences and ideas.

◆ Groupware collaboration in the development of new products or services.

◆ Training programmes that companies develop and share.

◆ Shared product catalogues accessible only to wholesalers or those in the trade.

◆ Project management and control as part of a common work project.

Insight

Marketing campaigns are most effective when they integrate different techniques to gather and convert customer data into potential new sales. That can mean combining offline, indirect methods – such as television advertisements – with online, direct tools, such as web banners and search engine optimization. And we can now add to this mix the fastest growing form of web-based direct marketing – online lead generation.

In July 2007, online sales were 80 percent higher than the same month the previous year. This means that the web is an ideal place to gather marketing data and capture leads. (www.utalkmarketing.com)

The Internet has established itself as an effective marketing tool, and that is reflected by the fact that 71 percent of businesses have established multi-channel sales and marketing operations – using multiple forms of advertising and contact media.

The online lead generation industry is expected to double in size between 2007 and 2009, and it is proving successful as it enables retailers to use the Internet to contact consumers who express an interest in their product.

Online lead generation uses a lead and data network of thousands of website publishers to host a consistent campaign across the Internet. Each publisher has a stakeholder interest in each individual campaign. They will generate the leads and then pass them back through the host's central system for cleansing, verification and forwarding to the client.

Instead of a database sitting at the back of a company's own website, collecting the data submitted by visitors, online lead generation proactively and automatically captures consumer details, and sends them through for sales agents to convert.

Nevertheless, for all its qualities, no one marketing tool will ever be 100 per cent efficient on its own. The way to achieve the best results is to realize that many methods have their own individual benefits, and create an effective mix that forms a genuinely holistic marketing campaign.

Source: Simon Wajcenberg, CEO of Clash-Media

Intermediaries and communication

Value-added activities

Examples of the kinds of value-added activities that intermediaries can undertake are: analysing information such as sales data, evaluating channel activities, co-ordinating advertising, personal selling, promotions and so on, facilitating communication, maintaining relationships between manufacturer and retail outlets, and providing advice, technical support, after-sales service and warranties.

Channels perform most effectively when they co-operate, co-ordinate and integrate their activities. Vertical channel management is where two or more channel members are connected by ownership or legal obligation. Marketing mix activities are more integrated, and often more effective because of this. Horizontal channel integration is the merging of organizations at the same level of channel operation under one management, for example, through mergers and takeovers.

Consumer and business-to-business marketing communications

The importance of B2B communications is underpinned by buoyant Internet-based marketing communications compared with relatively slow growth in the B2C market.

The most important difference, however, is that organizational buying decisions are taken by groups of people rather than individuals. A key issue is to identify the individuals who comprise the decision-making unit.

Communications in marketing channel networks

A planned, channel-orientated communications strategy should contribute to and reinforce the partnerships in the network. There are many factors that can influence channel communication strategy, for example:

- **Power** – Are some organizations more important than others?
- **Direction** – Are communications one-way or two-way?
- **Frequency** – How often should messages be sent?
- **Timing** – Should messages be sent to all members simultaneously or serially?
- **Style and content** – Should messages be formal/informal? What must be included?
- **Distortion** – Will messages be received, stored and acted upon as the originator intends?

Review and evaluate the effectiveness of communications activities

The apocryphal quote that 'half of all advertising is a waste of money but it is not clear which half' serves as a reminder that measuring the success of communications activities can be difficult. However, there are techniques that can be used for different purposes.

Evaluating channel effectiveness

It is essential that having selected an appropriate distribution channel and intermediaries, their efficiency, effectiveness and performance are continually managed.

Key performance and evaluation measures include the following:

◆ Regular reviews

◆ A forum for problem review and solution

◆ Monthly, quarterly and yearly sales data analysis

◆ Average stock levels

◆ Lead and delivery times

◆ Zero defects

◆ Customer service complaints

◆ Marketing support – achieving marketing objectives, level of marketing activity, sales promotions, distributor incentives

◆ Spot-check of distributions further down the supply chain

◆ Annual performance audit.

From an Internet perspective, typical evaluation methods of marketing effectiveness might include the following:

◆ Number of leads

◆ Increased sales

◆ Customer retention

◆ Increased market share

◆ Brand enhancement and loyalty

◆ Customer service.

Many organizations measure the effectiveness of their marketing communications, and there are a range of techniques and procedures available. Increasingly, it is the synergy that derives from effective co-ordination of all activities that determines overall success. Single elements of the communications mix are not used in isolation. Different parts of a campaign can be assessed and the evaluation process can be carried out at different stages of a marketing campaign, that is, before, during and after a campaign has been launched. However, the overall impact of a co-ordinated marketing communications campaign and the degree to which the promotional objectives have been achieved are key measures that interest stakeholders.

Whilst the primary focus is upon ascertaining whether objectives have been met and the strategy has been effective – efficiency is also of interest. There should be a strong emphasis on 'efficiency', 'effectiveness' and 'value for money', which means making the best use of the available resources to achieve the best possible outcomes. However, some aspects of marketing are notoriously difficult to evaluate; for example, advertising. Whilst communications is one element of the marketing mix, the other elements should be evaluated as well.

Pre-testing is about showing unfinished advertisements, often to focus groups to gather their reactions and to understand their reasoning. Post-testing is concerned with the evaluation of a campaign once it has been released. A typical measurement is the number of enquiries or direct responses elicited by a single advertisement or campaign. Recall and recognition tests are common post-testing procedures for advertisements.

Tracking studies involve collecting data from buyers on a regular basis in order to assess their perceptions of ads. Sales promotion evaluation includes methods such as consumer audits and general sales information, retail audits including, for example, changes in stock levels, distribution, market share and so on immediately after a promotional campaign. Salesforce feedback is also a common measure.

Voucher/coupon redemption – Usually coded so that the different response rates in different media can be tracked.

Calculating ROI

Obviously, the power of metrics diminishes if the information is merely distributed, and not intelligently assessed and acted upon by management. Return on investment is the most critical measure of marketing programmes for making decisions that will help maximize company profits. In its simplest form:

Return = Net profit (pre investment) – Net profit (post investment) – Investment

RoI = Return/Net Profit (pre-marketing investment)

Insight: Communication evaluation

Australia: State of Victoria Government communication evaluation guidelines key principles:

◆ Evaluation involves assessment of the degree to which an activity's objectives have been met as a result of the activity.

◆ Evaluation is an internal part of all communications projects, not an optional extra.

◆ Evaluation should be planned at the outset of a communications project.

◆ Evaluation must be properly budgeted for. As a rule of thumb, 10 per cent of a project's budget should be allocated to evaluation.

A good test of the usefulness of an evaluation is to ask the following questions:

◆ Does it effectively identify the success/failure of the project?

◆ Does it effectively identify the reasons for success/failure of the project?

◆ Does it effectively identify the cost-effectiveness of the project?

Broadly speaking, evaluation can address the following:

◆ Activity – what was done (e.g. wrote, designed and produced brochures).

◆ Output – what communication took place (e.g. distributed each brochure to 1000 people).

◆ Outcome – what was achieved in terms of knowledge, attitudes and behaviour. Outcome evaluation is far more important, useful and relevant than activity or output evaluation. All significant projects should be evaluated on their outcomes.

Source: www.dpc.vic.gov.au

Evaluation tools

Methods commonly used to measure project outcomes and outputs include:

◆ Surveys

- Focus groups
- Web statistics
- User feedback.

The choice of method in any case depends principally on the objectives and the budget.

1 **Accountability** – The evaluation should identify an individual, responsible, office holder who is accountable for the overall programme/activity.

2 **Situation analysis** – This should provide sufficient rationale for the programme purpose and objectives. It should include background to the activity, including the source of the original reason for the project.

3 **Rationale for approach** – Research/evidence should be cited in support of the approach taken, its form and extent.

4 **Aims and objectives** – The overarching aim from the original project plan should be provided.

5 **Target audience/s** – Target audience should be identified, and a rationale provided for them.

6 **Communications activities** – All project communications activities should be listed and a rationale provided for the choice.

7 **Selected media** – Media used should be listed and a rationale provided for the selection.

8 **Key messages/creative** – Key messages/creative should be cited/described, and a rationale/evidence provided for their selection.

9 **Output/outcome measurement tools** – Tools used as part of the evaluation should be specified and a rationale provided, if necessary.

10 **Evaluation findings** – Findings should be clearly stated, and address the objectives.

11 **Key success factors** – Factors critical for the success (or failure) of the activity to achieve its objectives should be identified.

12 **Recommendations** – The evaluation should make recommendations for the future, reflecting learnings gleaned from the evaluation.

13 **Budget** – Budget and expenditure figures should be provided, and a statement should be made in respect of the cost-effectiveness of the activity.

Customer service

Customer service can be interpreted as any contact, whether active or passive, between a customer and a company that influences customer perceptions. Customers make positive or negative judgements according to whether companies meet or exceed their expectations, wants and needs. This involves more than the face-to-face contact or direct service that a customer receives. It includes all the elements that are part of the production and distribution of products and services.

The Institute of Customer Service describes excellent customer service as:

◆ Delighting the customer, satisfying all their needs and giving them something extra to remember you by.

◆ Making every customer feel special, giving them the impression that they are your No 1 priority.

◆ Giving every customer a memorable experience, ensuring they will be pleased to return to you next time.

◆ Treating every customer with respect, satisfying all their needs and exceeding their expectations.

◆ Putting customers first – prioritizing their needs and delivering a swift, friendly and efficient service.

◆ Anticipating and exceeding all customers' expectations.

◆ Being there for your customers – to provide a rapid, reliable and unbeatable service to them.

◆ Showing customers you care about them; being professional at all times.

◆ Adding value to their lives through your dedication, skills and professionalism in satisfying their needs and resolving any difficulties.

◆ Making the difference for all your customers so they will return to you through choice.

◆ Establishing a valuable relationship with your customers based on trust, reliability, empathy and your ability to deliver your promises every time

◆ Making a commitment to your customer and keeping it.

◆ Being personable, precise, proactive and professional at all times and in all your dealings with customers.

◆ Showing you care enough to make the difference for every customer.

◆ Satisfying customers' needs in a way that shows you genuinely care about them as individuals.

◆ Welcoming and handling well a customer's enquiries or complaints so that the customer becomes an advocate.

To be successful and to prevent customer frustration businesses need to:

◆ Actively listen to the customer – rather than just hearing them.

◆ Make the right people accountable for improvement.

◆ Fix the things that make a difference to customers – addressing root causes not symptoms.

◆ Measure projects and operations with the same success-indicators – so it is clear what makes a difference to customers.

◆ Collaborate end-to-end across the business, to ensure the frontline can deliver what the customer wants.

◆ Track what happens and make sure the customer can see the difference.

◆ Put in a consistent process, not a one-off.

Source: www.insightexec.com/cgi-bin/item.cgi?id=131008

As industries mature and companies can no longer easily differentiate themselves by attributes such as products or pricing and technological innovations are widely available, customer service becomes a critical competitive advantage. Service and support interactions are often the only direct contact the company has with the customer and the quality of those interactions has a significant impact on long-term success. Organizations are facing increased pressures to do more with less. Many are being asked to provide service to more customers and/or support a wider range of products and services as budgets are reduced or remain flat.

There is a growing emphasis on the common management of diverse customer service communications channels, which include the phone, e-mail and the Web. Managing the channels as separate 'silos' makes it difficult to integrate information and gain a holistic view of a customer's preferences and purchasing profile. Organizations are looking for ways to treat all incoming service requests as a single, manageable queue so they can optimize efficiency.

An integrated customer service process can reduce cost, save time and improve profitability. Linking customer service information with sales data improves business scheduling and helps target potential customers. It helps to avoid duplication of effort and presents a unified, informed image.

The benefits of good customer service

The whole of an organization is implicated in customer service although some companies have dedicated customer service departments. Customer service is a link in a chain between buyer and seller and one of a series of links between stages in a marketing channel.

Increased customer retention rates

It has been repeatedly shown that good service leads directly to increased customer retention rates but the service has to be of a high standard to genuinely keep customers.

Reduced costs of running the business

Increased customer retention rates means the resources associated with setting up the customer's details are reduced to only one over a long time period, compared to a constant stream of new customers coming in as others leave. Regular customers can be serviced more efficiently. Good service means lower complaint rates, and therefore less time and cost involved in dealing with such complaints.

Reduced marketing costs

Many studies have shown that it costs around three to five times as much to attract a new customer compared to making the same sale to an existing customer. Customers can take on part of the marketing function by making recommendations and referrals. Personal referrals are one of the strongest influences on service adoption, and hence the strongest form of marketing.

Stronger position in the competitive marketplace

Companies identified as being good service providers tend to have higher revenue growth compared with poor service competitors. Customers that stay with a company for a long time are more profitable. They are more likely to make repeat purchases of the same goods and services, more likely to purchase other products or services, and often maintain higher balances/accounts.

Improved internal communication, staff relations and morale

Employees who receive positive feedback from their interactions with customers and a reduction in the number of complaints are bound to feel more satisfied with their work than working in a hostile climate. In turn this contributes to better customer service, and a virtuous circle is set in train. Being part of a service that is recognized as poor is damaging to morale.

Essentials of customer care

The culture of the organization is the basis of good customer service because it embodies the values of the organization, including how customers and employees should be treated. Motivated and valued staff is the basis of good customer care. Customers may interact with a number of different people during any transaction. The pre-transaction, transaction and post-transaction activities are the customer's chain of experience. An organization committed to customer service should try to understand and gain feedback about the customer's chain of experience.

Insight: Developing customer service

Sometimes, customer-care training focuses on superficial issues such as 'have a nice day' and doesn't look at the underlying causes of poor service, for example management style, lack of empowerment of customer-facing staff and lack of continuous training. If you are truly a customer-centric organization, you will literally live and breathe your customers' needs. Every activity should be tuned into making profit for all stakeholders, particularly customers, by maximizing the benefits available to them throughout the delivery and post-delivery processes. That means you have to work towards improving the 'life' of the individual or organization, and this also requires a system of needs and business improvement prioritization across the supply and value chain. So, Hood explains, you first of all must undertake a needs definition analysis of both your organization and customers. The next step is to ascertain which activities are going to have a greater impact on ROI for all of your stakeholders, which activities are necessary and in what order they must be achieved according to their potential impact and benefits. So measure not just inside your company, measure the customer too. Customer-centricity has to enhance the value of the relationship to create a win/win situation otherwise it isn't customer-centricity. The question is: how are you going to become customer-centric? To be customer-centric, you need to manage your total marketing – taking a broader, holistic approach to profit and strategy-making.

Source: Graham Jarvis, Editor, CIMTech International, www.insightexec.com

Customer audit

◆ Who are your current customers?

◆ What proportion of the business does each represent?

◆ Who is the 'buyer'?

◆ Are their needs satisfied?

◆ How can the service offered to them be improved?

If employees are expected to deliver high-quality customer care, their views should be canvassed for ideas about how customer service could be improved. They also need access to good quality training in areas such as dealing with telephone calls and managing customer complaints efficiently and effectively. A website can be used to give customers the services and information they want. A good database can also help with the organization and planning of customer contacts.

Implementing a customer care programme

Successful customer care means making the customer want to return and getting them to recommend products and services to others. Customer care should be about focusing staff energies on offering value, getting it right first time and continuous improvement. A formalized customer care programme with involved leadership helps to give a clear focus to roles and responsibilities.

Excellence depends on knowing customers' needs and expectations. Anticipating needs can provide a competitive advantage. A range of approaches can be used, including:

◆ Feedback direct from customers and staff

◆ Direct discussion with customers

◆ Analysis of customer complaints, enquiries and thank-yous

◆ Attitude surveys and questionnaires

◆ Visits to premises

◆ Focus-group discussions and customer audits.

Customer care involves a host of elements that contribute to genuine care and value for the customer. Focus the recruitment process on customers and ask questions at the interview stage, covering, for example:

◆ Candidates' experiences with customers

◆ Service levels and customer expectations

◆ The prioritization of customer needs over in-house organizational activities

◆ Incentives to motivate front-line staff

◆ Include customer care in the induction programme.

Communications need to be right and the right message needs to be conveyed to all staff in the right way. If internal communications are not working then external communications will not be successful either. Communications have to be reliable, consistent and regular so that all people receive and interpret messages in the same way.

Insight: Handling complaints

All staff should be familiar and comfortable with the organization's procedure so that they are prepared to receive complaints and are able to deal with them promptly and accurately.

◆ Let the customer air the grievance without interruption.

◆ Acknowledge the customer's viewpoint – even if you don't agree.

- Apologize – say sorry if a mistake has been made, but there's no need to overdo it.

- Find a solution – establish what needs to be done to rectify the problem.

- Keep the complainant informed – lack of ongoing information can exacerbate the problem.

- Reach a conclusion to resolve the problem for the customer quickly – a more permanent solution may take longer to find.

- Follow up – check that promised action happens.

Prompt and sympathetic handling of complaints can turn an unhappy customer into a loyal one.

Monitoring and evaluating customer service

A number of issues that impact upon quality measurement are as follows:

- The difference in perception between employees and customers

- The inseparability of production and consumption

- The individuality of employees' performance and customers' perceptions.

There is a proposed formula for measuring these components:

- Customer expectations – service organizations' perceptions of customer expectations

- Customer experience – service organizations' perceptions of customer experience.

The following are examples of processes that can contribute to the monitoring and evaluation of the service that customers receive:

- **Marketing research** – gather information about services, and delivery of them

- **Observation** – observing customer–staff interactions as the latter receive a service

- **Interviews** – to understand perceptions and expectations versus their experience

- **Customer satisfaction surveys** – questionnaires to monitor customer satisfaction

- **Mystery consumer experience** – include a mystery person in the delivery of the service

- **Evaluating dissatisfaction** – examine the main causes of customer dissatisfaction

- **Monitoring image** – how is the image of the service perceived

- **Performance appraisals** – of staff involved in the delivery of a service

- **Employee group discussions** – internal marketing practice.

SERVQUAL

Measuring customer satisfaction is important for many organizations. The SERVQUAL methodology was developed originally by customer satisfaction researchers Valarie Zeithaml, A. Parasuraman and Leonard Berry (*Delivering Quality Service*). The methodology helps organizations to better understand what customers value and how well their current organizations are meeting their needs and expectations. SERVQUAL provides a benchmark based on customer opinions of an excellent company, on your company, on the importance ranking of key attributes, and on a comparison to what your employees believe customers feel. It provides a detailed information about: customer perceptions of service (a benchmark established by your own customers); performance levels as perceived by customers; customer comments and suggestions and impressions from employees with respect to customers' expectations and satisfaction.

GAP 1   What managers and customers see as important;

GAP 2   What managers see as important and the specifications;

GAP 3   The specification and the delivery;

GAP 4   The delivery and the claim/promise;

GAP 5   Expectations and perceptions.

Examples of the kinds of questions that can be asked are shown in the table opposite:

◆   **Desired level** – The excellence level of service desired. Please consider the level of service you would desire for each of the statements below. If you think a feature requires a very high level of service quality, choose 9 in the second column. If you think it requires a very low level of service quality, choose 1 in the second column. If your requirements are less extreme, choose an appropriate number in between.

◆   **Perceived level** – Your perception of the service quality (see third column). Please use the same 9-point scale to evaluate the level of service you perceive.

Ways to improve customer service

Personalize communications – For example, greeting a customer by name, personalize the e-mail addresses of customer-facing employees.

Create opportunities for feedback

Find out from new customers why they chose the company over the competition. Ask existing customers what could be better. Enable online feedback by putting an e-mail response form or newsgroup on the website. Encourage complaints, as only one in ten dissatisfied customers bothers to complain, usually dissatisfied customers just take their custom elsewhere. Carry out occasional customer satisfaction surveys. Contact any customer who has stopped buying and keep a record of customer feedback to help identify problem areas.

Establish a customer hotline, and make sure the number is on every piece of paper sent out.

◆   Monitor and analyse the contact you have with customers.

◆   Use software to discover which web pages are most popular.

With regard to	My desired service level is: Low 1 2 3 4 5 6 7 8 9 High	My perceived service level is: Low 1 2 3 4 5 6 7 8 9 High
1. Providing services as promised		
2. Dependability in handling client's problems		
3. Performing services right the first time		
4. Providing the service at the promised time		
5. Keeping clients informed of when something will be done		
6. Prompt service to clients		
7. Willingness to help clients		
8. Readiness to respond to clients' requests		
9. Personnel who instil confidence in their clients		
10. Making clients feel assured		
11. Personnel who are always courteous and considerate		
12. Personnel who have the expertise to look after clients' needs		
13. The individual attention that clients get		
14. Personnel who deal with clients in a caring fashion		
15. Personnel who have the clients' best interest at heart		
16. Personnel who understand the needs of their clients		
17. The modern equipment and apparatus available		
18. The visually appealing facilities		
19. Convenient office hours		
20. How would you rate the *overall quality of service* provided?		

Differentiate between different customer segments

When marketing, if appropriate, differentiate between different market segments.

◆ Potential customers who have not yet purchased anything. For example, someone who has made an enquiry as a result of an advertisement where the aim is to build interest in what you have to offer.

◆ Another segment is customers who have already made a purchase, where your aim is to increase the frequency of their buying and to sell them other products and services.

◆ Premium customers who already make regular purchases. Sometimes, a few large customers generate a high proportion of profits and it is important to make sure that their needs are being met. Invite key customers to special events. Try to reinforce the idea that they are valued customers but without being unduly obtrusive or obsequious. Above all, don't be like Uriah Heep who was ever so 'umble'.

The loyalty ladder is a shorthand way of assessing customer value.

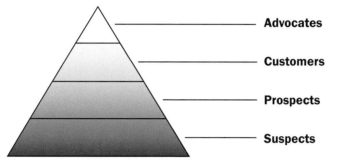

— Advocates

— Customers

— Prospects

— Suspects

Advocates – These are loyal customers who are enthusiastic about your products or services, and who recommend you to others. This group is the most valuable group of customers.

Customers – When prospects buy from you, they become customers. You now need to convince them to continue to buy from you.

Prospects – These are suspects who have responded to your efforts and have shown an interest in you.

Suspects – These people may or may not be interested in your products or services. They may be reached by advertising, cold calling or mail.

Added-value schemes

A successful loyalty scheme pays for itself by encouraging more frequent purchases. The most common loyalty schemes are based on offering rewards to loyal customers. Several businesses can collaborate to support the same loyalty scheme. An accounting system may need to track the purchasing activity of each customer and recognize when discounts have been earned. The following case study is an example of service standards and also shows how customers with special needs are catered for.

Customer management in action: Manchester United

Manchester United is a global sports/media organization with interests in retail, media and financial services. The importance of having a strong relationship with customers is even more important when the customers are also fans. The Club has an estimated 75 million supporters in 24 different business markets. It is a complex business ranging from retail with sales of shirts and memorabilia through to magazine subscriptions and credit cards and mortgages. The Club faces a significant challenge in interacting with its supporters, understanding their needs and communicating with them in order to ensure the maximum advantage for the club's commercial interests.

The Club needed a coherent customer relationship management system and embarked on a worldwide programme. The first phase was to further develop channels in order to connect to its supporters around the world. The second phase was to convert supporters into customers and maximize the potential of the Manchester United brand directly and indirectly through its partner network. It has been pulling together information from multiple databases, including Membership, ticketing, www.manutd.com, the Manchester United Museum and financial service partners. The Club has developed a data warehouse and the next step is effective segmentation of that data. The Club is moving towards the stage of trying to predict what people would buy if they were offered products and services at the right time. Having a comprehensive view of a customer is critical to the level and nature of the service the club can offer. The relationship with the supporters is the lifeblood of the business. The important thing is that this is being driven by the needs of the Club's business strategy.

Source: www.insightexec.com/

Plan for introducing better customer service

1   Review other organizations with good reputations for good customer service. Look at how this compares with practices in the target organization.

2   Agree what customer service means and how it will be interpreted in the target organization.

3   Agree customer service standards and procedures.

4   All staff should participate in the process of change. Establish a working group or project team that has representation from all the parts of the organization that have an influence on customer service.

5   Review strengths and weaknesses.

6   Agree and communicate customer satisfaction performance targets.

7   Develop plans to implement changes, including an internal marketing plan.

A training programme aimed at everyone who has an influence on customer service should be devised or outsourced and implemented.

Customer retention management

There are a number of techniques for measuring customer satisfaction linked to profitability. Established customers tend to be more profitable because:

◆   They place frequent, consistent orders, and cost less to serve

◆   They tend to buy more

◆   Satisfied customers may sometimes pay a premium price

◆   Retaining customers makes it difficult for competitors to enter a market or increase their share

◆   Satisfied customers often refer new customers to the supplier at no extra cost

◆   A higher retention rate implies fewer new customers need to be acquired.

Customer retention in business-to-consumer (B2C) markets

In consumer markets, customer retention schemes are focused around loyalty cards. Loyalty schemes are based on accessing information from customer databases, and making use of direct response media such as direct mail and telemarketing. Product-based sales promotion advertising is more widely used by retailers who do not use loyalty schemes.

Retaining customers in business-to-business (B2B) markets

The basic principles that a B2B market should consider in relationship development:

◆   **Technical support** – providing added value to clients in industrial markets

◆   **Technical expertise** – providing expertise can be a good selling point **Resource support** – making available a range of cost-effective resources to support the relationship

◆   **Service levels** – these appear to be of growing importance and will relate in particular to time, delivery and product quality

◆   **Reduction of risk** – using exhibitions, trial use and product delivery guarantees.

Relationship marketing

Key dimensions that provide a basis for a relationship:

◆   **Reliability** – ability to perform the promised service dependably and accurately

◆   **Responsiveness** – willingness to help customers and provide prompt service

◆   **Assurance** – knowledge and courtesy of employees, and their ability to inspire trust and confidence

◆   **Empathy** – caring, individualism, attention the firm provides its customers

◆   **Tangibles** – physical facilities, equipment and appearance of personnel.

Gronroos (1994) defined relationship marketing as identifying, establishing, maintaining, enhancing and, where necessary, terminating the relationship with customers and other stakeholders, at a profit. Relationship marketing is focused on maximizing the lifetime value of desirable customers and customer segments. Strategies need to enhance relationships with key markets, including internal ones as well as external relationships with customers, suppliers, referral sources, influence markets and recruitment markets. A relationship marketing approach aims to bring the elements of quality, customer service and marketing into an integrated relationship. This helps marketers to focus on maintaining and enhancing customer relationships. The types of interactions that take place between buyers and sellers can be viewed on a continuum, ranging from transaction to relationship.

Transaction marketing	Relationship marketing
Focus more on single sale	Focus more on customer retention
Orientation more on product features	Orientation more on product benefits
Comparatively short timescale	Comparatively long timescale
Little emphasis on customer service	High emphasis on customer service
Limited customer commitment	Higher customer commitment
Moderate customer contact	Higher customer contact
Quality is primarily a concern of production	Quality is the concern of all

Relationship marketing and mass customization

Mass customization enables companies to focus on what customers want, rather than what the company can produce. It also allows companies to produce individually tailored products. There is a longer history of using this approach with services such as banking on stockbroking rather than with products. Mass customization is also more common in B2B markets and the simplest approach is to design a product that buyers can customize themselves. Dell Computers allows the buyer to design an individual computer and then track it through to delivery. Much of Dell's production, up to the point of final assembly, is outsourced which means that suppliers at every link in the chain need good timely information about what customers want, and when. Speed and good communications are essential if mass customization is to work.

Case study: Dell's business model

While other PC makers rely on resellers, retailers, and other agents to carry much of the burden of marketing and sales, Dell has to reach out to customers largely through its own efforts. And while other PC makers can run high-volume assembly lines to achieve economies of scale, Dell must tailor each order to meet customer specifications, a process that puts heavy demands on shop floor employees, suppliers, logistical and information systems. Direct sales means that Dell must reach out to potential customers, either through its own sales force or through advertising and other marketing efforts. Its use of the direct approach provides it with detailed knowledge about its customers, and also allows Dell to identify customer trends early so it can respond with the desired products before its competitors can. Build-to-order requires Dell to have very close coordination between its sales and manufacturing arms and with its suppliers. It achieves this by refining its business processes, developing close relationships with a limited number of suppliers, and using IT to facilitate communication within and outside the company. The build-to-order production system is the focal point of Dell's business operations, the common contact point for sales, procurement, logistics, manufacturing, and delivery. Build-to-order production, or mass customization, should also gain footholds in more industries as companies look to differentiate their products and avoid pure price competition.

Insight

There is no doubt that information technology is transforming the way that business is conducted and hence how marketing needs to adapt. In Chris Anderson's book *The Long Tail: Why the Future of Business Is Selling Less of More*, the 'long tail' refers to marketing that treats consumers as individuals with unique interests and needs. It indicates smaller and smaller volumes of each of an ever increasing number of niche products. Products that are in low demand or have low sales volume can collectively make up a market share that rivals or exceeds the relatively few current bestsellers and blockbusters, if the store or distribution channel is large enough. By lowering search costs, information technology could substantially increase the collective share of niche products, thereby creating a longer tail in the distribution of sales. According to Chris Anderson, economics has taken on a new shape. Websites and online retailers offer countless market opportunities for those who cast a wide net and de-emphasize the search for blockbusters. Really successful consumer product businesses will be unlike their predecessors. They will win not by investing in the blockbuster that makes them a fortune, but in smart mechanisms that allow a multiplicity of consumers to find different products for very particular tastes. These mechanisms minimize cost by allowing millions of users to do for free what companies would otherwise have to pay for; for example, it enables eBay to run the world's busiest auction house without any of the overheads and Wikipedia to produce a vast encyclopaedia without paying a single contributor.

There are three driving forces behind this revolution:

◆ **Tools of production:** Hardware and software put product creation into the hands of everyone. Software empowers people to share their knowledge, leading to an exponential explosion in niche products. This makes it easier to create and produce but it must still be a high-quality product.

◆ **Internet aggregators:** Aggregators pull 'products' together, one offer all in one spot. For example, iTunes aggregates music, one offer to consumers. Google AdSense pulls publishers together, on offer to advertisers. Some of the most successful Internet businesses have leveraged the Long Tail as part of their businesses. Examples include eBay (auctions), Yahoo! and Google (web search), Amazon (retail) and iTunes Store (music and podcasts).

◆ **Filtering software that connects supply and demand:** This enables consumers to find those niche products. The Top 10 searches at Google account for only a small minority of its searches. Half of the 200,000,000 searches per day are unique. The competitive threat from these niche sites is reduced by the cost of establishing and maintaining them and the bother required to track multiple small websites. However, these factors have been transformed by easy and cheap website software. There are some reservations about the theory, particularly its applicability outside the media industries.

In Christopher et al. (2002) the relationship marketing strategy is developed around six key market domains underpinned by the view that marketing can no longer be seen as the responsibility of a single departmental function.

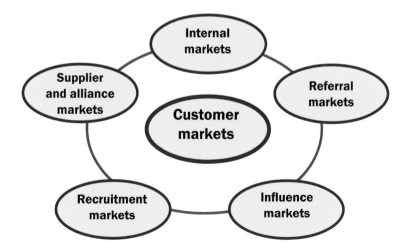

Relationship marketing challenges organizations internally to support cross-functional change management and externally to support a shift to long-term relationships with a broader range of stakeholders, among which the customer is of central but not exclusive importance. An action taken in one domain, say the customer market, can affect the supplier market and probably the internal (employee) market, with perhaps wider environmental impacts that require careful management and planning. This approach is not just a way to think about delivering value but about the value-creating possibilities of working within relationships. The six markets model encourages a systemic approach to planning... businesses from one end of a supply chain to the other are embedded in loose-knit stakeholder networks that might be better described as 'value constellations' of related interests.

Source: Peck et al. (1999)

The book argues that although customers are central to relationship marketing, the term itself doesn't necessarily imply that an organization should seek intense interactive relationships with all its customers. To be properly customer-facing it will have to move from 'vertical' to 'horizontal' management structures and dealing effectively with all the organization and culture change issues associated with this is critical for successful relationship marketing. A corporate culture that recognizes that delivering stakeholder value is the primary purpose of the business underpins any successful relationship market strategy. In the authors' view, relationship marketing has been one of the key developments of modern marketing science and the emphasis on relationships, as opposed to transaction-based exchanges, is likely to continue to redefine the marketing domain. They believe it should lead to a new general theory of marketing, as its fundamental axioms explain marketing practice better than other theories.

Source: Christopher, M., Payne, A. and Ballantyne, D. (2002)

Summary

As Fill (2002) clearly states, choosing a combination of media and attempting to 'generate synergistic effects' is difficult, but advances in technology and the growth of the Internet now means that other media have to be considered. The main classes of media according to him are as follows:

- Broadcast
- Print
- Outdoor
- New
- In-store
- Other media classes.

Within each of these six classes there are a range of media types. Moreover, within each medium, decisions have to be made on the precise media vehicle preferred.

There are a variety of approaches to planning the design, implementation and evaluation of communications campaigns. Marketing communications are used to develop relationships or communicate with a range of stakeholders including the provision of support for members of a marketing channel. There are also a variety of ways to review and evaluate the effectiveness of communications activities.

Hints and tips

◆ Integrated communications is a typical example of the task that faces the professional marketer. Not only must the right things be done but they must be done in the right sequence and at the right time.

◆ It needs a firm grasp of the nature of the communications issues and proposes a number of justified activities. Some innovative suggestions are made. Both 'push' and 'pull' elements are covered.

◆ Application of knowledge requires practice; candidates are strongly advised to practise and develop their skills on past case studies. The specimen answers available on the CIM website are intended to be a guide to aid in the process. Specimen answers are not 'textbook' answers to be learned and reproduced in the next exam.

◆ Each exam case study has a different context and will need context-specific application of marketing theory. The need is to develop skills in this process.

◆ Candidates are advised to practise applying their marketing skills in various contexts, not only to gain good exam grades but also to develop their professional competence.

◆ Candidates should also read around the current marketing press and journals. Aspects of marketing such as e-commerce are changing fast, and textbooks only a year old may already have become dated in some of the faster-moving areas.

Sample questions

June 2006

The International Federation of Aroma Trades has decided to organize its first international conference to be held in New City in June 2007. You have been recruited to the role of Events and Marketing Manager to assist in the marketing and planning of the conference.

Question 2

a.   What information would be needed to develop a successful conference programme and how might this be obtained?

(15 Marks)

b.   This is the first conference for the International Federation of Aroma Trades. What information should be collected from delegates to plan for an even better conference next time and how might this information be obtained?

(10 marks)

Question 3

How might 'e'-based methods be used to promote the International Conference within the context of a co-ordinated communications mix?

(25 Marks)

June, 2005, Question 3

Outline and justify the integrated marketing communications activities required to promote the launch of '@ Medi Wrap' in 'New Territory'.

(25 marks)

December 2004, Question 3

Outline the integrated marketing communications activities required to promote the online digital image processing service.

(25 Marks)

Bibliography

Anderson, C (2006) *The Long Tail:Why the Future of Business Is Selling Less of More*, New York: Hyperion

Beamish, K. (2007) Communication strategies and planning, Marketing Communications, Harlow: Elsevier Butterworth-Heinemann. (NOT FOUND)

Beamish, K and Ashford, R, (2007) *Marketing Planning: 2007/08*, Elsevier Science, 4th edition

Birch, A., Gerbert, P. and Schneider, D. (2000) *The Age of E-tail*, Milford, CT: Capstone 4th European edition

Carlzon, J. (1987) *Moments of Truth*, Harper

Christopher, M., Payne, A. and Ballantyne, D. (2002) *Relationship Marketing: Creating Stakeholder Value*, Oxford: Butterworth-Heinemann

Fill,C, (2002) *Marketing Communications : Contexts, Strategies and Applications*, Hemel Hempstead: Prentice Hall Europe 3rd Edition,

Gronroos, C. (1994) From marketing mix to relationship marketing: towards a paradigm shift in marketing. *Australian Marketing Journal*, Vol 2, August, 9-29

Kotler, P. (2006) *Marketing Management*, New York: Prentice Hall, 12th edition

Parasuraman, A., Zeithaml,V.A. and Berry, L.L. (1998) SERVQUAL: A Multiple-Item Scale for Measuring Customer Perceptions of Service Quality, *Journal of Retailing*, Spring, 12-40.

Peck, H., Payne, A., Christopher, M. and Clark, M. (1999) *Relationship Marketing: Strategy and Implementation*, Oxford: Butterworth-HeinemannZeithaml, V.A., Parasuraman, A. and Berry, L. L. (1990) *Delivering Quality Service - Balancing Customer Perceptions and Expectations*, New York: Free Press

Appendix Feedback and answers

Unit 1

Activity 1.1

There are often problems in translating high level policies into the daily lives of managers, especially when they are dealing with competing pressures. Many managers would like to be better at what they do but sometimes work pressures can mean that aspirations are not realized. However, this doesn't mean that this has to be accepted and regular feedback from team members is one way of staying in touch with what needs to be adjusted and changed.

Unit 2

Activity 2.1

Were you able to answer this question easily, or did it take a long time to think about the whole range of stakeholders involved with your organization? Your list should have included internal and external people. In some organizations, the expectations of different parts of the organization will be explicit but, in others it may only be implicit. Sometimes there is a disdainful view of other parts of the organization that contribute to the overheads but whose contribution to frontline activities is not so visible – for example, what is your view of personnel/HRM? finance? – Were you able to identify your key stakeholders' expectations of your team? Who did you identify as your customers? – Do you see people internal to the organization as your customers?

Activity 2.2

In what areas does your team work well and in what areas does it need to improve? If you identified any barriers to effectiveness, how much of this is within the power of the team to overcome? Usually, teams can improve if one of their goals is to improve how they work together. However, this may not be spoken about even though there may be a recognition that the team does not work well.

Activity 2.3

The list is very long. Managers in this situation need to make sure that they are briefed on protocols. Awareness of self and of context as well as cultural empathy are attributes that will serve managers well in all kinds of situations irrespective of particular cultures. Diplomacy works as well in a domestic situation as it does in an international one.

Activity 2.5

Employee specification:

Factor	Essential	Desirable
Attainments	Degree preferably in a media or marketing discipline	CAM qualifications to Diploma level
Specific professional skills	Written composition and presentation skills. Media and communications strategies	–
Experience	5 years or more in a media/PR role	Preferably in a non-profit organization or consultancy
Reasoning abilities	Capacity for strategic media analysis and event management	–
Personality	Calm, proactive, assertive, confident, representative personality. Empathy with NHS values	–
Aptitudes	Networker, promoter, persuader, win rapport with clients. Create and develop promotional material	–
Physical make-up	Professional, well-groomed image. Stamina and good health	–
Circumstances	Weekend and evening work	–

Essential – Attributes essential for adequate job performance. Job cannot be performed unless these factors are present.

Desirable – Attributes that are not essential but if present will enhance effective work performance.

Adapted from: http://sol.brunel.ac.uk/~jarvis/bola/jobs/mediajob/perspec.html.

Unit 3

Activity 3.1

Polarising people and situations is rather false because usually people are a mixture of these opposites, and their behaviour can vary in different contexts and situations and at different times. However, making stark contrasts is useful for encouraging reflection and for synthesising aspects of different approaches. It isn't so much a case of either/or, rather it is a case of what is fit for purpose in any given set of circumstances

Activity 3.2

Were you able to identify your team's development needs and any people in the organisation that could help? Will you need any assistance to be able to access this help? Is your line manager likely to be supportive or will he or she see this as a threat because they may feel any weaknesses makes them look like a poor manager ? Or is your line manager more secure about themselves and likely to be more supportive?

Activity 3.3

Many organisations now see coaching as an integral part of a line manager's responsibilities. Working with others and developing people are key aspects of the manager's repertoire of skills and, in terms of impact on performance, it is a more effective way to develop people compared to sending them away on a generic course and expecting them to implement whatever they have learned.

Unit 5

Activity 5.1

How easy was it to devise a Gantt chart? Did you find it useful? Can you think of examples of how you could use it at work?

Activity 5.2

There should be a lot of examples where a project management approach may be useful in a marketing context, such as developing a communications campaign or working with external agencies, for example in market research projects.

Activity 5.3

Examples of the key areas could be as follows:

The project timetable, with particular reference to critical event times and potential bottlenecks. There should be feedback on activity times achieved and their effect on the whole project. If network analysis is used, then it is vital that the network is reworked and updated to take into account the actual performance achieved.

The project budget; budgetary control procedures can be used as in respect of any other form of budget.

Quality and performance standards; these need to be monitored against the original project specification subject to changes agreed with stakeholders in the course of project development.

Unit 6

Activity 6.1

These are examples of the kinds of questions that can be asked. Developing and maintaining an MkIS system can be expensive so it is important that it is fit for the purpose and meets the identified needs. An MkIS system should serve the whole company, not a single department, and integrate data from across business functions and from many sources. Data often exists already in an organization but not in a form that is useful to marketing.

Activity 6.2

Were there any gaps, that is, information you would like that is not available? How could this information be obtained from other secondary sources?

Unit 8

Activity 8.1

Are there any conclusions or criteria that you would draw from the campaign that you identified that could be used in other campaigns? What kind of appeal was being made through the campaign? Was it appealing to 'the rational' or 'the emotional' you? Were you able to associate the product or service with the campaign? Often, we seem to be able to remember advertisements but cannot remember the brand that is being sold.

♦

Index